I0798849

KETEBE

ketebe.co.uk

1st Edition, September 2025
2nd Edition, November 2025

Original Title *: Why History Matters?*
Reviving Faith through the Lens of History

Published by Ketebe Publishing
UK | Türkiye

ISBN: 978-625-5888-79-2

Cover design by Yasin Çetin
Interior design by Nilgün Sönmez

Printed in Türkiye

For permissions or inquiries:
books@ketebe.com

Copyright © 2025 by Ketebe Publishing
All rights reserved. No part of this publication may be reproduced, distributed, or transmitted in any form or by any means, including photocopying, recording, or other electronic or mechanical methods, without the prior written permission of the publisher, except in the case of brief quotations embodied in critical reviews and certain other non-commercial uses permitted by copyright law.

Why History Matters?

Reviving Faith through the Lens of History

YAKOOB AHMED

KETEBE

Yakoob Ahmed

Dr. Yakoob Ahmed holds a PhD from SOAS, University of London, and formerly served as an Associate Professor at Istanbul University's Faculty of Theology and Islamic Studies Institute. He also spent a year at the University of Tokyo's Institute of Advanced Asian Studies. A specialist in Late Ottoman and intellectual history, Islamic constitutionalism, and nationalism, he regularly features on The Thinking Muslim Podcast, including episodes such as "Ottoman Decline & Muslim Collective Amnesia" and "10 Ottoman Myths Debunked." He is now an independent researcher, preparing his new book on the late Ottoman ulama.

CONTENTS

SECTION II
THE QUR'AN AND SĪRAH AS A SOURCE FOR ANALYSIS AND INSPIRATION FOR HISTORIANS

SECTION III
AN ISLAMIC ETHOS TO KNOWLEDGE PRODUCTION

SECTION IV
PATTERNS AND PARADIGMS

SECTION V
STUDYING ISLAMIC HISTORY FROM A CIVILISATIONAL APPROACH

SECTION VI
THE BLURRING LINES BETWEEN FICTION AND REALITY

و

بِسْمِ اللهِ الرَّحْمٰنِ الرَّحِيْمِ

Bismillāh-ir Rahmān-ir Rahīm

(In the name of Allah, the Rahman, the Rahim)

"Say (O Prophet) O Allah! The Lord of the Possessor of all things/of sovereignty, You give the sovereignty to whom You will, and You take the sovereignty from whom You will, and You endue with honour whom You will, and You humiliate whom You will. In Your Hand is all good. Verily, You are capable of everything. You cause the night to pass/merge into the day, and the day to pass/merge into the night (i.e. increase and decrease in the hours of the night and the day during winter and summer), You bring forth the living out of the dead, and the dead out of the living. And You give wealth and sustenance to whom You will, without limit (measure or account).

—TQM, *Sūrah Āl 'Imrān* 3:26-27.

O Allah, send prayers upon him ﷺ.

O Allah, send prayers upon Our Master Muhammad ﷺ.

O Allah, send prayers and peace upon Our Master Muhammad ﷺ and upon his Family.

O Allah, send prayers and peace upon Muhammad ﷺ and upon his Family and Companions.

O Allah, let Your Blessings come upon Muhammad ﷺ and the family of Muhammad ﷺ, as you have blessed Ibrahim and his family. Truly, You are Praiseworthy and Glorious.

O Allah, bless Muhammad ﷺ and the family of Muhammad ﷺ, as you have blessed Ibrahim and his family. Truly, You are Praiseworthy and Glorious.

To the People of Gaza,
I am sorry we failed you.

ACKNOWLEDGEMENTS

All praise is due to Allah, the Only One worthy of worship. May peace and blessings be upon our Master Muhammad ﷺ, who was born as a mercy to the worlds and sent as a guide for all of humanity.

Before anyone else, I must express my deepest gratitude to the scholars of our tradition—those giants upon whose shoulders we all stand. From the Companions of the Prophet ﷺ to the jurists, theologians, historians, poets, and thinkers across centuries: you preserved, clarified, and expanded a vast and beautiful intellectual legacy. Your sacrifices, sincerity, and brilliance shaped the soul of this ummah. My work is but a drop in the ocean made possible by your dedication. May Allah reward you all and allow us to be faithful inheritors of your knowledge.

Writing acknowledgements is, in one sense, the easiest part—because I am certain that everything I know is not my own, but a gift from Allah. It is also a product of the knowledge passed down, the wisdom of teachers today, and the many individuals—my village—who shaped who I am. But in another sense, it is the most difficult part to write. To name everyone who has supported me feels nearly impossible, and both memory and these pages fall short. Still, I shall try, in no particular order, to acknowledge those who made this project possible.

This book was born during a time of grief and helplessness—a time of genocide—when all I could do was gather my scattered thoughts and write. It is, in many ways, a work in progress. I am grateful to those who encouraged me to begin, however modestly. I hope these reflections will inspire conversation, spark thought, and be built upon by others. I only ask that the ummah be gentle with me—for this heart is easily bruised, and always sincere.

I am especially grateful to Ömer Faruk Yeni, who gently encouraged me to share my thoughts when I felt unready. His support helped me realise that I must do more for this noble ummah. My thanks also go to the entire Ketebe team for believing in this work.

There are many remarkable individuals whose names deserve mention:

Abdurrahman Mahmoud, Hamza Gondal, Fawaz Abdul Salam, Muhammad Zeino, Tariq Fattahi, Elis Gjevori, Noor Saadeh, Umer Sheikh, Wajahat Husain and the Al-Qasas family, Ali Khuwaja, Sabur Khan, Shaykh Asif Hirani and the Texas community, Ebad Rahman and his son Ibrahim Rahman and their family.

Also, Ahmed Ibrahim, Abdulsamad Haffejee, Muhammad Asif Khan, Abdullah Selim, Ismael Elkhateeb, Tugay Taşçı, Owais Khan, Rashid Dar, Alyssa Mazlan, Ayman Azlan, Sunbul Sayyid, Fahad Shahzad Wariach, Fuga Kimura, Naoki Yamamoto, Jaan Islam, Yusuf, Valit and Abdullah Nazari, the Kırmızı family—especially Müfit, Vera, and Nevra.

Further thanks go to Elif Özge, Muhammad Alkhateeb from Gaza, Burcin Mustafa, Omar and Khurrem Sharif, Shaykh Humza Maqbool, Shaykh Asim Timur, Professor Wan Mohamed Nur Dawud, Itrisyia Dayini, Qasim Albadry, Tariq Tamimi, and my colleagues at Istanbul University's Ilahiyat Faculty.

A special thanks to my dear friend and brother Muhammad Jalal, and to his incredible late wife, Farhat Amin, who amplified my voice at a time when I felt unworthy of being heard.

To those whose names I have unintentionally omitted: please forgive me. I pray that Allah, who never forgets, rewards you abundantly.

Lastly, my deepest gratitude is reserved for my family: my mother, Zebunnisa Ahmed; my father, Mohammad Taib Ahmed; and my beloved sister—my heart and soul—Noorjhan Ahmed. I hope I am making you proud.

ب

INTRODUCTION

I began my journey as a historian after earning a PhD in Ottoman History from the School of Oriental and African Studies in London. It was a long and demanding path, during which I constantly asked myself whether studying Islamic history—and doing so as a Muslim—would ultimately bear any meaningful fruit. By 'benefit,' I do not mean success in my career or personal life, but rather whether the knowledge I gained in this intellectual pursuit could truly serve my community. My fascination with history has always been strong, and it deepened further as I travelled across the Muslim world and witnessed the enduring imprint of Islam in every place I visited.

I spent some of my best days in Damascus before the war. I would pray often at the famous *Masjid al-Umawī* (Umayyad Mosque). I paid my respects at the tombs of *Ṣaḥābah* like Bilal (ra) and to the great *ʿulamāʾ* of Islam, such as Imam al-Nawawī and Ibn Taymiyyah. I often frequented the tomb of the great Salahuddin al-Ayyubī after the *jumuʿah* (Friday) prayers and reflected the Ottoman architecture all around me, especially as I would have to go through a market called *Sūq al-Ḥamīdiyyah* (The Hamidian Market) named after the late Ottoman Sultan Abdulhamid II. Islam was everywhere in

Syria, and the history of Islam fascinated me the most—there was so much to experience, and I knew so very little. My experience in Syria forced me to ask myself what it means to be a Muslim, what it means to be a part of not only my *ummah* but the historical *ummah*, and what about the *ummah* of the future? I chose to approach Islam not simply as a religion but as a civilisation that influenced politics, art, science, architecture, and so much more. The only way to learn about this holistic way of Islam's impact on the world was to study the history of Islam. My time in Syria was the first step.

Since then, I have travelled extensively around the Muslim world. I have been to some of its major centres, like Mecca, Medina, *Bayt al-Maqdis* (Jerusalem), Cairo, and Istanbul, as well as Konya, Sarajevo, Karachi, and Kuala Lumpur. While each city was different and had its own geographical specialities, environmental differences, culture, language, and food, there was, nonetheless, a commonality that I inherently understood. While Islam in these cities was a lived experience, these cities were also historical—Islam had left its mark evidently on them. I felt a part of this world, and I wanted to know more. I hence moved to Istanbul, the last centre of the Muslim *Khilafah* (Caliphate). In Istanbul, I could sense Islam's influence on power and how that power supported the Islamic message and community. With its incredible mosques and the breathtaking calligraphy inside them, Istanbul, once an Eastern Roman centre, had become a major centre in the Muslim world for 400 years due to the Ottomans. I travelled extensively throughout the ex-Ottoman domains and became fascinated at how this empire ended and captivated at how it all began.

I became intrigued by how the Ottomans were able to reign over the Balkans, Anatolia, the Arab world, and North Africa. Istanbul felt like a microcosm, not only of the Ottomans but the Muslim world at large. While the diversity of the Muslim world formed a rich tapestry, there was nonetheless similarity and familiarity, which made sense to me. The Muslim world was pluralistic in every way imaginable, but there was a shared paradigm regarding this life and the next. Islam was that paradigm.

It became clear to me that, as Muslims, we have something important to tell. We possess a rich and meaningful story—stories—of Islam, of Muslims, and of a civilisation that has left a lasting mark on the world. This conviction is what led me to pursue the study of Islamic history. I chose to undertake a PhD at a time when very few Muslims were visible in the field. Needless to say, it was a challenge. I soon realised that being a historian required far more than a love for history or an inquisitive mind. It demanded a broad set of skills: learning languages, mastering the art of reading and interpreting historical documents, and developing the ability to form well-reasoned and honest intellectual judgments. The absence of Muslims undertaking history in the Anglophone sphere with the intention of teaching the community became an increasing concern for me. History was seen as a privileged space, a vocation where very little financial gain could be attained. Coming from a working-class background, I noticed that the subject I had started to fall in love with was a space where people who looked like me, thought like me and hailed from a world like mine were missing. There were indeed Muslims studying history, but they often disappeared into the academic world, writing books for the academy which very rarely filtered down to the communities. When first embarking on this journey, I was once told, "Who is going to pay you to think? Why not get a proper job?" I did not miss the point—indeed, any practical person would have made such a statement. But I continued, and I quickly learnt that the absence of good Muslim historians was extremely detrimental to the Muslim community. Yes, by going into the fields of science, technology, engineering and math, we were making money—even contributing to society, perhaps—but we were losing our collective self.

As I continued to operate within the academic space, I started to feel very strange that my tradition, culture, *din*, and *ummah* were being spoken about as merely an abstract object. The vibrant history of the Muslim world, which is still alive today, did not resonate: my lived experience and what was being produced in the academy, at times, felt worlds apart. Do not get me wrong; many of my colleagues are indeed stellar thinkers and academics, and they have enriched my mind and ideas in ways I could not imagine. But what was missing in many ways, I guess, was that connection to the tradition of Islam I felt should have been there in the works I was reading and producing.

I felt that works on Islamic history, firstly, should not always feel abstract; and secondly, a Muslim historian should also produce works of history that can help Muslims make sense of their place in this world and how that is connected to the next life. My point is that morals and lessons were missing, and as a Muslim historian, I believe these are important. I mentioned academia in this section because while Muslims are studying, teaching and producing historical works, the majority of historical research and knowledge production takes place within academic modes of learning that have been inspired by secular 'Western' academic models. There is no doubt that since the nineteenth century, Western academia has paid special attention to history as a vocation in a way that the Muslim world has not. As a Muslim historian and academic, it is my hope to find a way where I can take my academic training and find a way of making it more in conformity with the values of the knowledge tradition of Islam so that Muslims can, firstly, relate to their history as something which is not simply abstract; and secondly, help them think beyond simply events and ideas, but rather values of being good, learning from the past and, as I mentioned, trying to get closer to Allah and His Messenger ﷺ.

One might ask: is that really the role of academia? Simply put, no. But then, what is the role of a Muslim historian if they are not engaging with history through an Islamic lens? I was conscious of not losing myself in the academic whirlpool—producing knowledge for the academy that might incidentally benefit Muslims, yet never speaking directly from an Islamic perspective. I believe Muslim historians have much to offer when they approach their craft with both scholarly rigour and a rooted Islamic worldview. As a result, I started working at Istanbul University's *Ilahiyat* (Theology) department, where I taught Islamic history full-time in the hope that maybe I could be in a space where I could find a way of bringing my skills from academia and my knowledge of the Islamic tradition closer together in my knowledge output. Most of my students were Muslim, and we engaged with Islamic history as something that could educate us and enrich our understanding of our faith and collective identity. Throughout my time in academia, I spoke to a number of my colleagues who were also Muslim from around the world about this. Some felt that the way I was teaching did not fit the academic framework and that I should reconsider teaching in this manner.

The question was, "Why?" Simply put, I dared to place Allah at the centre of the conversation. I taught my students to learn from the lessons of the past so that we do not make the same mistakes again. I tried to provide morals, lessons, and values to the way we did history. My instinct was telling me that I was not wrong in what I was doing—it was just different. I was possibly trying to open a third space in studying history, in which I was able to use the various skills that Western academia had provided and try to apply them with a series of trial-and-error methods to a framing that was conducive to Islam and Muslims.

After being asked to present on a few Muslim podcast shows, as well as teaching around the world at mosques, *madrasahs*, and online, I came to realise how little of Islamic history the global Muslim community was studying—in Ottoman history, my area of speciality, I felt even more disappointed. I learnt very quickly that outside of Türkiye, the Muslim understanding regarding Ottoman studies was not at the level that I had hoped. The dislocation of 600 years of Ottoman history simply felt like Muslims had forgotten, as if there was a collective amnesia. In fact, one thing that has concerned me more, due to the impact of social media and its relationship with consumerism, is what is known as "Agnotology". Agnotology is the deliberate production of ignorance, which is hampering our communities deeply. It was not that there was ignorance in our communities, but more disturbingly it was being facilitated.

While teaching around the world, a common question that I faced, mainly from Muslim parents, was: "What books do you recommend that we read or teach to our children?" I would often find myself stumped at that question, as I would provide a list, but with many caveats. The reason was, firstly, the parents were not trained in the way a historian would be to navigate works written by historians. They were always under the impression that history works were neutral and not value-laden, but it was, in fact, quite the opposite. Secondly, I came to realise that Muslims who were aware of this fact nonetheless lacked alternative literature on Islamic history, or even history in general, that could give them meaning, as Muslims, for both this life and the next. It was this accumulative experience that encouraged me to write this small book as a conversation and work of *nasīḥa* (advice) on what Islamic history is, why we need to study history in general, and whether it is possible to study it Islamically.

This simple effort starts off with the premise that Muslims should be studying not just Islamic history but history in general. The study of people is an exercise in learning about all peoples and societies, which we, as Muslims, can greatly benefit from. Historically speaking, Muslims have never been worried about the question of learning from other nations, people, or civilisations, as long as what we were learning was in conformity with the *ʿaqīdah* (creed) of Islam. This practice of knowledge production permitted Muslims to interact with philosophy, art, science, and technologies from various traditions and cultures. When history was written by earlier Muslim historians, they did not shy away from writing about many societies who were not Muslim. The Qur'an itself is filled with evidence of Allah speaking of people who are not Muslim so that we may learn from their lived experience, not only their mistakes.

An aim of this book is to help Muslims understand that a good "historical consciousness" is based on the notion that a "thinking Muslim" becomes a "contemplative Muslim" and that from this act of contemplation, one thinks deeply about their lives, their actions, the Qur'anic *nomos* regarding the people of the past and that can shape us as individuals, society, and civilisation. It is not only the history of Muslims that I encourage studying, but *all* history in general. Furthermore, it is my hope that this act of contemplation regarding the past can encourage people to become action-oriented as a way of trying to improve themselves and possibly our current predicament as an *ummah* and humanity by giving *dawah* and working to change our condition for the better.

In addition to this, this book will attempt to address three matters: firstly, why should we study history; secondly, why should we study Islamic history; and finally, is it possible to study history Islamically? While the first two points are straightforward, the final point is an exercise in starting a conversation about how we could find ways of taking ideas, concepts and skills from the academic world and make them applicable in ways that do not contradict the *ʿaqīdah* of Islam.

Islamic history and the history of Muslims can be seen as being mutually distinct, which is important for understanding the broader context of the *ummah*. Islamic history encompasses the principles, teachings, and practices of Islam as they have been lived out throughout the ages, including the lives of the Prophets, the Prophet Muhammad ﷺ, and the early Muslim community. This perspective focuses on the collective efforts to implement and uphold the teachings of Islam, reflecting a tradition of submission to Allah. Whereas the history of Muslims, while it may detail events, actions, and developments involving Muslims, can sometimes lack the contextual grounding in Islamic principles. Such accounts, if not connected to the overarching values of Islam, may align more with secular historical narratives. While these accounts can provide valuable insights and data, they may miss the deeper meanings and implications of those actions within the framework of faith. A truly Islamic history, in my opinion, is one that not only recounts events but also interprets them through the lens of Islamic teachings and values. This approach emphasises the importance of connecting the *ummah*'s experiences and challenges to the principles of Islam, fostering a holistic understanding of the community's journey. It highlights the idea that history is not merely a collection of events but a narrative shaped by the faith, struggles, and aspirations of a community bound by shared beliefs.

Studying history Islamically could, therefore, involve placing historical events within the framework of Islamic teachings and beliefs, and these historical events can be examined through an ethical lens reflected in the Qur'an and *Sunnah*, encouraging discussions about the moral implications of actions taken by individuals and communities, and how they align with Islamic values. Another point worth exploring is the collective experiences of the *ummah*, emphasising the unity and shared purpose of Muslims throughout history.

This fosters a sense of identity and belonging. When providing lessons, one could relate historical events to current issues facing the *ummah*, helping readers see the continuity of Islamic principles in addressing modern challenges. It is my hope that, when writing within an Islamic lens, these framings are considered by contemporary Muslim historians.

In that sense, my first proposal in this book is to encourage Muslims to study history and find ways to place history as a staple subject within our institutions of learning. I believe that Muslims ought to study, for example, the French Revolution and how it has shaped the world we live in, or even the history of China and Japan. Often, we continue to make reductive declarations in our works regarding many parts of the world or people who are not Muslim, which is often due to a lack of study. Their histories give us a sense of how previous peoples negotiated their place in the world and also how this impacts us directly as Muslims. This not only helps us to understand other people but also how to give *dawah*. As a result, while much of this book will provide examples from Islamic history, I want to stress that we should also be studying the history of all societies and people.

Naturally, much of this book shall focus on Islamic history and what that *is*. Islamic history, for me, is the history of the people and lands that have submitted to Islam. The point of studying Islamic history is to understand how Islam has been practised, implemented, and spread all over the world. It gives us a sense of what Islam as a civilisation offered people. Islamic history is not just a study of the *fiqh*, *kalām*, or *ʿilmī* traditions of Islam—it is also the study of power in Islam: the configuration of governance, the role of learning in the form of the *ʿulamā* and their institutions, and finally, the *ummah* as a networked community of believers, locally *and* globally. It is a study of the Islamic and Muslim world. And so, this book will attempt to show how ideas, thoughts, and institutions in Islam have been important in representing Islam as a lived experience. It may seem pretty obvious in that sense, but I want to stress that Muslims need to study their own history, not only so that they can aptly place themselves in the timeline of history but also so that they can build their own identities, knowing they are part of a long genealogy that goes back not just to the Prophet Muhammad ﷺ, but all the way to Prophet Adam ﷺ.

Finally, a key theme of this book is to ask the question: *can* history be studied Islamically? This book will make the case that both the Qur'an and *Sunnah* not only direct us to the need for history writing but also shape the way we produce our knowledge. Fundamentally, the primary objective of *'ilm* is to know Allah—and any *good* form of knowledge production by a Muslim would, in both style and substance, naturally include a reminder of Allah and of the reader's salvation in this life and the next. In this book, I explore themes from the Qur'an and *Sunnah* and ask if they can be applied to what one could call a methodology or theory in writing history that is not only in conformity with Islam and its principles but also provides meaning for the reader and scholar. Can the history of Islam, while indeed speaking of the *Sharī'a*, the *ummah*, and the Muslim experience, be considered as history *being done Islamically* if it is devoid of Allah? While I recognise that writing from a humanist approach is vital in providing *insān* (human beings) agency in the writing of history, with this book I ask: do we as historians have a responsibility in our knowledge production of putting into our writing the agency of Allah? What I mean by this is, can I use the Qur'an and *Sunnah* as evidence to explain the notion of patterns and repetition mentioned by Allah in the Qur'an or indicated in the *Sunnah* or *Sīrah* of the Prophet ﷺ as proof when giving historical analysis? I would argue that, even if possible at all, this is very difficult within the secular paradigm of knowledge production. Thus, we ought to be aware of this and strive to put Allah's ultimate agency in our works. And *this* is the new third space I propose: I feel Islamic history ought to be an attempt to understand the meaning of Islam within the framework of how Islam presents itself.

I call it a third space because I recognise that there are many universal, ideological ideas, methods, and practices that we can incorporate in our contemporary history works. We can also apply ideas, methods, and modes that are in conformity with our tradition to the point that history can be written Islamically, which is intellectually robust, rational, and yet *ākhirah*-oriented. In the past, Muslim historians may not have felt the need to create a framework or methodology for writing history from an Islamic perspective simply because Islam was the dominant ecosystem from which many of them wrote. Al-Tabari (fourth century AH–tenth century AD), Ibn Khaldun (ninth century AH/fourteenth century AD) and Alim Ahmet Cevdet (fourteenth century AH/nineteenth century AD) were all experts in *tafsīr* and had either found ways of incorporating the Qur'an into their works, or had written works that were part of a whole tradition of learning that included books on *tafsīr* and history. For example, when Ibn Khaldun was writing, he provided methods of how a Muslim historian ought to produce their work, criticising some of the methods used by previous historians. However, contemporary ideologies would not have been part of Ibn Khaldun's imagination. Cevdet attempted to find a middle ground by using the new methods that were emerging from Western Europe, but still writing in a way that would provide meaning to Muslims. When examining the history works of Cevdet, it is evident he was trying something new; nonetheless, he too did not tackle the question of methodology.

I am willing to concede that this book may not be able to comprehensively address this question, as this type of project is not something that has been embarked on by Muslims who have chosen to be Western styled academics. That is not to say that Muslims have not written or engaged in such questions in the Muslim world. I have engaged with such people, who have been influential in my thought process.[1] These types of questions have emerged within the traditional field of *'ulūm al-Dīn,* but history writing is often still considered a secondary vocation rather than a possible supplementary one. This book, however, is mainly aimed at all those who, having attended my talks, classes, and interviews, tend to ask me how we can study history Islamically. The attempt of the book is to highlight the ethos of *'ilm* in Islam, how we practice it, how the Qur'an and *Sunnah* can help provide meaning, and what historians should do so that all these points are understood. I have mentioned on many occasions that our trained historians tend to relegate their focus solely to the academic world, and as such our community is stuck with storytellers or bullet-point historians.

Finally, I make the case in this book that a sense of historical depth for Muslims can be helpful in other fields of study, such as political science and international relations, or in fictional works as well. When we understand that politics is not something outside Allah's domain, an Islamic perspective of writing history can inspire the way we anticipate the future from an Islamic lens. Muslims ought to be future-oriented, and even more so in the field of politics. While there is no need for a historian to be a political scientist, a *good* political scientist, diplomat or thinker is required to have a good grounding in history. It should come as no surprise that the likes of *Alim* Ahmet Cevdet, who was justice minister to Abdulhamid II, and Khayruddīn (Hayrettin in Turkish) al-Tūnisī, who was the *Bey* of Tunis and Grand Vizier for Abdulhamid II, were historians. Even in the USA, the likes of Bernard Lewis, who

---

1 One example is *al-Tafsīr al-Islāmī lil-Tārikh* by 'Mad al-Dīn Khalīl.

shaped much of US policy post-9/11, and Foreign Policy advisor Henry Kissinger were also historians. In that sense, I think it is imperative that Muslims who go into the field of politics study history, too, and Muslim historians need to be part of the wider discourse regarding politics and the community.

As for fiction writing, which was part of the Muslim tradition and is very popular in many traditions and cultures, it too requires historical depth. Ideas and imagination do not come from a vacuum but are, instead, built on those that came before. Allah taught Adam ﷺ the names of things; all knowledge is built upon this first interaction. Works of fiction, often perceived as simply works of one's imagination devoid of any truth, are, in fact, based on previous experiences. While many fiction writers and producers may produce fiction just for entertainment, many others produce these works as a way of speaking truth by using narrative, analogy, and metaphor as mediums to be able to express the human experience and bring people closer to the truth. Fiction writers, who are not restricted by the need to adhere to evidence or data, have the creative freedom to speak truth more than the academic at times, as the imaginative space provides a greater scope for interpretation. I will make a distinction in this book, however, between works of fiction and history, as I believe that while many in the Muslim community are critical of fiction, they have also reduced history to storytelling—in this way, they have diminished both history and fiction at the same time. My criticism of storytelling is not that it cannot be helpful, but that simple storytelling is not what we historians do. The concern here is that either storytelling becomes an act of academic inquiry, or that historians are nothing more than storytellers—both of which I disagree with.

Nonetheless, I argue that the field of political science and fiction requires history, as we continue to learn from the past. Both fields can be of benefit to the *ummah*, and studying history can be helpful in these fields too. Thus, this book shall also explore this point. By the end of the book, it is my hope that this conversation can encourage Muslims to explore whether we can do history not just differently but *Islamically*.

For this reason, I request that people do not take shortcuts when studying history. Anyone can read information about the past but cultivating a critical and creative mind is a long process. I am aware that some aspects of this book may be challenging and other parts repetitive. But I have written each paragraph hoping that it may encourage you to think and discuss, hoping we can revive the Islamic tradition of the discipline of history. I repeat points as a way of trying to instil ideas into memory—*your* memory. Throughout this book, I will show how Muslim historians can, in the modern world, take refuge in the Qur'an and also inspiration from it regarding how the vocation of Islamic history ought to be taught and studied.

I ask Allah to inspire me, and any and all benefits that come from this humble attempt are solely from Him, *al-Ḥakīm* (the All-Wise), *al-'Alīm* (the All-Knowing).

THEMES OF THE BOOK - AN ISLAMIC APPROACH

The ʿilm of history, while numbered among the literary arts, is also one of the means to the sciences of the Sharīa. It helps one gain the proof of experience, and it sharpens the thought of the learned and skilful so that he can compare the cases of compliance and satisfaction to what happened in the past and see the causes and consequences as well as the events and what grows out of them. But for history, the virtues would die out with the death of those possessing them. This would lead to them being ignored. The benefit is not disowned if the stories are told, the exceptional are tied down in writing, the deeds are transmitted, and the actions of those who did them remembered.

-Ahmed Abi bin Diyaf-

• Epistemic Re-Orientation:

This book consists of a series of essays in which I aim to share my thoughts on how history can be written from an Islamic perspective, specifically for the average reader. The intention behind this work is to emphasise that history writing is not merely about recording past events but rather a serious endeavour to uncover the truth. It seeks to highlight the importance of approaching history with a deeper understanding of its significance and how it should be framed in a way that resonates with the values and principles of Islam.

The first important component of an Islamically-oriented history writing project is that historiography should be conceptually filtered through the prism of the Islamic *ʿaqīdah* (Creed), which extends to the tenets of *īmān* and *iḥsān* which I shall explain later. Since the advent of modern history writing, finding a space where Islam as theory has been aptly incorporated into the writing of history in comparison to other ideologies has yet to find a space that I am satisfied with. Some historians, both Muslim and non-Muslim, may disagree on whether that is necessary, but I will argue in this book that this ought to be considered, even if the idea is at an early stage. Works in accordance with the *ʿaqīdah* of Islam recognise the reality of the world Allah created and that He is the creator of it. Central to the Islamic *ʿaqīdah* is the concept of monotheism, and that the practice of monotheism should be done in accordance with the manner that Prophet Muhammad, the final Prophet ﷺ, practised it as an example to humanity.

As a result, an Islamically-oriented, or more specifically, an *īmān*-oriented work, should consider and support this in the writing process. Many historians, including Muslims, may suggest that works produced in a secular paradigm within Western academia do not contradict and contravene the Islamic *ʿaqīdah*; thus, why is there a need to specify specifically an Islamically-oriented approach? I would respond by suggesting that while most works will indeed fit the general principles of Islam, a deeper Islamic-oriented approach is one in which the tenets of *īmān* and when needed the tenets of *iḥsān* are highlighted in the investigative process, as well as in style and final output. This means that a Muslim historian ought to provide meaningful solutions and lessons to get close to Allah, as that is the Islamic mission, especially now.

This is because we have clear concepts of *ḥaqq* (truth and reality) and *bāṭil* (falsehood) in Islam. We also equally have concepts that differentiate between *īmān* (certified belief) and *kufr* (disbelief), as well as *ʿadl* (justice) and *ẓulm* (oppression). It is imperative for Muslim historians, whenever they can, to write in accordance with these concepts as a way of bringing the reader closer to Allah and making the case that Islam advocates principles, ethics, values, commands, and obligations that regulate the life of a Muslim. These are not just for the individual but for communities, societies, and nations. The Qur'an ought to be made a clear source of reflection and guidance in the writing process. I would suggest that, when possible, it should also be considered in the historical analysis for the reader to see Allah's guidance and divine commands in the historical moment being mentioned. As a result, Allah and the centrality of the Qur'an not only educate and guide the reader from the perspective of what Allah has ordained but mention of Allah is also on the pages.

In an *īmān*-oriented approach, one must also see the Messenger of Allah ﷺ, who was chosen by Allah to complete and perfect the mission, as a source of guidance. The belief in the Qur'an and the Prophet ﷺ are central to Islam and to *īmān*. As a result, it is not only the *Sunnah* of the Prophet ﷺ that I recommend being consulted and included in the intellectual endeavour, but as I shall mention later, the *Sīrah* (life-story) of the Prophet ﷺ should also be seen as an example and guide when examining people of the past, as he ﷺ was a guide for the whole of humanity. In that sense, I would extend by suggesting that the *Sīrah* ought to be seen as a source of consultation for the Muslim historian so that the Muslims can, firstly, get close to and love the Prophet of Allah ﷺ and secondly, and equally importantly, to take lessons from his life-story as a point of analysis that can help us understand the schemas of societies, and the notion of what is good and what is evil in accordance with Islam as that is a principle Allah expects from humanity of which the *din* of Islam is the framing for.

By examining human societies via this prism, we learn how the believers behaved and how the opponents of the message throughout Islamic history have responded. This can show us a particular consistency about Muslim societies throughout the civilisational history of Islam, which can hold true up until today. It can also highlight how Muslims have maintained how to adhere to Islam's principles that shaped our civilisation. Additionally, it is not only Muslim societies that we can learn from, but other societies too, and understand how societies configured, organised, succeeded and failed. This means that via this approach, we are expected to understand the nature of societies, peoples, and their creeds in order to understand the Islamic call in relation to it. This type of approach helps us not only understand the failures of those who opposed Islam during the time of the Prophet ﷺ and the contestation between *ḥaqq* and *bāṭil* but also how Muslims endured periods of collective hardship. By doing so, we can examine how the Muslims behaved in trying to adhere to the principles of Islam as the world discursively changed but we can also examine the impact of a society or nation, whether that be Muslim or non-Muslim, who did not adhere to the general principles that can be found in Islam, such as justice and what that meant for humanity in the long term.

The life of the Prophet ﷺ should not only be compared to what came after him ﷺ but also what preceded him, as he ﷺ is the point of reference for all humanity, nations, and human relations. While the *Sharīa* that was completed by the Prophet ﷺ was a completion of the Prophetic missions that started with Adam ﵇, the point here, however, is that his ﷺ life journey can be compared to that of Mūsā ﵇ for example, or any society and nation in human history as a way of examining the constituency of the divine plan, and the concepts of justice and ethics that are integral to Islam.

Another point for a work to be *īmān*-oriented is that the author understands the Islamic concept of *ummah* (the community of Muslims). The notion of belonging to this *ummah* means that we are all bound by the same belief in Islam and that we all testify to the precepts that are found in our *Shahādah* (Testimony of faith), and that we subscribe to the tenets of *īmān*. As a result, the notion of brotherhood in Islam means not only do we belong to an extended fraternity that is the *ummah* but also have a sacred responsibility to safeguard this community and its interests and make sure that the community adheres to the principles of Islam, which includes upholding justice in accordance with the divine command and upholding the ethics and morals inherent in the notion of justice that Islam so evidently propagates. In doing so, as a Muslim, it is imperative to enjoin what is good and abstain from that which does not follow what the Qur'an has laid down as a foundational principle. This means that as a Muslim historian, when writing, this notion ought to be explored as part of the Islamic mission. As Muslim historians have done in the past, we must attempt to guide the reader through the moments in human history where tensions between the *ḥaqq* and *bāṭil*, and between *īmān* and *kufr*, were on display and how Islam continued to be the *raison d'être* of the *ummah*. As a result, this endeavour is one in which we attempt to learn and establish the truth, and this is important as Islam has a clear position on the notion of what is the truth.

Furthermore, Muslim historians should also make their work an open invitation to Islam as an act of *da'wah* (invitation). When I mention being action-oriented in this book, what I mean is *da'wah*, in which the Muslim invites and encourages the reader to read about the Islamic call of goodness and the message that justice and good ethics are foundational principles of this *ummah* and that this way of life is for the betterment of humanity, not just the Muslim, as Islam is the divine guidance for humanity from Allah via His Messenger ﷺ. As a result, a work that is *īmān*-oriented has to uphold this value when writing. Thus, I argue that a Muslim historian who endeavours to produce work based on the Islamic *ʿaqīdah*, should be striving for *iḥsān* themselves as an act of getting close to Allah, and being rewarded by Him as well as encouraging the reader to do the same, as Allah says in the Qur'an, "Truly, Allah is with those who fear Him (keep their duty unto Him), and those who are *Muḥsinūn* (good-doers)."[1] (*Sūrah al-Naḥl* 6:128)

History writing, as any other endeavour of knowledge-production, for the Muslim should epistemologically adhere to the general criteria of knowledge production in Islam and conform to the Islamic *ʿaqīdah*. Hence, an *īmān*-oriented historian must approach historical knowledge as a field of information that induces both rational thinking and spiritual cognition, which altogether draw both the historian and the reader closer to Allah and the Prophetic ethics. This principle should dictate the subject matter studied and the style of writing chosen. Viewing historiography through the lens of Islam, and by extension *īmān* and *iḥsān*, ensures that historical narratives are not merely factual recounts but are imbued with spiritual significance. This approach fosters a deeper understanding of how divine principles influence human actions and historical events. When a knowledge producer or reader is primarily dealing with or producing works that are detrimental to this balance, it can have an impact on the spiritual aspect of a person in which they may assume that matters of spirituality have only to do with worship or knowledge about religious rules. *ʿIlm* in itself, however, is an endeavour to get closer to Allah. The *Ṣaḥābah* (Companions of the Prophet ﷺ), Hudhayfah Ibn al-Yamān, reported that The

1 A person who internalises and practices *Iḥsān* is a *muḥsin* and the plural is *muḥsinūn/muḥsinīn*.

Messenger of Allah, ﷺ said, "The virtue of knowledge is better than the virtue of worship, and the best of your religion is conscientious piety."[2] In this *ḥadīth*, what is being affirmed is not obligatory worship, but optional. But the point is that the *ʿilm* we produce must inspire the same ideals regarding the principles of faith.

An *īmān*-oriented approach respects the complexity of life, integrating both spiritual and material dimensions. This dual focus provides a richer narrative that reflects the realities of the human experience, affirming that faith is integral to understanding history. In Islam, the pursuit of knowledge is not just an academic exercise; it is a means to understand Allah's creation, fulfil one's responsibilities, and cultivate a deeper connection with Him and the Messenger ﷺ. By explicitly connecting historical events to Islamic teachings, scholars can challenge the implication of secularism that Allah is absent from modern life or from the experiences of previous generations. It allows for a richer narrative that respects the complexity of human existence, integrating the spiritual and material aspects of life. By doing so, Muslim historians can help restore the significance of faith in public discourse and inspire individuals to recognise the relevance of Allah in all aspects of life. This approach not only enriches the field of history but also reaffirms the centrality of faith in shaping human experience and understanding.

While academics have challenged Orientalism, modernity, and coloniality, as well as other forms of intellectual ideologies that are anti-Islam, an alternative Islam-based approach has yet to be fully actualised within academic studies. This may not be possible at this time, but that does not mean an academically trained Muslim historian cannot undertake this type of writing. I emphasise the need for a transformative

2 al-Mu'jam al-Awsaṭ lil-Ṭabarānī 3960

approach to scholarship that integrates divine agency into the analysis and interpretation of human experience. Works explaining this approach must be written to pave the way for future generations of scholars to explore and articulate the relevance of *īmān* in their research, fostering a deeper understanding of the interconnectedness of faith, history, and society. If Muslims continue to write in the secular domain and not challenge it or write in a third space, not only will their knowledge production, over time, submit to secular paradigms, but so will their souls, as individuals and as a collective. This kind of rational contemplation leads to emotional and spiritual tranquillity, and this is a significant point for a Muslim scholar to seriously reflect on.

• History as an Auxiliary Form of ʿilm

Once the epistemic objective of history has been reoriented, I would argue that Muslim historians must start to pedagogically and methodologically integrate history within the larger curriculum of the Islamic sciences. Teaching history Islamically requires developing methodologies that help Muslims feel rooted in and connected to the past. Hence, the discipline must be re-conceptualised as one of the "*ʿulūm al-āla*" *or* auxiliary sciences that serve as a tool to strengthen one's *ʿaqīdah*. In this sense, its relationship with other Islamic sciences must be re-established as a discipline whose insights endow the Muslim with the ability to appreciate Allah's *Qudrah* (power), *Jamāl* (beauty), *Raḥmah* (mercy), and *Jalāl* (might) as they manifest throughout time.

From a Qur'anic paradigm, the science of history must then be re-conceptualised as the science that cultivates human memory of Allah's creations and actions. It is a science of remembrance. This conceptualisation should guide Muslim historians in choosing which subject and historical questions are worth pursuing and investigating, or which narratives are worth critiquing and engaging with. Pedagogically, this can form a guideline for Muslim historians to think about how and in which language their knowledge is produced.

Once philosophically connected to the other branches of Islamic sciences, Islamically taught history would always indicate that Allah is the creator of this universe, and human beings would centre this in our historical contemplations. However, this must not imply a simplistic historical paradigm where "Divine intervention" is considered but not analysed. Instead, the events of the past and their analysis should help direct our focus to the underlying laws that govern human action and the natural environment. This acquired insight would indeed have a spiritual effect on the hearts and minds of Muslims. These kinds of holistic historical paradigms are not new. Marxist historiography was based on the philosophical principles of dialectical materialism that aimed to explain human history as the expression of contradictions resulting in the socioeconomic material conditions of human societies. Additionally, in nineteenth century Britain, a historiographical school known as the "Whig historians" also favoured a historical reading of the past based on the philosophical and ideological principles of liberalism and constitutionalism. This historiographical school posited that a holistic reading of the human past only indicates "universal progress" towards societies and political systems underpinned by the progressive values of Protestant liberalism.

- **Historical Subject Matters Expounded on with Islamic Sensibility**

Once these steps are taken, a project of an Islamically-oriented history will need to address the philosophical questions of meta-narratives and temporal change, which both are embodied in the concept of the "historical narrative".

• **Narrative**

Islamically, the study of history should be carried out in a manner that will provide Muslims with relatable historical narratives about human nature, civilisation, economic forces, social formations, the *ummah*, etc, which altogether lead to a better understanding of Allah's *Sharīa*. Moreover, these narratives should and must rely on useful methodological tools both from the Islamic and Western epistemic traditions in order to bring the ideological underpinnings of historical narratives within an Islamic fold. Such a narrative that draws from the Qur'an and *Sunnah* would allow Muslims to appreciate and find meaning in subject matters that concern belonging to the *ummah*. This form of narrative writing can be helpful in re-evaluating what it means to be human in a post-modern and even post-humanist world.

• **The Logic of History**

An *īmān*-oriented object of history writing should thus be continuously elaborating on Qur'anic themes by analysing historical material, themes, paradigms, etc. Just as grammarians elaborate and simplify language logic, historians must elaborate and simplify the logic of time to the believers. This requires a re-orientation of the objective of historiography and not necessarily a drastic reformation of the methodology. The elaboration on Qur'anic themes requires the Muslim historian to produce historical narratives that take into account the uniqueness and contingencies of historical events as well as the cyclical nature of history. As historians, our task goes beyond identifying patterns in the past; it involves analysing the information available to us and discerning how these patterns inform our understanding of human behaviour and societal change. Each interpretation is shaped by the evidence we gather, and our theories inevitably reflect our historical outlook. This book shall examine the importance of meta-narratives and how understanding time and societal evolution as part of a larger process can help us better understand our place regarding our collective experience. Finally, the influence of Ibn Khaldun's approach to cycles will naturally be examined and whether such thinking can be approached today.

Meta-narrative writing can highlight that Muslims have been through extreme moments of success and then extreme moments of failure. Meta-narratives emerged in the past in the West but still exist today in a different garb. Marxist, feminist, and environmentalist histories tend to produce meta-narratives through their focus on gender dynamics, class clashes, and human-nature relationships. Hence, Islamically-minded history writing can be established methodologically by choosing to focus on particular themes or human dynamics apart from the state/dynasty for instance, and instead examine themes that are a part of our Islamic tradition and culture.

Thinking of our experiences and lives as part of a larger process connects us to the past and future. It requires rediscovering certain concepts, which are not necessarily statistics but provide a process-like, process-driven mindset. Such concepts are passed down generationally in order to achieve change and can help the reader understand that they are still connected to a process that precedes them. This is different from a progress-driven approach. In a progress-driven approach, the main focus is on achieving tangible outcomes, moving forward, possibly disconnecting from the past and reaching milestones. The emphasis is on results and measurable advancement rather than strictly following a set process. This approach is more goal-oriented and typically more flexible, adapting methods as needed to ensure continuous progress, but in doing so, it abandons traditions. In a process-driven approach, the focus is on following a set methodology or series of steps to reach an outcome. This approach emphasises consistency, standardisation, and assuming that the best outcomes are achieved through reliable processes. The process approach is to understand that the ultimate outcome and victory are in the hands of Allah while adhering to the tradition of Islam.

The main objective of the Muslim historian is to attain the inner meaning of understanding the human condition. The historian must establish subtle explanations of causes and present a deep knowledge of how and why things happened. The archetypal nature of historical narratives in the Qur'an heavily influenced the Muslim historian Ibn Khaldun's theory of human history. His theory asserts that every nation ultimately declines, usually as a result of moral decay. It also involves analysing patterns among nations to identify consistent themes within this process. Khaldun uses the word *ʿaṣabiyyah* (group solidarity/bonds) and how they are impacted by conditions that show the strength and weakness of such bonds and what happens to them as they go through a life cycle. These are:

· ***ʿAṣabiyyah* (Social Cohesion)**: A strong sense of social cohesion and solidarity forms among the community, often rooted in kinship, shared identity, or common interests. This unity is crucial for the formation and success of a new society.

· **Emergence of a Ruling Group**: Strong *ʿaṣabiyyah* allows a new ruling group or dynasty to emerge, often led by a charismatic or capable leader. This phase is marked by territorial expansion and economic growth.

· **Consolidation and Prosperity**: The dynasty consolidates power, establishes institutions, and experiences cultural and economic flourishing. The society enjoys stability, high living standards, and security.

· **Weakening of *ʿAṣabiyyah***: As prosperity increases, *ʿaṣabiyyah* begins to weaken. Luxury, complacency, and internal divisions emerge, leading to a decline in governance quality.

· **Moral and Cultural Decline**: The ruling elite may grow detached from the populace, causing dissatisfaction. Economic decline and exploitation can lead to unrest and conflict.

· **Collapse and Renewal**: The weakened dynasty faces internal revolts and external threats, eventually collapsing. A new group with strong *ʿaṣabiyyah* rises, often from marginalised groups, and the cycle begins anew.

- **Invest in Narrative as a form of History Writing**

Muslim historians need to cultivate their literary abilities in order to relay and explain their historical analyses and arguments in the form of micro-history, which requires a great deal of interpretative creativity. The merit of this form of history writing is that it allows the reader to relate to the historical subjects and the various interlinked contexts in which they lived, thought, and socialised. This form of history writing will allow Muslim historians to harness the tools of fictional writing and literature to bring life to their subject matters without compromising the historicity or the pieces of evidence upon which their argument is based. In other words, Muslim historians need to harness the tools of literary and fictional narratives, i.e., character construction, plots, thick description, and constant oscillation between micro and macro events, when they interpret the whole corpus of historical and primary sources. This is all the more important because, more often, scholars and academic historians might underestimate the relationship between form and content. That is, an economic or demographic historian whose monographs consist of various statistical tables explaining certain economic or demographic trends might be at a disadvantage when trying to really explain the meaning or significance of these trends to non-specialists. This is where the role of narrative techniques—upon which various works of historical fiction are based—comes into use. Thus, this book is an attempt to examine a host of points I think are necessary for a new generation of Muslim historians and students, that don't simply follow the framing within the academic space but work to be multi-disciplinary by adhering to the precepts of Islam while learning from other disciplines like literature. The series of essays in this book is designed to encourage this thought process.

ب

SECTION I

WHY MUSLIMS NEED TO STUDY HISTORY?

Why The Need to Examine the Current Approach?

When I first started teaching Islamic history, I noticed the empty stares of my students, uninterested in the class before I had even begun. I sat wondering why they did not share the same enthusiasm as I had about matters concerning our faith.

I knew the answer of course. Just like them, I too was taught history as memorising dates, facts and events when I was young.

Instead, to elicit a response from my students, I asked them, "Why do we do history? What is the point of it? Do we need it? Should Muslims study the history of Islam and Muslims?" Of course, all my students agreed that studying history *was* important, but they were stuck on *why*. I would often get the well-drilled answer that we study history to learn from the mistakes of the people of the past.

Of course, there was truth to that statement. As human beings, we inherently feel that we tend to repeat offences—too many examples in our everyday lives prove that. But is that the only reason we study history? Pushing my students a bit more, I then asked, "Why else do we study history? What value does it have?" The class went quiet as they looked down at their desks in the hope that I would not see them—but, of course, I could see them. I smiled and told them,

"It's okay, this is not a trick question." I then told them that for the next term or so, we would not only be studying Islamic history, but throughout our time, I want them to think about why history is important.

In the modern period, although we have so much access to information, there is, in fact, a crisis regarding our collective memories. I have written before about the *ummah*'s current predicament and the collective amnesia we suffer regarding our Islamic past(s). I say 'amnesia' deliberately to address the notion of forgetting and collective memory. I want to stress the point that because it is part of our tradition, we need to remember that the idea of complex memory is what separates *insān* from other creations of Allah: as intelligent beings with reason and thought, we exercise memory as part of knowing. Memory is of both the human mind and soul, of the intellect and emotion. Yet it is also natural for human beings to forget, as memory is fallible.

Why is memory fallible? The minute information enters the mind, it is already declining towards forgetfulness—as a result, we require many mechanisms to remember or, at least, not forget. But indeed, we will forget some things in parts and others in totality, for if the human mind never forgot anything, it would become overwhelmed. The loss of memory is part of the challenge that historians attempt to address. Knowing that they are always going to forget, human beings have found a variety of ways of leaving behind clues or forms of documentation—sometimes knowingly, other times by accident—for future generations.

Today, human beings have an array of ways in which they document their lives. Just as people in the past had various ways to document their lives and existence. The digital age has transformed how we share and access information. Today, our lives are often documented through social media, mobile apps, and online services, creating a digital footprint that can be vast and intricate. This abundance of information offers both benefits, like enhanced connectivity and access to resources, and challenges, such as privacy concerns and the potential for misinformation. For historians, the abundance of information available today is both a treasure trove and a challenge. The rise of digital communications—emails, text messages, and social media posts—offers historians new avenues for understanding social dynamics, cultural trends, and political movements.

In the past, people too had ways of leaving behind traces of their lives, which we can call documentation. These are what is known in the field as archival sources. Archival sources can appear in many forms, such as state documents, letters, memos, memoirs, memorabilia, and so on. When I say "documentation", I want to stress that this is not only official records or things written down—stamps, coins, architecture, tombstones, to name a few, are all forms of documentation that previous people have left behind. As time goes by, sometimes those documents become less attainable for people; sometimes people pay little attention to them, or forms of power allow or even encourage documentation of a previous people to disappear. Historians tend to make use of these archival sources or objects, artefacts, or documents to remind people of the past. Historians are well aware that people forget or, at times, are made to forget. This can happen on an individual basis or collectively as well.

Being a natural disposition of human beings, forgetfulness is, therefore, a mercy from Allah—imagine never being able to forget? Yet remembering is also a human exercise to find meaning and belonging. Hence, life is all about, on the one hand, the fallibility of memory and, on the other, the exercise of recollection. While we recognise that we will forget things and that this is indeed a mercy from Allah, it is nevertheless a requirement that people work to remember things and use investigative approaches when learning about the past, as that is needed in order to reflect on peoples of the past.

In fact, reminding people of the past is very clear in the Qur'an itself: Allah points to such examples so that people are aware of what happened to their predecessors in order not to fall into similar situations. When making the case of the need to remember, Allah does not simply mention reading and writing as a way of remembering—He also encourages people to reflect and *contemplate over* previous peoples and civilisations when people travel to foreign lands. In *Sūrah Muhammad*, Allah says: "*Have they not travelled through the land and seen how was the end of those before them? Allah destroyed [everything] over them, and for the disbelievers is something comparable.*" (TQM, *Sūrah Muhammad*, 47:10) and again in *Sūrah Yusuf*, Allah says, "*And We sent not before you [as messengers] except men to whom We revealed from among the people of cities. So, have they not travelled through the earth and observed how the end of those before them? And the home of the Hereafter is best for those who fear Allah; then will you not reason?*" (TQM, *Sūrah Yusuf*, 12:109). In both *āyāt* (signs/verses)[3], Allah is making the case that people should reflect and contemplate about people of the past and the countries they go to regarding this matter. In this sense, we should always be paying attention to the places we travel to and remembering and reflecting on the people who lived there. This brief mention of travelling and paying attention to the plight of previous nations and civilisations, in my opinion, stresses the importance narrative plays in helping people remember.

But why is narrative important? As a good historian will remind you, it is the most potent form of maintaining one's memory and is hence also one of the tools at a historian's disposal

3 I mention the word *āyāt* to mean sign as each *āyāt* is to be reflected over. However, as the known convention is verse, I shall use that throughout this book. However, I would like to stress that the idea of reflecting on life, nature, and the cosmos requires signs something I believe that the Qur'an also does, hence why each verse as *āyāt* being known as a sign is also worth noting.

to help us remember. It is an important tool which a historian uses through which we maintain a solid historical awareness. Narrative plays a crucial role in shaping and preserving memory for several reasons. Narratives—essentially, stories—provide a framework for organising information. By placing events in a sequence with a beginning, middle, and end, narratives help us make sense of complex experiences and recall them more easily. When we connect emotionally to a narrative, we are more likely to retain the details and the lessons it conveys. Narratives, in this regard, are essential for passing down knowledge and values across generations. They encapsulate cultural identities, beliefs, and traditions, helping to maintain a sense of belonging and continuity. Whether as written history or fiction, narratives actively rely on thought, memory, and imagination. A *good* historian recognises all these, as it is for this reason that complex memory—especially regarding the collective memory of nations—is instrumental to storytelling.

The act of storytelling engages multiple cognitive processes, such as imagination and critical thinking. By providing structure, evoking emotion, and facilitating cultural transmission, narratives engage our cognitive processes into forging a deeper connection to our memories. The narrative visualising of events, while undoubtedly enhancing retention and understanding, helps us derive meaning from our experiences—they allow us to interpret and contextualise events, providing insights that can guide future decisions and actions. Shared narratives contribute to collective memory, shaping how communities remember their history and identity; they unite individuals around common experiences and shared values. In essence, narratives are powerful tools for memory, helping us not only to recall information but also enrich our understanding of ourselves and our place in the world.

Ultimately, narratives do more than preserve information: they enrich our understanding of ourselves and our shared histories, guiding us as we navigate our lives. Most academic historians primarily write to an academic audience, but they are also trained to write in narrative form to speak to a wider public too. I remember once listening to the Palestinian academic Rashid Khalidi, who said that the historian's job was to educate the masses about matters that were important to the community but had now escaped their collective memory. In essence, Khalidi was not simply making the case of evoking memory—he was also making the case of how it is done.

I have mentioned in many of my interviews that the current crisis of memory suffered by the modern human being has led to a crisis in identity and the notion of belonging. Human beings require a sense of belonging, and in seeking it out, forming groups and the tensions that arise are inevitable. However, othering and belonging are natural parts of the civilisational outlook of human beings. We will continue to choose to be in one group and make a distinction by abstaining from another. People will identify with race, nation, ethnicity, language, religion, and anything else they can identify with.

The need to identify with a group, while partly an issue of belonging, also provides meaning. The most wholesome way that human beings can identify is to belong to a culture with deep, authentic roots in the past—we have come to believe that this gives validation. However, with the advent of modernity and the modern schooling system, most people are educated to internalise their identity and, later, the values of the respective nation-states to which they belong. What this ended up doing was dislocating us from a deep historical past and, instead, binding us to the collective memory and experience of the nation.

The national identity hence became the most dominant way of identifying and belonging from the twentieth century onwards. Never before had human beings possessed such a rigidly defined understanding of themselves, as their sense of belonging was now grounded in the nation's history. Modernity removed, or at least marginalised, the past and focused on progress, detaching peoples from their traditions, cultures, dogmas and doctrines and replacing their whole existence with the "here and now". In doing so, dislocation becomes a tragic reality for many—for Muslims even *more* so, as they have a rich past with great historical depth. The absence of a historical mindset within the community leads to the absence of belonging to this long, rich historical past, now simply understood in periods, events, dates, and time-stamps.

History is a discipline. It is not just writing about the past but also how the historian interprets, constructs, and reconstructs their interpretation of the past into a narrative that provides meaning to those invested. Why should we care about the past? Why does the past *matter*? It matters because human beings require belonging; to make sense of their world, they need to feel part of a past. Knowing the past not only allows us to make sense of the world we are in currently but also permits us to imagine the future. We are generational and have lineages, cultures and traditions; we belong to lands, languages, ethnicities, religions, and corpora of knowledge. We require knowledge of these aspects of our humanity to feel human. Being dislocated from the knowledge that connects us to the past leaves us disorientated, isolated and unable to understand how to navigate the terrain we call life.

The best historians are the ones who can navigate the complex sources that help build the world of the past and then provide not only an accurate explanation of that past but tell it in a way that gives us meaning. People who have faced extreme subjugation due to colonialism will say to you that, at times, what was worse than losing their lives, homes, land, and resources was the attempt to remove their memories and, in doing so, their right to imagine possible futures. The human memory is more complex than any living organ in this cosmos. Memory gives us meaning—it is an intrinsic part of us, and not simply that which one has experienced. Memory can be generational and passed down from person to person to give deeper meaning.

For me, this is an essential point regarding history. It rests on the knowledge of how human beings remember and how they cultivate those memories to give them meaning. In doing so, human memory requires understanding the past, present, and future, making it a phenomenon attached to both the human mind and the soul. For the Muslim, then, history is a vocation that attempts to address the rational intellect and the soul. A good historian, aware of this, will not simply be obsessed with sources alone, but with how to bring the ideas of the past to life.

Of course, I am not the first to ask why history ought to matter to Muslims, and whether there is a different approach to history writing that can once again be meaningful to the *ummah*. In the nineteenth century, Muslims recognised that due to the changing world conditions, the introduction of new technologies, and a different culture of writing history which was emerging in Europe, they also needed to adjust how they started to produce their literature. In the Ottoman Empire, for example, we can see this new trend in the *ʿālim* (and later statesman) Ahmet Cevdet, who was commissioned by the Ottoman state to write a history of the Ottoman Empire from the end of the eighteenth century.

In 1853, during the advent of the Crimean War, the Ottoman government requested the *Encümen-i Daniş-irade-i Seniyye* (Council of Scholars/*ʿulamāʾ*) to commission a writer to work on a history of the Ottoman Empire that began in 1768. That scholar was Ahmet Cevdet, who would be appointed the official state chronicler so that he could document the political events of his time. The first three volumes of his work on history, *Tarih-i Cevdet,* date the beginning of the events in 1774, during the signing of the Treaty of Küçük Kaynarca, and its end in 1826, when Sultan Mahmud II disbanded the Ottoman institution of the Janissary. During this time, Cevdet was asked to complete the works of the *'ālim* Pirizade Mehmed Sahib Efendi's incomplete translation of the *Muqaddimah*[4] of the fourteenth century Muslim jurist and historian Ibn Khaldun, who popularised the theory of the rise and fall of dynasties. Cevdet also published the life-story (*Sīrah*) of the Prophet Muhammad ﷺ to take inspiration from and undertook a project of doing the *tafsīr* of the Qur'ān.

Cevdet exercised his position as a historian to learn from the past to change the fortune of the Ottoman Empire. His endeavours ought not be seen as a sum of individual projects but rather as part of a whole, as all his projects were interconnected. Ibn Khaldun's influence on Cevdet led to him making the case of finding ways to maintain the harmony between the Ottoman-Muslim tradition and the changing times, suggesting that Cevdet felt that a more balanced approach regarding Islam and the changing world was needed. In fact, the children of the palace, which included Sultan Abdulhamid II, would study Cevdet's Ottoman history, which encouraged the Sultan to make Cevdet one of his close policy advisors.

It is evident from Cevdet's early endeavour into history that he was also interested in learning lessons from the Ottoman and Islamic past. Cevdet believed that history could be the key to helping the empire learn from past mistakes, and as such, it was action-oriented to change its future. In addition to this, new technologies that included print culture exposed Cevdet to writing styles that were emerging from Western Europe. Cevdet was aware that a new medium—the emergence of print capitalism culture—and increasing literacy meant that a transition was needed in writing history that moved away from the established tradition of transmission

4 Turkish: *Mukaddime*

culture or works that promoted legend and folklore. Cevdet, like Ibn Khaldun before him, was critical of the way previous historians had written about the past but was also aware of the direction Western modes of writing history were taking and so sought to create a synthesis between the emergence of the Western tradition and the ideas of Ibn Khaldun and the Ottoman tradition that inspired him. It is evident, when reading *Tarih-i Cevdet,* that he was still of the opinion that history should provide lessons and have moral evaluations by the writer who can inform the reader of what is morally right and wrong. On closer inspection, this synthesis was a reflection of Cevdet's thought process; whether it was his writing of history, ideas on institutional reform, or the *Mecelle* (Ottoman Civil Code) project, Cevdet was a person who was trying to create a new medium of communication that was in line with the changing world but maintained its Islamic character. What Cevdet did not do, however, was articulate a theory or methodology of writing history for Muslims from an Islamic perspective. Perhaps this was because Cevdet did not feel it necessary, or maybe he did not think about it, as history was not a vocation pursued by many during his time.

Another was Khayruddīn al-Tūnisī, the Prime Minister of Tunisia in 1873-77 before he was dismissed and then later the Grand Vizier of the Ottoman Empire under Abdulhamid II in 1877-78. When reading the works of Khayruddīn al-Tūnisī, one can see that al-Tūnisī, too, was attempting to craft a way of writing history that was in conformity with the new styles of writing along lines that worked within the Islamic tradition. In his book titled *Aqwam al-masālik fī ma'rifat aḥwāl al-mamālik* (The Surest Path to Knowing the Condition of Kingdoms), he wrote in attempting to address the needs of reform in Tunisia and Ottoman domains. The work, which was written in both Arabic and French and later translated into Ottoman Turkish, was a work of history and politics that was addressed to the political class and *ʿulamāʾ* of both Tunisia and the Ottoman centre. Al-Tūnisī was clearly inspired by Ibn Khaldun when writing this book, as well as the *ʿulamāʾ*. It is not surprising that the first decade of Hamidian rule, which was probably the most stable, had thinkers who also had historical depth as advisors, such as Cevdet and al-Tūnisī. But like Cevdet, al-Tūnisī did not endeavour to write about the possibilities of establishing a methodology for writing history for Muslims.

It was not only in the Ottoman world that Muslims concluded the importance of history and how the *ummah* requires the vocation of history as part of its intellectual tradition. In India, we see the emergence of Muslim historians in the *Darul Uloom Nadwatul ʿUlamā* in which *ʿulamāʾ*, such as Sayyid Sulayman Nadwi and Shibli Numani, to name but a few, emerged. While these men were *ʿulamāʾ*, it is remarkable that they are most known for their foray into history writing. The concern for these *ʿulamāʾ* was the fact that history was being taught in the Western-style university setting in India under the British colonial occupation. This led to the *ʿulamāʾ* of *al-Nadwa* believing that Muslims needed to write history for themselves. As a result, Indian Muslim historians of the eighteenth and nineteenth centuries started to ask how history should be written and for whom. These scholars came to believe that there was a need to write Islamic history in general, the history of Muslim personalities and Indian history of which Islam was a feature, firstly for Indian Muslims, and secondly in a contemporary manner that was from the Islamic tradition but also applicable to audiences at the time. By recognising that readers had changed, especially after the introduction of print press culture and new forms of print writing formats, a new theme was introduced by some of the Indian Muslim historians. Rather than establishing an Islamic methodology for writing history, different approaches to different audiences would be taken. This meant, for example, when writing for Muslims, increased Islamic terminology and references were given added to the notion of providing lessons. However, there was also a need to address the academic circles and write in a manner of confronting problem areas that were emerging from orientalist writers. Hence, responding to these writers meant being able to also write in an academic style in accordance with the rules the secular academy had set. It was an approach of writing in different styles to different audiences; one audience was internal, and the other required an edifying engagement.

Other concerns arose, of course. One of them was whether history writing can be seen as an act of *dawah* or not, and another was whether the purpose of writing is to inform or invite people to Islam. The paradox was that, on one hand, there was a need to defend the Islamic tradition and Muslims from historians from a colonial tradition, but on the other hand, there was also a need to present Islamic history as an ethical civilisation that reflected Islam's moral principles as a whole. Shibli Numani, probably one of the more famous Indian Muslim historians of the period, felt that the traditional Islamic history culture in India, which was usually the recording of events, was reflective more of a Persianate tradition of writing and ought to be adjusted to develop a new way of writing history for the Muslims of India. While that new way was not established by Numani, he nonetheless started to focus on the historicity of Indian history, as negative impressions of Islam were being presented from a historical point of view. For Numani, studying the past was about discovering or rediscovering human societies but also dispelling falsehoods about Islam and Muslims.

Additionally, a concern of the Indian *'ulamā'* of *Nadwatul Ulamā* was that Muslims in India were facing severe challenges, firstly regarding self-identity and how to place themselves both within the greater tradition of Islam and the *ummah* that went beyond time and space, and secondly of being Indian Muslims that shared space with Hindus, Christians, and other peoples under British occupation. As a result, the attempt was to address this by having new thought producers, produce publications, books, textbooks, journals and newspaper articles, and then build curricula, syllabi and institutions for Muslims. In that sense, the Muslims of India went for an approach of both macro-history and micro-history writing, in which works on the *Sīrah*, previous Muslim dynasties, and the history of Islam and Muslims in the Asian sub-continent were written.

It is somewhat interesting to note that some of the concerns of Muslim thinkers during the eighteenth and nineteenth centuries still resonate today, as while many of these actions were initiated by the nineteenth century, by World War II, many of these initiatives faded away as worthy projects of investment as Muslim concerns moved to other matters. Muslim thinkers during the colonial period were concerned about the loss of a memory of the Islamic tradition from the minds of the Muslims as a result of colonial violence, occupation, and disruption. Furthermore, these disruptions created breaks in links to the past, links to traditions, memory, culture, and education, all methods by which Islam was passed down from one generation to another. As a result, the imperative to revive history as a vocation was on the minds of many at the time.

What does a Historian do?

While I have mentioned the importance of narrative, historians are not simply storytellers or merely people who talk about the past. As learning is an act of acquiring knowledge that already exists, one could naturally argue that everything we learn is about the past. As a result, it is easy to understand why, to some degree, we all tend to think we can dabble in the act of writing about the past. But the job of the historian is not simply to speak of the past but to be as accurate as possible, applying the correct sources, whether primary or secondary, examining them in the appropriate manner, and framing the details so that they are reflective of what actually transpired.

Additionally, a historian needs to attain a level of learning where they can effectively analyse the sources and interpret the past in a way that not only gives meaning to us today but also is the best representation of the point that they are explaining. The historian is not simply trained to examine the sources but to be able to verify their validity, their biases and their flaws and place them within the correct context. Historians thus deal with two types of sources, archival sources and secondary sources, and attempt to examine the validity of both.

Archival sources are pieces of evidence for the historian but are not necessarily proof. People often use "evidence" and "proof" interchangeably because, in everyday conversation, they both relate to showing that something is true. When someone presents evidence, they might feel it's strong enough to prove a point or argument, even if it isn't conclusive in a formal sense. The distinction between the two terms can seem blurry when someone has gathered compelling evidence, making it feel like they have already proven something. In casual contexts, the nuances between the terms aren't always emphasised, so people may use "proof" when they mean "evidence" or vice versa, especially when they believe the evidence they have presented is strong enough to convince others. However, while evidence consists of facts or information that support a claim, proof is the final conclusion drawn from evaluating that evidence, establishing the truth beyond a reasonable doubt.

Evidence supports a claim, while proof establishes its certainty. There are primary sources that can serve as proof of a particular issue. For instance, we have conclusive proof that the Prophet ﷺ was the final Messenger and Prophet. In contrast, sources like *ḥadīth* provide evidence on practices, such as whether to pray with one's hands folded or by the side. However, these are evidence, not conclusive proof, as they do not definitively establish one method of praying as more valid than the other. Similarly, historians may rely on archival material and need to be aware of whether primary sources are an indication of proof or are evidence to point to one's interpretation. For example, showing that the Ottomans occasionally banned coffee and coffee houses. However, the reasons behind these bans remain unclear, leading historians to speculate that they may have been motivated by religious, political, or social factors. As a result, historians must be cautious in distinguishing between what constitutes evidence and what is conclusive enough to be regarded as proof.

Some historians may argue that all three examples mentioned above regarding the banning of coffee are reasons which act as proof, but the act of interpretation is required by the historian for why they think the way they do regarding any piece of evidence they use. Historians can often have the same evidence but still disagree on what the evidence actually indicates. Sometimes historians have to deal with the act of the absence of proof or evidence, for example, a popular assumption is that Sultan Beyazid II had a *fatwa* declared to ban the printing press. While this assumption has become an internalised narrative, there is neither concrete proof nor evidence of the existence of the *fatwa*, apart from a claim that has stuck. In such cases, historians would ask for the evidence to be able to substantiate the claim. While many will argue that while the evidence cannot be found, they will justify the claim based on outcome by suggesting the fact that the Ottomans were not using the printed press during the time of invention and that this is the proof that it is likely that it was banned, even if the supposed *fatwa* that is often mentioned does not exist.

As for secondary sources, these are usually works written by historians who have undertaken research. They may have used archival sources in their work. Historians would often also cross-examine the works that are published in secondary works, as different historians may vary in opinion. Thus, the trained historian does not simply take both archival sources or secondary sources as fact but scrutinises both.

As a result, the historian has to deal with two matters here. The first is the need to have evidence in order to make a definitive claim, and the second is that if there is no evidence, to be clear that the position held is speculative. As a result, the historian is not simply trained, for example, in learning languages to understand the written text that they may be reading, but will need the skills to interpret other sources, such as maps, photographs, and inscriptions. For example, we do not have historical concrete proof with regard to the existence of Ertuğrul Gazi, father of Osman Gazi the founder of the Ottoman Empire. But we do have a coin that has the inscription "Osman Gazi, son of Ertuğrul Gazi". We take from this that we know that a man named Ertuğrul existed and that he was the father of Osman, simply because minting coins was undertaken by a political authority. In fact, minting coins, especially in the Islamic tradition, was more often a reflection of the right of a Muslim authority, leader or government, which suggests that there is evidence for the existence of a man named Ertuğrul. Historians will also verify the validity of the coin to check if it is forgery or not, and in this case, the coin seems to have been verified to be coined during the time of the early Ottoman *beylik* (principality).

It is not only archives that historians examine but secondary literature too. Much of what we do as historians is to make meaning from the evidence available to us. The only way we can do that is to depend on existing literature or a corpus of works that, via some form of consensus, provides the additional information and places the evidence within a historical frame. Secondary sources are, therefore, seen as pieces of work that have gone through some form of vigorous examination by fellow historians regarding the validity of the ideas that have been presented. By going through such a process, it is assumed that the work produced has at least been based on the premise that evidence was provided. That does not mean that the works of individuals or even a collective cannot be compromised for whatever reason, and historians may disagree with a claim, interpretation of a piece of evidence provided, or a general narrative that is held by a wide range of scholars.

An example of the reinterpretation of a piece of evidence is that for decades many historians of the Ottoman Empire placed the *Gülhane* Edict of 1839 as a document that was inspired by the ideals of the French Revolution due to the notion that the Ottomans were attempting to reform their empire in the image of the Western European nations. While the document, which started with the *Basmala,* made mention of the *Sharīa* and addressed the Muslims, earlier historians of the Ottoman Empire claimed that these were simply attempts to place an Islamic veneer to appease local public opinion. Additionally, when the document suggested that it was the responsibility of the Ottoman government to protect one's life, religion, property and honour, historians argued that this was proof of the *Gülhane* taking ideas from the French Revolution. This was the dominant interpretation until the works of the Palestinian Christian academic Butrus Abū Manneh and later others, showed that there were a host of drafts of the *Gülhane* written by the *ʿulamāʾ*, that many of the architects of the document were religious Muslims, and that the ideas of protecting life, religion, property, and honour were principles found in Islamic works that predated the Ottomans. This new reading by Manneh impacted many Ottoman historians to re-examine the once-held collective position and influenced many historians to revise their interpretation of the *Gülhane* document and the way that the late Ottoman Empire was framed. Of course, not all historians accepted Manneh's interpretation; there was even pushback, but the point here is to suggest that even positions that have been verified by a fraternity can still be challenged. Historians are aware of this and do their best to not only examine different forms of evidence but also secondary sources.

As historians, we do not only examine sources, of course. Additionally, there are other matters which historians should take into consideration when examining the past. Indeed, the past should resonate in order for us to feel connected and attain meaning, but the past can also be a distant place that is very different in comparison to today. It is important to make sure we do not see the past anachronistically, meaning we do not see the past through today's lens. Our job as historians is to understand the past, not necessarily place a moral judgement on it, even though one can, of course, critique what had happened. The idea is to not obscure our understanding of the past no matter how abhorrent it may be or how nostalgic we may feel about it, because in doing so, we speak of the past with what we feel should have happened rather than what actually did.

I see that in many Muslim circles, we do not often pay attention to the whys and hows of history, but rather to the "what ifs". This leads to what some historians have called "present-mindedness". Historians need to be careful not to create unwarranted continuities with the past as they attempt to join the dots from the past to the present. One of the pitfalls is when people do not appreciate the past for what it was but rather what it ought to have been, from the prism of how we see the world now. This can influence the historian to sometimes incorrectly join dots that are not related, or to ignore evidence that is contrary to their claim, or to include or interpret evidence that is weak or unrelated. While I do encourage many of my students to use their imagination to examine "what if" a particular act, event or phenomenon had or had not happened, to encourage their creative thought process and try to encourage empathy; nonetheless it is still important to be able to appreciate what happened, why and how so that we can better make sense of it. As a result, the historian's responsibility is to attempt to interpret the past in a manner that best reflects the conditions of that time.

Additionally, as I have mentioned, the past is a distant place. Thus, for example, it is important to understand the social and geographic nature of Arabia during the advent of Islam in order to appreciate how different it is from today, or how the populations were far different in the past than today or how the technology we have today makes the world starkly different to a world that was devoid of the technology we use. Concepts such as freedom in the nineteenth century may have a different meaning to the way we understand it today, and a world where there was no nationalism is quite different from the world we live in today. In that sense, a key objective of the historian is to establish the **continuities** and **changes**, how societies, ideas, politics, and technology, for example, have continued from the past and where and how they have changed.

As we continuously refine our understanding of the past, we are also shaping our present knowledge. In this sense, we are constantly influencing our past, present, and future, much like time travellers. Similar to many science fiction stories, altering events in the past has consequences for the present and future. A good example of this is the long-held belief that the Ottomans banned the printed press, which was accepted for decades, only for contemporary historians to disprove that claim. This shift not only changes the historical narrative of the Ottoman Empire but also alters our current understanding of it. As a result, future generations may view the Ottomans in a different light compared to how previous generations did.

In addition to this, a good historian will be able to examine the ideas of **cause** and **effect**. If one is to learn from experiences of the past, the trained historian will be able to tell you that the cause of an event, act or moment, would have consequences, thus an effect. But the cause-and-effect study requires a real detailed examination. Sometimes these could be single events; for example, Selim III's creation of a new army called the *Nizam-i Cedid (al-Niẓām al-jadīd)* caused a Janissary reaction. But at other times, a cause could have happened, and its effect would have been felt a long time later, and on other occasions, historians may examine multiple causes that created a particular effect.

This leads to my next point: when examining the past, we historians are aware that **context** matters. Too often, people will make the claim that the Ottomans banned the printed press, or that the Ottomans abandoned the *Sharīa*, or that they were in decline. We fail to give context, nor do we appreciate the **complexity**. I will come to complexity soon, but I want to address the idea of context. Context matters, as it provides the details of otherwise rather abstract statements, such as the ones I have just mentioned about the Ottomans. In particular, we historians stress the context, as we are aware that in the contemporary world that we live in, politicians, journalists, and people on social media make statements about a given event but provide no real context. The absence of context, in many ways, is designed to reduce the complexity of any given historical moment. Some may even mention the situation is complicated, but by not providing context and, in fact, use the notion of complexity to avoid providing any details. As a result, historians should attempt to provide reasons, choices, circumstances, the prevailing worldview, or convictions people had when something in the past took place. Context provides the much-needed layers and details for people to understand matters in a more profound manner. To provide and explain the context is to place the historical event in its rightful place regarding all the attained information related to it.

This leads us to the need for **complexity**. More recently, *imams* and untrained Muslim public figures as storytellers have started to present history as simply the act of storytelling the past. While they may have correctly recognised that people find this method well suited for them to be invested in history, what they ignore, at times, is complexity, as that act requires extensive research. When telling stories, the need for complexity is seen as not important, where people simply want to either be entertained or lack the required historical depth, and so storytellers will simplify history in order to adhere to the needs of the audience—on many occasions very large ones, especially on the Internet—by giving them a reduced narrative of the past. While storytelling has its place, it must be subject to the historical sensibilities and questions of the trained historian. The historian may not so much "provide complexity" but understands how to navigate the complexity of historical periods, causes, and effects, to provide a coherent narrative and interpretation. For example, a storyteller may argue that the Abbasid Revolt against the Umayyads occurred because the Umayyads were corrupt. This type of framing may or may not be true, but what it does is reduce the narrative to one which says that the Umayyads were corrupt, and so they were bad, and the Abbasids revolted against them, and so they were good. This type of storytelling, which we see in the movies and by politicians, and now more and more by *khaṭībs* (Muslims who deliver sermons) and social media content creators, is devoid of any complexities. It is very possible that the Umayyads had become corrupt, but does that mean the Abbasids were good? For most historians, they would examine this type of framing by trying to understand the tensions the Umayyads had with succession, the emergence of a new group of Muslims called the *Mawali*, the rapid extension of the Muslim world, fiscal tensions, outside threats from the Eastern Roman Empire, and the emergence of new ideas that eventually created the conditions for the Abbasids to revolt. Historians may also argue that the Abbasid revolutionaries were not a homogenous bloc, and just like all revolutionary groups, they were an umbrella of different factions who moved against the Umayyads for different reasons. By presenting history in this manner, the historian attempts to raise the level of thinking of the audience and perhaps give them a more profound and more nuanced understanding of the Abbasid Revolution. Once we learn the complexity of a situation, while one may still want to present one side as good and the other as bad, in reality, this question is not as significant, and instead, it can be possible that neither side is good nor bad, and, in fact, the conditions are simply complicated.

Another matter that historians deal with is the matter of **human agency** and the choices people make. On occasions, especially in many fields where methodology, discourse or paradigms are central to the construction of the ideas of a writer, human agency tends to become secondary, to the point that an inevitability is presented where people are given little to no agency. This means that due to a particular action(s), an inevitable outcome is projected. But such inevitability is only realised when we have the advantage of hindsight. But at the time, the outcome may not have been inevitable, as human beings do have agency. Just like how a weak sports team plays a superior opponent in a cup final, one may suggest that the better team is likely to win, but suggesting their victory is inevitable denies a fundamental principle in human behaviour, which is that the outcome is unknown and is not inevitable. What untrained and, at times, trained academics may do is that once they know the result, they may project the inevitability of the outcome, but as historians, we are trained to be careful in such projections on the past. An example in a historical context is when people talk of the decline of the Ottoman Empire. What is known as the "decline paradigm" implied that the Ottomans were inevitably in decline, and there was no way to stop it. In doing so, human agency is either removed or presented as being unable to make changes or stop the trajectory of events, as their agency is not important. But much of what happens, whether in the past or now, is dependent on the choices and actions human beings take. Historians are careful not to fall into the trap of fatalism, and while we have the vantage point of being able to see the consequences of people's actions, a good historian is also aware to not diminish or ignore the notion of free will that Allah has provided us.

Additionally, one of my main concerns is that not only do people at times take away human agency, but they equally ignore the **agency of Allah**. While I accept that it is much harder or even impossible to prove Allah's support, or guidance in any given matter or moment, independent of when He mentions it in the Qur'an or when it was mentioned by the Prophet ﷺ, nonetheless, it is still important to acknowledge at least that Allah not only has agency but has the ultimate agency. It is important to be aware of this point since history has been presented as a science in Western academia, and the mere mention of Allah is perceived as being unscientific.

By centring human beings while denying Allah's agency, we risk adopting a perspective that reduces our understanding of the past and present to mere human constructs, often shaped by ideologies like modernity. This secular framework can strip away the spiritual dimensions that give meaning to our experiences, treating time and history as if they exist independently of divine influence. Such an ideology may inadvertently place humans in a role that overlooks their relationship with the divine, leading to a fragmented view of existence. Recognising Allah's agency allows for a more holistic understanding of history, where human actions are seen as part of a larger divine narrative. It invites a perspective that respects both the spiritual and material dimensions of life, offering a deeper sense of meaning and purpose. This interplay between divine and human agency is crucial for a comprehensive understanding of our place in the world and the significance of our choices.

The Ideology Behind History Writing

Two main issues that emerge regarding the vocation of history are, firstly, the writing of history itself, where people often contest the validity of an event, idea, or narrative. The second issue is the practice of history writing. This issue often refers to the "objectivity" and "subjectivity" of the vocation and/or the historian. The contestation surrounding historical narratives is significant. Different perspectives, cultural backgrounds, and ideologies can lead to varying interpretations of the same event. This can result in debates over validity, where individuals or groups advocate for their version of history. These disputes often reflect broader societal conflicts and can influence how history is taught, remembered, and understood. As such, the writing of history becomes a dynamic process, shaped by power relations and the contexts in which historians operate. The question of objectivity is central to historical practice. While historians strive for accuracy and truth, complete objectivity is challenging, if not impossible. Every historian brings their own perspectives, biases, and interpretations to their work. This subjectivity can enrich historical narratives by introducing diverse viewpoints but can also lead to selective interpretations. The interpretive nature of history means that personal and cultural contexts inevitably shape how events are understood and presented.

Ultimately, while historians aim to uncover truths about the past, the vocation itself is deeply intertwined with both subjective experiences and the ongoing dialogues about what constitutes history. This recognition invites a more nuanced approach to understanding history, acknowledging the interplay between evidence, interpretation, and the historian's role in shaping narratives.

All human endeavour is limited to human effort. History writing and historians are not immune to this. There are many reasons why historians may get things wrong, and it was for this reason that Ibn Khaldun criticised Muslim historians who were prone to error, knowingly or unknowingly. But ever since the nineteenth century, when the modern vocation of history was perceived as being a scientific endeavour, people who read works of history have had the expectation that what they are reading is the closest to the truth based on the premise that the archival and empirical data are entirely factual and objective indicators of the truth. However, even primary sources require interpretation and are at the mercy of the way the historian understands the evidence available to them. Historians can make errors for many reasons, such as misunderstanding evidence or misunderstanding the reality and context. Some may be partisan, whereas others may take previous ideas and works as a given. It is rare within the academy that a historian's attempt to be "objective" is questioned, as the field expects that this is the least a secular historian ought to do. Objectivity is expected from the style that we produce and write. I would argue, however, that even the so-called objectivity within the academic space requires scrutiny, as a secular approach to history is not objective but rather from the viewpoint of secular ideology. However, more recently, criticism from Muslims towards the vocation has increased due to ideological undertones, such as Orientalism, Eurocentric framings, or Marxist ideologies, to name a few, that are present in the knowledge process. As a result, many Muslims today ask whether the history that emerged from the Western Academic space is fair to Muslims and Islam.

Primarily, this leads to the question of how Islam is conceptualised. For Muslims, Islam is the *din* (religion) which provides them a route to salvation, both in this life and the next. As a result, Muslims evaluate Islam from within, where the sacred is central to their knowledge output. Western academia, however, inherently subscribes to a "secular consciousness" within its culture of knowledge production. As a result, "secular objectivity" simply looks like an evaluation of the sacred by the antithesis of the sacred worldview. This raises the question: who writes for Islam and Muslims, and is it possible for Western academia to be able to fairly write about Islam and Muslims? This is because while presumed secular objectivity is perceived as being neutral, it is nonetheless antagonistic in essence towards religion and Islam. Secular objectivity rejects the truth of Islam and rather places it under the notion of just another religious "truth-claim". Its epistemic paradigm often prioritises empirical evidence and rationality, which can dismiss and overlook the spiritual and cultural dimensions that are central to many religious narratives. As a result, historical interpretations from a purely secular standpoint may not resonate with or reflect the beliefs and values of religious communities; this is the case regarding Islam. It is for this reason that Muslims have not been surprised that Orientalist, Zionist, Eurocentric, Nation-state narratives and Marxist critiques of Muslims and Islam are seen as far more noxious, as they can portray Islamic history and cultures through a lens that emphasises Western superiority or distort complex realities, leading to a one-dimensional view of Islam.

Needless to say, there have been a host of academics who have written valuable works on Muslims, Islamic history, and Islam. Many of whom have been Muslim. It is not for me to question their sincerity or contributions that have furthered our understanding of the past. However, it does still point to the question of whether history can be written from an Islamic perspective that can give meaning to Muslims, especially as, since the nineteenth century, history writing has tended to be dominated by Western secular methods, while there may be no room in the corridors of academia for an Islamic approach or experiment. As a result, it is worth examining not only some of the problem areas that were raised by Ibn Khaldun regarding the traps that could lead to error for the Muslim historian but also how contemporary history writing also has its own set of traps that a Muslim reader and/or a historian ought to be aware of.

As I have just mentioned, I have no need to doubt whether a historian, a book, or a project has *attempted* to be objective in accordance with the secular tradition. But whether the criticism is from within an Islamic framing or one from academia itself, there is something to be said regarding the modern discipline of history and how Islam fits within it. The historian and critic of modernity, Eric Hobsbawm, is correct in making the case that much, if not all, of the Muslim world is under the ideological yoke of nation-state narratives. Hobsbawm made the case that nationalist narratives tend to forget history, or rather, manipulate it, in order to facilitate their own fictitious claims to a "national" historical narrative and memory. What these "official" historiographies do is that they relegate or ignore their own histories prior to the creation of the nation-state. This is what is called the "founder paradigm", in which history before the founding of the nation-state is seen as decadent. Some historians have called this the "decadent thesis", in which the histories prior to the emergence of the nation-states are seen through a host of negative propositions. There is no disputing that the various national narratives were ideological, and while, on the one hand, they attempted to present themselves as movements that escaped the colonial yoke, on the other hand, they presented previous moments as either irrelevant or decedent.

Some thinkers have thus suggested that this was due to the dominance of Eurocentric impressions and interpretations of the Muslim world, in which, from the nineteenth century onwards, Muslim societies were seen from a Eurocentric lens—what Edward Said popularised as Orientalism. Whether Orientalism as a term is appropriate in describing this phenomenon is up for debate, as there were many Muslim and non-Muslim thinkers who had criticised how Western Europeans viewed the "non-West". But what is worth noting about Said's framing is the suggestion that nationalist and liberal thinkers in the Muslim world did internalise certain tropes that reflected a "self-Orientalisation" as thinkers attempted to place themselves and their national projects within the framework of belonging to the group of civilised nations, which in the nineteenth century was seen as being Western European, and today can be seen as being led by America. However, while in the Muslim world, thinkers may have internalised and perhaps instrumentalised a host of Eurocentric tropes about their historical past, it should be noted that Orientalist academics have provided ample works on the Muslim world and Islam, and this has not found an equivalent project in the Muslim world regarding Islamic history. That is not to say that works in Islamicate languages have not been undertaken, but unfortunately, many works in Arabic, Ottoman Turkish and the like still require to be translated for an English reading audience to be able to benefit from. Both Orientalist and nationalist works are influential because they are the primary works visible. While many Muslims have internalised certain tropes, Muslim critics of nationalistic fabrications and Orientalists' untruths have led other Muslims to question to what degree the practice of history can be reflective of the Muslim experience and Islam, more specifically, and Muslims would not be wrong to have such sceptical positions.

The Muslim Malaysian thinker, scholar, and philosopher Sayyid Muhammad al-Naquib al-Attas, when speaking about how Islam came to the Malay Archipelago, made the case that Orientalist historians, when writing about this subject matter, deliberately overlooked, if not outright missed, many matters that their worldview would negate. Al-Attas' concern was that most historical works on the Malay people were written by Orientalists. For al-Attas, the criticism towards Orientalists had merit—however, he was far more interested in the roots of Orientalist discourse. For him, to which I agree, Orientalism was simply a product of a secularist outlook on Islam and the world. Al-Attas argued that while there is much truth that can be attained from writing history within a Western academic framework, the issue of knowledge being secular meant that many indigenous ways in which Islam may manifest are negated. In the case of Malaysia, al-Attas critiqued how Orientalist thinkers focused on tradesmen bringing Islam to the Malay world, suggesting that the interests of the people primarily lay in their worldly benefits and very little else. Al-Attas does not reject that Muslim tradesmen who arrived from places such as Yemen had an impact on the region, but al-Attas also goes on to explain that members of the *ʿulamāʾ*, Sufi shaykhs and peoples of notable families also came with the sole intention of spreading Islam. He also stresses that beyond the empirical data, if one examines folklore, marionette puppet stories, mythologies, poetry, and other mediums beyond law and trade, one may see how Islam was creatively being presented to the people in unique and indigenous ways.

A final point worth noting about al-Attas is that he also includes the idea of intuition as a tool of a good historian, which is ignored within academia. There is no doubting al-Attas' thoroughness in examining archives and going beyond the plain and obvious; he is a grounded thinker. In fact, for someone like al-Attas, the need to be twice as thorough becomes important simply due to the possibility that Western secular academia, from its own restricted paradigm, may choose to reject the propositions he put forward. Furthermore, as I just mentioned, the idea of intuition, which is hard to substantiate in a simple setting, is worth negotiating with in regard to Muslim thinkers who write about their past. As Muslims, we seek inspiration from Allah and make it very clear to ignore/reject inspiration from *Iblīs* (the devil). Intuition is not mere speculation where one places blind trust. Intuition is a concept which includes sincerity, spirituality, and sensory knowledge and experience to help them investigate a particular claim, especially if their lived experiences can be informative in understanding a particular reality. For example, as a Muslim historian knowing the culture and knowledge of Islam, my intuition has led me to search for answers beyond the obvious: answers found beyond just written documentation, but perhaps in oral traditions, cultural practices, art, or architecture. As a Muslim, I have often found academic claims based on a secular understanding of the Muslim to sound improbable, resulting in me scrutinising the claim. The Muslim historian must turn to Allah for inspiration and—if out of sincere hope that inspiration is given—must then be open-minded in recognising that answers may be found in places that may not be considered "scientific" in the Western sense but *'ilmī* in the Islamic sense: where experience, knowledge of Islam and Muslims, and one's senses provide one with an intuition to investigate certain claims.

This leads to my next point, which is how the writing of history is seen as a positivist-scientific exercise. Since the internalisation of secularism within the Western purview, scientific knowledge is perceived as being the highest form of knowledge, in which "facts" as truth can only be found through the scientific method. The idea of scientific knowledge is based on observable and measurable phenomena which rely on data gathered through experiments, observations, and investigations, and that scientific findings should be reproducible by others using the same methods. This consistency helps ensure the reliability of the results and leaves very little room for interpretive thinking. Since the nineteenth century, the vocation of history in the West has also been heavily influenced by this type of thinking. In historical inquiry, the validity of claims often hinges on the availability of empirical data, such as documents, artefacts, and eyewitness accounts. Historians seek to construct narratives based on evidence, but this evidence can be incomplete or subject to interpretation. In the humanities, including history, the notion of truth often involves a broader understanding of human experiences, contexts, and meanings. Not every aspect of human life can be distilled into empirical facts, and interpretations may vary based on cultural, philosophical, and emotional dimensions. Whereas scientific knowledge is often based on the idea or attaining facts, in the humanities, the notion is based on attaining truth as not every matter can be a fact.

On a rudimentary level, the main difference between fact and truth is that a fact is seen as an objective statement that can be verified and is based on empirical evidence. For example, "Water boils at 100 degrees Celsius at sea level" is a fact because it can be tested and confirmed. While facts themselves are objective and verifiable truths, their interpretation, presentation, or omission can be influenced by ideological perspectives. This manipulation often occurs in subtle ways, allowing individuals or groups to shape narratives that align with their worldview or political, religious, or social agendas. There are many ways that facts can be manipulated, some of which include selective readings, confirmation bias, and the manner in which facts are framed, just to name a few. Truth can be seen as more subjective and can encompass a broader range of beliefs, interpretations, and perspectives and often reflects a deeper understanding, context, or moral consideration that goes beyond mere data. While empirical data and facts are foundational to both disciplines, the humanities embrace a more nuanced understanding of truth that considers the complexities of human experience, culture, and interpretation. This distinction allows historians to explore the richness of the past beyond mere data points. However, it goes without saying that empirical evidence and all other forms of testable evidence or proof are necessary to make a claim about truth.

The question is whether history writing and the endeavour of the historian should be based on being factual as a reflection of attempting to establish what is true? Part of the problem with this way of thinking is that it creates a narrow purview for the historian where many forms of knowledge may be rejected simply because these forms are not seen as being scientific or scientific enough. In these cases, religious texts are rejected, and so are people's experiences. Making moral judgements such as citing that a particular *ʿālim* was sincere in his endeavour to write a book will be seen as irrelevant as this is not scientifically observable. I want to stress it is not that historians do not deal with writing about factual matters, as this is indeed a form that historians deal with, but it is also important to recognise firstly, when one makes a claim that something is a historical fact, that is it indeed a fact or an attempt to represent the truth. Too often, historical narratives will be presented as if they are fact in order for them not to be questioned, and yet on closer inspection, the point made may not be a fact at all. Additionally, due to the popularity of scientific knowledge and its vocabulary, people often tend to forget that in the humanities, historians also deal with other methods apart from just empirical data.

It is not only with regards to data in which this idea is applied; it is even in terminology and ideas that fit the scientific framing about life that have impacted the way we historians write about the past. Ideas such as progress, modernity, and innovation are seen in a positive light. Why does the idea of something being new imply that it ought to be desirable? In many ways, when writing history, contemporary historians tend to write about the historical progress of a given nation or people and then judge those people based on how progress is viewed. By placing history within the purview of it being a scientific endeavour, there is greater emphasis on data gathering over narrative, although narrative writing can be viewed as an act of fiction, perhaps. As a result, it is better to view historians who will attempt to provide the best interpretation of reality based on the tools, evidence and personal skills available to them. Their works will then be put into the public space for testing.

While academia has mechanisms of criticising Marxist ideology, Orientalism, Coloniality and so on, these are nonetheless self-criticisms of knowledge writing that still belong to a secular worldview about life. How does the Muslim historian write about Islam? My case at this point would be to ensure that the production of knowledge be in conformity to the Islamic *ʿaqīdah* and the Qur'an and *Sunnah*. Ibn Khaldun was aware of the challenges that interpretive knowledge has when writing about the past. The "*ʿilm*" of history in Islam is not the same as the "science" of history in Western academia. *ʿIlm* in Islam, while loosely translated as science in English, does not understand knowledge in the same way secular knowledge has understood scientific knowledge. In Islam, Allah, the principles of the Qur'an and *Sunnah*, the ethics and morals of Islam, and the reason for truth-seeking are based on a different set of "scientific" principles. As a result, the key to writing Islamic history for the Muslim is to have a consciousness of *Tawhid* over the secular. That ideology, narrative and language must be subservient to the *ʿaqīdah* of Islam.

Interpretive writing requires an endeavour to be objective and truthful and requires responsive writing that provides ideas and thoughts from the historian; otherwise, the works have very little meaning and are an exercise in data collection. Interpretive writing strives for objectivity by grounding interpretations in evidence, and while aiming for objectivity, interpretive writing also seeks to convey truth in a broader sense. This involves acknowledging the complexity of human experiences. Subjectivity plays a crucial role in the interpretive writing process as each writer brings their own perspectives, emotions, and insights to the narrative, which can enrich the interpretation. This subjectivity allows for a deeper exploration of a host of meanings. It is for this reason I argue that the binary of objective truth and subjective experience being compared as if secular objectivity is the only quest for truth, and any Islamic objective in the subject is seen as a biased enterprise, negating the realisation that the two need not be in contradiction. Objectivity does not equate to truth but rather a process of truth-seeking, and subjectivity does not equate to falsehood but rather experience that can help the reader.

Another point worth mentioning is the issue of narrative. Narrative and ideology are closely linked. While ideology shapes the given assumption about Islam, a group of people, or events, it is narrative which provides the emotive ability to join the dots to create a thesis. Narrative, in many ways, can be far more influential and dangerous when it comes to the manner in which Islamic history is written, as people rarely challenge narratives in the way they do ideology. There has been much criticism of ideological trends within the academic world, but criticism of narrative construction less so. A part of this could be due to the fact that the theory of narratives is discussed in other disciplines, such as literature, translation studies, or media and communication studies.

However, narrative writing is a central theme within the field of history. The danger of narratives is that people are often unskilled in challenging established narratives, as it requires, at times, emotive attachments to narratives because the narratives provide meaning to those who choose to believe in them. Whereas ideologies can be challenged regarding the particular beliefs within a given ideology, with narratives, historians are often asked to disprove deeply held assumptions that have taken root because they have just been repeated over and over. The main difference between ideology and narrative is that ideology refers to a system of beliefs, values, or ideas that shape how individuals or groups understand and interact with the world, whereas a narrative is a structured account of events, experiences, or stories. A narrative can be fictional or non-fictional and is often used to convey meaning, context, or lessons. Ideologies are often more rigid and systematic than narratives. They can encompass a wide range of beliefs, from political ideologies to cultural or religious ideologies. Ideologies can shape narratives by framing how stories are told and what is emphasised or marginalised. They often seek to establish a dominant viewpoint, which can limit the diversity of narratives that are recognised or valued, but narratives also have the capacity to challenge or subvert ideologies.

The key here is to understand that people very rarely challenge assumptions in the narratives. Firstly, because they do not appreciate that the narratives carry implicit assumptions about values, beliefs, and perspectives. These assumptions shape how the story is told and what is considered important or relevant. Secondly, people are often not trained to deconstruct narratives—that requires trained historians. As a result, people adopt narratives as they perceive them as being believable. The fact that many people may not realise that narratives have built-in assumptions leads them to accept them at face value. This can prevent critical engagement and deeper analysis, allowing certain viewpoints to dominate without question. A skilled historian is able to deconstruct narratives by presenting evidence or highlighting—which is more common—the absence of evidence, as people are rather attuned to believing what is plausible rather than to critically examine evidence. Cognitive biases also play a role in how people process narratives. Confirmation bias, for example, leads individuals to favour information that aligns with their existing beliefs, making them less likely to question the underlying assumptions of a narrative. Part of being a historian is to continuously challenge the ingrained beliefs of a given narrative by challenging assumptions in narratives. This is vital for developing a more nuanced understanding of history, culture, and society. Encouraging critical thinking and awareness can help individuals recognise the complexities and biases within narratives, leading to richer discussions and interpretations.

Historians do not have to simply deal with narratives on a meta-level; rather, at times, there are a host of embedded narratives that are created within a given meta-narrative. The challenge with narrative is that while ideologies provide the belief system to a group of people, narratives provide context and meaning, which are rarely questioned. When there are meta-narratives within, historians are forced to put out multiple fires. An example is the meta-narratives that the late Ottomans were anti-technology and fell behind regarding the Industrial Revolution. This meta-narrative then has other narratives layered within it, where people assume that the Ottomans banned the printed press, that the Calligraphers were anti-technology, that literacy rates were low as a result, and so on. Most of the time, a historian's time is wasted in dispelling these narratives that have been internalised by the community without much resistance and have shaped how they see the past and themselves now. Then, Muslims demand that Muslim historians deconstruct each and every one of these narratives to validate their positions. It is for this reason that I want to highlight how narratives, especially those based on falsehoods that have created believable assumptions, need to be taken into consideration by students of history.

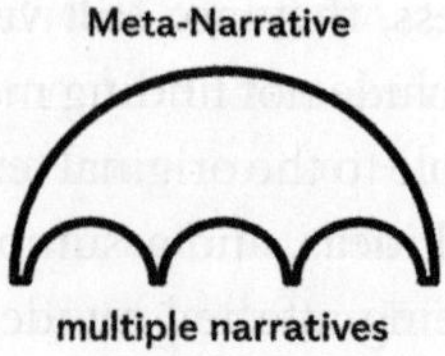

Finally, I want to stress the importance of ideology in translation. Translation is not a simple practice where one just translates a word or idea from one language to another. Languages belong to a family of languages; they are part of cultures, they shape and have been shaped by traditions, and languages evolve and change over time. The exercise of translation is a loaded exercise in which many faculties are required, as very rarely do languages translate with ease or smoothly. It is true that some languages translate from one language to another smoother than others, but the act of translation is something most historians engage in, as primary and even secondary texts are often found in multiple languages.

Fundamentally, there are two ways that one could translate a sentence; the first is to do a literal translation. This can often be done with simple sentence constructions. However, with more complex ideas, proverbs, and idiomatic expressions, the idea that one can make a literal translation is just not plausible. This leads to the second method, which is that the translator exercises a pattern of thought in which they derive meaning. This is the act of the translator doing their best to try to attain the best translation possible and reach the essence of the text. But this is no easy exercise, and one text could be translated in multiple ways by various translators. In fact, translation is such a laborious process that translators will go through many translations to arrive at the best meaning of a given text.

While one would hope that a translator is objective and does their best to find the closest meaning of the text that they are translating, nonetheless, they are still vulnerable to a host of challenges that can include not finding meaning in the translated language comparable to the original text, to being influenced by ideologies, cultural ideas, and assumptions. Translators are not excluded from being affected by ideological assumptions. This is why when you pick up a copy of the English-translated Qur'an, you may find multiple different translations, not simply of the whole Qur'an but each *āyāt*. Translators who go through this process must determine what they think is the best translation of the original. This process provides agency to the translator who may translate a given text in the way they understand it. While some thinkers place much on the amount of agency a translator may have, other thinkers have argued that many contemporary translators have very little agency if they fall victim to ideological paradigms in which practices become attached to accepted norms and how ideas ought to be understood. In that sense, as historians, we are well aware of such challenges and how this must be navigated, something many people take for granted. I also argue that while some people argue whether one Qur'an translation is the best or another, in fact, when working with Qur'an translations, one quickly learns that sometimes an *āyah* in one translation may sound more applicable to them and then the next *āyah* in the other translation. The point I'm making is that taking a translation as a whole as the "best translation" does not really solve the problem of translation. In fact, with the use of AI, people have become sloppy, as they simply access the translation fed into the data sets on the Internet. This can be even more dangerous, as many people will absolve themselves from participating in the translation process and simply give up their agency to a translation which is deemed authentic by the AI software. What the process does not tell you is that even the AI process is influenced by ideology.

I also want to make one last point here, which is that it is worth noting that there are inherent translation issues between languages which are deemed Islamicate, meaning languages that have submitted to Islam and what are deemed "modern" languages such as English, French and German. When I say that Islamicate languages have submitted to Islam, what I mean is that Arabic, first and foremost, submitted to the Arabic of the Qur'an. While the Arabic in the Qur'an is different and superior to what is called classical Arabic, and now Modern Standard Arabic, nonetheless, the Qur'an set the tone for grammar and vocabulary that was later popularised and given meaning by the *Sunnah*. The Arabic of the Arabs pre-Islam gradually submitted to the forms that Islam brought to the world. As Islam spread around the world, the culture of *'ilm* influenced many languages of the Muslim world, where they started to use the Arabic script and either embraced vocabulary from Arabic or established translations in their own language that, over time, reflected more or less the meaning of the Arabic terms. Examples of such languages include Farsi, Urdu, Jawi and Ottoman Turkish. When it comes to what are known as Modern Western Languages, such as English, French and German, they did not submit to Islam in both form and culture, and instead when examined, are languages that actually reflect the secular tradition. As strange as it may sound, these languages were unable to attain the indigenous meaning of words in the Islamic culture. An example would be that the word *Salah* in Arabic (the act of praying five times a day) would translate as *Namaz* in Persian, Turkish or Urdu, in which the meaning is captured very closely. However, in English, the word used is prayer, which somewhat misses what *Salah* is. Thus, while all translations contain some act of cultural specificity, Islamicate languages, due to their adherence and submission to Islam, do not have the same challenges as Modern Western Languages do. The act of translation is an ideological act as it involves cultural interpretations, acts of omission, and political context, not to mention that languages also carry ideologies where certain expressions, idioms, and structures reflect worldviews.

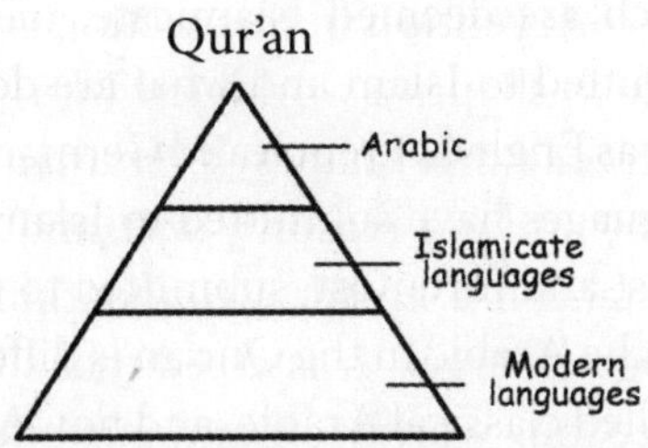

A Muslim historian must be aware that when examining Western academia, it is not as simple as rejecting what was written because it is not in conformity with an Islamic framework of writing history. Ibn Khaldun was clear in pointing out that even Muslim historians can be prone to error, which could be due to methodological or personal reasons. But Western academia poses a different challenge, something Ibn Khaldun did not have to contend with, which is that Western academic history writing is written from deep ideological paradigms that have not emerged from the Islamic worldview about life. As a result, these ideologies, which present themselves as being value-less are, in fact, value-laden, in the sense that they place judgements upon Muslims and Islam. Furthermore, these ideologies facilitate a host of assumptions about Allah, the Prophet ﷺ, the Qur'an and *Sunnah*, and Muslims, and consequently provide the basis of narratives where the assumptions are rarely, if ever, challenged. Syed Naquib Al-Attas is correct in suggesting that while critiquing ideologies, and by extension, ideological narratives, can be an important exercise, the main issue is one of *'aqīdah*, which is that the way Islamic history is written is from a secular consciousness, in which writing from an *īmān*-centred perspective becomes somewhat impossible. It is from the framework of the six tenets of *īmān* that a Muslim thinker should think. They are not simply tenets of faith but a framework that future generations of young Muslim historians could use.

Thus, my final intervention in this section is to make the case that all *ʿilm* which shapes a worldview (*din*)[5] is dependent on the *ʿaqīdah* (creed) that shapes it. Human beings generate thoughts (*afkār*) and use reason (*ʿaql*), and then those series of thoughts establish a creed, a foundation from which all other knowledge emerges. It is creed that shapes our knowledge and, hence, our worldview and our interaction with the *dunyā* (world) in it. As I will explain in the next section, the *ʿaqīdah* of the Muslim is based on Allah's existence, *tawḥīd*, and *īmān* in all things He has commanded us to believe in. In the secular world on which academic works are predicated, Allah's existence is rejected, and each stage is shaped without consideration of Allah. This then can have detrimental consequences for the Muslim who is engaging with history in general, but Islamic history more specifically.

5 I have chosen to use the word *din* for worldview in this case regarding the point I am making—I am well aware that *din* can also mean 'religion'. I have used the word *din* to refer to a way of life, religion, or system of beliefs that can encompass not only spiritual practices and rituals but also ethical, social, and moral dimensions that inform how one interacts with the world.

The Current Dilemma of the Muslim Historian

I want to explain some of the concerns I have regarding how Muslim communities that I have been teaching have been interacting with Islamic history. There is no doubt in my mind that, more recently, I have noticed an upturn of interest in learning more about our past and people wanting to study history. However, I still have concerns in regards to how our communities have a reductionist approach to history learning rather than understanding that history can be an intellectual endeavour. As I have just explained above, history is a sophisticated vocation, and there are a host of matters that we historians engage with regarding our knowledge production. It has become even more concerning for me that while interest in learning history has increased, the quality that is reaching the communities, whether that be in Islamic schools, our mosques or even the Internet, is not of the standard that the community deserves. It is for this reason, rather than having a stop-gap person teach history in our communities, that we instead seek Muslim historians who are trained to engage with the communities.

Historians, like detectives, need to sieve through sources, make sense of the world in the time they are investigating, make sense of the world they currently live in, and provide meaning in the form of a narrative to an audience. The narratives historians create hold value for society by fostering understanding, empathy, and critical thinking. They can challenge misconceptions and illuminate the complexities of human experience. By approaching their work with the rigour and curiosity of detectives, historians contribute to our understanding of the past and its relevance to the present and future. The historian in the Islamic tradition has been seen as part of the intellectual class who understood or tried to understand the human disposition, and sound statecraft was dependent on historians guiding state and society. This role has now been replaced by political scientists in academia, think tanks, journalists, celebrities, or influencers on social media.

The historian, now more than ever, is finding it difficult to survive in a world where narrative writing is being seen as secondary to information and data. Yet, I argue the world now more than ever requires moral and ethical historians, people who are mediums of narratives that create communities with a moral purpose and an understanding of the past, present, and imagination of the future. This is what I hope to encourage in the Muslim historian, who is aware of their moral obligations towards their readership. It is hoped that some of these historians or historical works can also provide a space for contemplation, providing a reading of getting close to Allah, and providing values for this life and the next,

The modern man's predicament is that we are creating a world in which a sensory overload of information and data is masquerading as knowledge. Both technology and ideology have facilitated this current difficulty. The modern agent has come to internalise notions such as that the past no longer provides us meaning, that nature needs taming and that the future need not be imagined. We do not think about the future but live in a "continual present" where the future is collapsed into the present. Information has become a part of consumption culture and is substantially offered to provide stimuli. In a time when rationality is stressed, an information-driven culture presupposes that the accuracy of information overrides how that information gives meaning. Contemporary society has abandoned the virtue of wisdom, where past experiences matter, where a body of knowledge offers us meaning. Instead, much of the information we consume is for entertainment and is absent of deeper reflection. I argue that while the information we consume can give us forms of understanding, often, but not always, this provides only the perception of knowing. Deeper learning, however, which takes time and requires investment, provides perspective. Perspective is the ability not only to know but also to understand the other. For the historian, we are not looking to merely attain a perception of what happened but to understand the perspective of the people of the past.

There is something to be said about the modern dilemma: easy access to information via AI, the Internet, social media, and current legacy news outlets has left us believing that we are more knowledgeable than the people of the past. The past has become a distant memory, in which through our attempts to "progress", we have become rather myopic in our understanding of the human condition and time itself. As a result, the critical mind required for the historian is becoming more of an aversion. Historians are needed now more than ever as the world becomes consumed with data camouflaged as truth for the rational mind; what is required is a sense of value, an ability to resonate and empathise with our fellow human beings not just now but also in the past. Human beings need to know what it means to be human. That experience comes from the knowledge of our humanity today and a more wholesome understanding that includes people of the past. It is for this reason I am writing this book. I want more Muslims to study history again. There is a need for the rational mind to also understand that narratives are part of the human condition. Now more than ever, the art of narratives is needed for people to understand complexity and nuance and that the human being is an agent that consists of patterns of behaviour that often reoccur. This is not the first time in human history that an excess of information due to technology has created societies that lack critical thinking. Easy access to data that is assumed to be factual has given mediums that provide information with an authority that has been detrimental to narrative experts.

This is why, again, I stress that historians are needed, as the most successful historians are the ones who tell the best narratives, who help preserve memory and help facilitate collective significance and identity. I come back to this point of narrative telling firstly to highlight how narrative telling or "storytelling" ought not to be done simply without training. Secondly, Muslim historians should recognise that presenting historical narratives within the discipline is just as important as our archival and language training. Finally, recognising the dangers of how narratives outside our tradition are making us internalise ideas about Muslims that require a counter-narrative. Good historians are not simply people who tell stories; however, as I have already stated, we are truth seekers and want to provide meaning to the readership of why the past should matter to them and how they can learn as a way of having a better present and future. For me, the primary meaning of a Muslim historian is to provide understanding regarding the *nomos* (a law, convention, or custom governing human conduct) of Allah found in the Qur'an for societies, nations, civilisations and humanity.

The best historians are the ones who can provide some idea of what is to be learnt from this moment of history and what meaning it can give the present. For Muslims, the primary aim is to attain moral value from the historical narrative. As

I have mentioned, narratives are needed to make sense of our world and are the most potent way to make sense of our human experiences. Our experiences need to be compared with the experiences of others to make sense of our value systems. During wars, news outlets will often talk of the number of dead in statistical terms, but it is narratives that humanise or demonise that resonate with people; it is frequently for that reason that perpetrators of heinous crimes construct counter-narratives to shape public opinion in their favour. The reason why narratives become so significant is that the reader becomes invested in making sense of and judging the actors' choices in the past, attempting to make sense of the choices that were made. It is usually during this moral quandary that we discover our sense of moral judgement and what we would have done had we been in the same situation. Likely, we are indeed in the same situation, as the past and present interact, making the narrative of the past meaningful in so many ways.

A good historian ought to be a truth seeker, and this pursuit of truth is fundamental to their work. I cannot stress this enough regarding the need for more truth seekers today, where much of our information is riddled with falsehood. A well-trained historian should strive to base their interpretations on evidence and gather data from various sources, including primary documents, artefacts, and testimonies, to put together a truthful foundation for their narratives. The search for truth involves critically analysing sources for bias, reliability, and context. The objective of a historian ought to be not about filling an academic gap but the quest for truth that I have just mentioned. If this is indeed the case, then the historian will be forced to reflect on the nature of humanity and existence. Historians assess differing accounts and perspectives, recognising that history can be complex and multifaceted. This, then, would be reflected in how they interact with society by highlighting to them the complexity of things. While historians aim for objectivity, their interpretations are influenced by their contexts and perspectives, and I believe that, in this case, Muslim historians who attain their experiences from Islam have much to offer here. Historians work to provide a balanced view, acknowledging multiple narratives and seeking a deeper understanding of events. The pursuit of truth in history is not static, and at a time when truth is under assault, it is needed more now than ever that the truth of Islam and the Islamic past is written within the purview of the Muslim community as this should matter to them. As new evidence emerges or as societal contexts change, historians may revise their understandings, and the act of revision is an act of establishing the truth, not simply revising something for the sake of it. This is a key aspect of scholarly integrity. Historians have an ethical responsibility to present their findings truthfully and transparently, and I would argue that this is even more so for the Muslim historian, as they should remember that they are to be held accountable by Allah. Misleading the *ummah* in such matters will not only have dire consequences through creating false impressions of people of the past, but it can also lead to disputes among people in the present; but furthermore, we will be held to account by Allah. When attempting to establish the truth, the exercise often points one to the past. In Islam, tradition, as well as the past, still has authority in the way we behave today. Misrepresentation or manipulation of historical data can lead to distorted understandings of the past, and the Muslim historian must be humble enough to know that they may make mistakes. They must recognise that this is a human endeavour and must not be flippant in the way that they present the past in case they misguide the *ummah*.

However, while putting together narratives which are based on sources, data, and other historians' interpretations, I want to return to the point that it must be stressed that historians are not mere storytellers. There has become a tendency on social media platforms teaching the Muslim community in the mosque space to provide exaggerated or misleading accounts of history as a way of either boosting the congregation's *īmān* or highlighting Muslim failure without sourcing the evidence of how such a conclusion has been established. This can be even more problematic when such stories are presented on social media around the world, with the impression that this is an endeavour to teach history. Whenever we are producing works of history, if we are writing from the perspective of Islam, a key matter is to help Muslims be aware of causality and how historical events and change always reveal something about the divine order of our universe. Most often, amateur historians will make mistakes, reinforce errors, or teach history as a storyteller would.

Post-modernist thinkers have criticised historians, suggesting that they make selective choices and subjugate the truth to ideological beliefs. There is no denying that every writer makes choices and, as such, has the power to control the narrative. However, this simplification suggests that the ideas of the historian are not subject to scrutiny by the fraternity of experts. Historians first belong to a large corpus of contemporaries that challenge, examine, and attempt to verify their ideas and works. In that sense, most historical narratives have undergone extensive vetting in the academy but have not found their way into the Muslim community.

For this reason, revisionism is essential in the writing of history. Human attitudes, shifting opinions, and new information coming to light always require the historian to re-evaluate narratives that, at one point, were the accepted norm. Like in any other occupation, new evidence and ideas can cast doubt on any given viewpoint or opinion; just like in a court case, for example, where new evidence can change narratives, historians can do the same. Thus, it is acceptable and expected for the historian to keep examining the narratives. An example of such a case is the notion of what we call a "paradigm shift", in which a complete transformation can take place when a set of assumptions, theories and methodologies that have been influencing a narrative, thesis or positions are forced to change to the discovery of new evidence, a flaw in the paradigm, or a new or different paradigmatic approach.

ب

SECTION II

THE QUR'AN AND SĪRAH AS A SOURCE FOR ANALYSIS AND INSPIRATION FOR HISTORIANS

In this section, I shall examine how the Qur'an and *Sunnah*, but in particular, the *Sīrah*, ought to be a source for writing works as an Islamically-oriented method for writing history. It is evident that the Qur'an, which is the word of Allah, and the *Sunnah* and *Sīrah*, which are sources regarding the Messenger of Allah, are indicated in the testimony of faith—the *Shahādah*. But these points are once again reiterated in the tenets of *īmān* by highlighting the belief in Allah, His books, and His Prophets. The Qur'an and *Sunnah* also point to the tenets of *īmān* regarding the *Qadr of Allah* and that everyone will be held to account, which is related to the Day of Judgement.

While we believe in the other books and previous Prophets, it should go without saying that the Qur'an and *Sunnah*, which includes the *Sīrah*, are the sources that I am referring to when speaking of an Islamically-oriented method of writing history, thus an *īmān*-oriented approach. The Qur'an contains narratives, lessons, and moral guidance that can help historians understand the values, beliefs, and societal structures of early Muslim communities. Its *āyahs* can provide context for historical events and the motivations behind actions taken by individuals and groups. The Muslim is not only interested in the material realm of what happened; however, just as this *dunya* (world) is a reality, so too is the *ākhirah* (next world). The fact that the Muslim is working to seek the pleasure of Allah and enter *Jannah* (Paradise) means that when writing history, a Muslim historian should write in accordance with helping the Muslims understand the notion of their existence. Needless to say, it is only Allah who can judge who goes to *Jannah*, but Islam has prescriptions that speak of justice, enjoining in the good, worship, being people of ethics, and so on that Allah mentions in the Qur'an and can be seen embodied in the Prophetic mission by the Prophet Muhammed ﷺ. It is my point to suggest that an Islamically-oriented approach to history writing should attempt to point to these references in the Qur'an and examples of the life of the Prophet ﷺ and then see how the lives of individuals, nations, and societies can be analysed in relation.

Thus, this section shall examine the ways in which the Qur'an and *Sīrah* can be a source for the historian to analyse events and patterns, as well as provide principles regarding Islam. In this section, I want the reader to appreciate that, at times, it is required to write about matters that can give the believers a sense of purpose in accordance with what Allah requires from the Muslims. Thus, writing history by using the sources of Islam to give meaning to Muslims is part of what I subscribe to in an Islamically-oriented approach.

The Importance of the Qur'an for the Muslim Historian

The Qur'an is exemplary in its use of narrative. It not only provides historical narratives but does two important things for the historian's critical mind. The first is that the Qur'an addresses the intellect of the reader. It stresses the need to think, reflect, and contemplate and addresses those who reflect, contemplate, listen, remember, question, and understand. In that sense, the Qur'an is very clear in the need to apply rationality, and the Qur'anic narratives do not go against this aspect of the human being. The second is that the Qur'an gives meaning to the reader. Hence, it provides value and recognises that the reader is also moved by emotion for memory. Narratives require a committed community of readers who subscribe to them. The narratives, in turn, shape the readers with values that they subscribe to. Thus, the Qur'an is clear that good narratives address the intellect and align with the values of those engaged in the narrative. The human being is a rational and emotional agent; separating one from the other is to the detriment of what it means to be human. In doing so, the Qur'an does another thing worth examining. The Qur'an, in telling its narratives, creates what is known in the field of literature as a 'narrative community', in this case, the community of believers—the *ummah*.

The modern mind has become reduced to thinking along the lines of the self. Individualism has become such a dominant characteristic of many societies that even when Muslims read the Qur'an, they take meaning from it in an individual capacity. However, in this case, the *ummah* is the 'narrative community' created by the Qur'an and its values and ideals are shaped by it. It is in the Qur'an that Islam is given its name, and it is in the Qur'an that the Muslim, *mu'min*, and *muḥsin* are identified.[6] It is not only Muslims who are identified but also those who are not. It is via historical narratives that Allah then identifies the *millah* of Ibrahim ﷺ as being Muslim, fashioning the idea of the *ummah*, which is one that followed the straight path. Thus, in *Sūrah Fatiha*, Allah says, "*It is you (Allah) we worship, and you we seek aid. Show us the straight path.*" (TQM 1:5-6).

What is worth noting in these *āyahs* is that the plural is used, where it says '*we*' and 'show *us*' the straight path. Thus, the Qur'an provides meaning in its narratives because it resonates with the experiences of the Muslim community as a collective and reminds us that previous believers have also gone through such an experience. The narrative community thus pays careful attention to the narratives, as Allah also stresses in the Qur'an that these narratives are for those who understand, indicating the need for attentiveness from the narrative community. In doing so, the community resonates and empathises, and their investment in the narrative is emotional and intimate. The community then recites these *āyāt* from the Qur'an in their *khuṭbahs* and lectures and, when speaking to the community, uses them in their written works. They reinforce the lessons of the narratives that continue to speak to generation after generation. It is this culture which Ibn Khaldun is influenced by when talking about the role of the Muslim historian. It is here where history writing for Muslims differs from academic writing. The ideas of the past are not for mere enquiry but must fit the overall culture of the

6 In the plural, the *Mumin* is *Mumineen*, and *Muhsin* is *Muhsineen*.

narrative community of finding meaning that concerns the objectives of belonging to the *ummah*. Thus, the Qur'an forces the reader to re-evaluate what it means to be human and what it means to be Muslim.

As a result, it is worth noting how the Qur'an ought to be a central source of inspiration for Muslim historians. Our pursuit of *'ilm* (knowledge) is based on the Qur'anic culture and model.

Everything good in Islam comes from the Qur'an. The Qur'an elevated the station of the Messenger of Messengers—the angel Jibril ﷺ. It was from the first Revelation of the Qur'an that Prophet Muhammad ﷺ started his Prophetic mission for humanity. The Qur'an makes this *ummah* unique, as we are a people of the Qur'an. Nothing that is associated with the Qur'an has not been elevated by it. The Qur'an elevated the Arabic language and, in turn, every other Islamicate language, just as it has done with everything else. The Qur'an has been the single most influential communicational medium in the history of humanity. As the word of Allah, the Qur'an is also very clear in its intentions and is the ultimate source for humanity.

When opening the Qur'an and turning to the *Sūrahs* that start with the *Ḥurūf al-muqaṭṭa'ah* (mystery letters of the Qur'an), you would more often notice that in the following *āyah* or sentences after the *Ḥurūf al-muqaṭṭa'ah*, the Qur'an is mentioned and confirmed as a source of guidance. Allah emphasises the supremacy of the Qur'an to the reader so that they can understand that this is indeed His speech. In *Sūrah al-Baqarah*, for example, Allah says, "*Alif-Lahm-Mim, this is a book [Qur'an], beyond no doubt, is a guidance for those conscious of Allah*". (TMQ 2:2). In *Sūrah Yūnus*, "*Alif, Lam, Ra, – These are the āyahs of the Book of Wisdom.*" [Qur'an] (TQM 10:1). In *Sūrah Yusuf*, "*Alif, Lam, Ra – These are the āyahs of the clear book [Qur'an].*" (TQM 12:2), or *Sūrah Yasin*, "*Ya Sin*

– *By the Wise Qur'an.*" (TQM 36:2). These are just some of the examples in which Allah starts by mentioning the Qur'an and its centrality to our lives and knowledge seeking. Each of these *Sūrahs* usually states that the Qur'an is a profound source of wisdom, clarity, and guidance for those who are mindful of their relationship with Allah.

In that sense, the Qur'an has already laid down the principles of communication between Allah and His creation. This is important because when Allah mentions a historical narrative in the Qur'an, there is a clear intention that Allah is dispelling falsehoods and misconceptions or providing a rendering of the unknown. By making it clear that the Qur'an is a book of truth and Allah is the source of all knowledge, *al-ʿAlīm*, the Qur'an becomes a primary source of all knowledge for the Muslims. Allah is in no need to prove what He has communicated, as when He revealed the *āyah,* He was challenging the reader/listener with the legitimacy of the truth, for Allah speaks nothing but the truth. With these Qur'anic principles in mind, it is clear that the Muslim historian should strive to search and write the truth, be inspired to write in a manner that provides wisdom, be able to examine the signs in history and provide guidance, as has been mentioned in the previous paragraph.

The First Sūrah Starts with a Tone to Contemplate the Past

Sūrah al-Alaq

Bismillāh-ir Rahmān-ir Rahīm

ٱقْرَأْ بِٱسْمِ رَبِّكَ ٱلَّذِى خَلَقَ ﴿﴾ خَلَقَ ٱلْإِنسَٰنَ مِنْ عَلَقٍ ﴿﴾ ٱقْرَأْ وَرَبُّكَ ٱلْأَكْرَمُ ﴿﴾
ٱلَّذِى عَلَّمَ بِٱلْقَلَمِ ﴿﴾ عَلَّمَ ٱلْإِنسَٰنَ مَا لَمْ يَعْلَمْ ﴿﴾

I shall explain that while history is often seen as an elective or optional vocation that can be of value but may not be necessary for students who study *'ilm* or any other subject, I would stress that, with today's intellectual challenges, history ought to be reconceptualised as one of the auxiliary sciences (*'ulūm al-ālah*) that bolsters all forms of knowledge, and that this can be seen in the Qur'an itself. Just as grammar (*naḥw*) is an indispensable science for understanding the language of the Qur'an, an Islamically-oriented science of history can be established within this curricular paradigm. The Qur'an provides a foundational framework for Muslim historians. Its teachings and narratives can guide historical interpretation, emphasising values such as justice, morality, and truth. The Qur'an also serves as a source of context for understanding historical events, cultural practices, and societal norms in

Islamic history. By aligning their research with its principles, Muslim historians can enrich their analyses and contribute to a more nuanced understanding of the past.

As a historian, I would argue that the study of history as a discipline should not be seen as merely superfluous but as an addition that elevates ideas by providing context to disciplines from philosophy, *kalām,* and *ḥadīth* to the study of science and technology. All knowledge is built upon the knowledge of the past, as Allah not only created mankind but also taught mankind. Allah taught Adam ﷺ the names of things, and as He provided him ﷺ, just like all the Prophets, with the divine wisdom of the mission that they were tasked with.

In the Qur'an—in *Sūrah al-ʿAlaq*—the first thing we are told is Allah created us and that He taught us. This was the first *Sūrah* revealed to the Prophet Muhammad ﷺ, and Allah implies that human beings have a tendency to forget. The *āyahs* revealed to the Prophet ﷺ in the cave of Hira by the angel Jibril ﷺ highlight that all creation and all knowledge comes from Allah. One could read *Sūrah al-ʿAlaq* and the narrative of the Prophet ﷺ in a simple manner, or one can appreciate how the interaction between the words of Allah and His beloved ﷺ was much more intimate and profound. It is narrated that when this first *Sūrah* was revealed, the Prophet ﷺ was contemplating in the cave of Hira in solitude when he ﷺ experienced his first interaction as an adult with Jibril ﷺ. Jibril ﷺ squeezed and shocked the Prophet ﷺ. This was symbolic of Jibril ﷺ waking up the Prophet's ﷺ heart for the first time, hearing Revelation and preparing him ﷺ for his mission. After this experience, the Prophet ﷺ needed time to reflect so that he ﷺ was ready for the testing road ahead.

The *Sūrah* starts with the word *iqra*ʾ, which means to read or recite. Some Muslim commentators suggest it implies specifically reading with understanding. The words *iqra*ʾ and Qur'an are derived from the root letters Q-R-A. The word *iqraʾ* is the imperative form of these root letters. Thus, it makes the case from the first word of Revelation that it is a book to read, recite, and understand. It is not simply that the Messenger of Allah ﷺ is being asked to read or recite, but that he ﷺ is being asked to do so and testify with knowledge. What is Allah commanding the Prophet ﷺ and, by extension, humanity to do? The word *iqra*ʾ, in its timeless form, is telling all those who read or hear these words that they are to testify in the way we do in the *Basmala*, that it is He, their Lord, who is the creator and that it is He, their Lord, who taught mankind knowledge. What is important to consider is that while he ﷺ was listening to the *āyāt* being revealed to him, it was also an act of reading and recitation. The Qur'an can be recited by listening and then being added to memory without actually reading from the *muṣḥaf* (Physical copy of the Arabic Qur'an).

In these verses, Allah tells the Prophet ﷺ via Jibril ؑ two pieces of information. The first is that Allah is the *Khāliq* (The Creator) who created humans from congealed blood or a clot. Here the word when Allah says, "*iqra*ʾ, in the name of your Lord who created," Allah states that He is the creator of everything and the One Whom the Prophet ﷺ was contemplating about when he ﷺ was receiving dreams preparing him for his Prophethood. The Prophet ﷺ is then told that humans were created from congealed blood or a clot. The *āyah* does not mention the creation of the Prophet Adam ؑ, the first human, but how humans are conceived. In Arabic, *ʿalaq* here means congealed blood, meaning the embryonic state in which parts of the man and woman form the human foetus. Not only that but by this, Allah also points to the humble form in which human beings come into this world.

The second part of this *Sūrah* revealed at this time, repeats the command *iqra*ʾ again and commands to testify that Allah is the most generous, as He taught human beings knowledge with the pen, that which human beings did not know, meaning that Allah has taught human beings all knowledge, and without it, we would be ignorant. Allah has taken human beings from the humble form of congealed blood and made them elevated beings, making them the noblest of creation because they were possessors of knowledge and were able to cultivate their intellect via the medium of writing. This point is not simply highlighting that the art of reading and writing is why knowledge can be passed down from one generation to another but also that the Qur'an shall be written down. The commandment in the *Sūrah* is thus clear, i.e., all forms of knowledge pursuit which begin with the act of reading must be anchored in the desire and objective to know Allah through His creation.

The Qur'an, which was revealed to the Prophet ﷺ, also addresses humanity, stating that those who understand must recognise that Allah is the ultimate source of creation and the ultimate source of human inspiration. The *Sūrah* revealed to the Prophet ﷺ was not simply making a statement about a sign of nature but stressing the need to **remember**. This was not simply an act of reminding human beings but for the thinking mind and the spiritual soul to testify to the truth that has been spoken of in the Qur'an. The Qur'an reminds the one who reads or listens to it that human beings are doing a disservice to themselves if they choose to forget or be ignorant of Allah's bounties. From the inception of Revelation, the Qur'an recognises the human plight of memory and the need for us to be reminded.

Muhammad Iqbal, the South Asian Muslim thinker and philosopher, makes the case that each *āyah* in the Qur'an is a sign of contemplation and that the Qur'an addresses humans by reminding them of the signs of nature and the signs of human history. In many ways, making the case of nature and history for Iqbal was to make the case that just like how nature has its laws, so do the rise and fall of nations and that life itself follows a course. Once life is understood this way, that there are norms to nations, civilisations and so on, then human beings can understand their place in it and how we can be agents of change to make our lives better.

When we examine Allah's names that He is *al-Khāliq* (The Creator), *al-Bāri'* (The Maker/Evolver), and *al-Muṣawwir* (The Fashioner/Maker), these attributes can easily be perceived when understanding the laws of nature. As *al-Khāliq*, Allah brings everything into existence as it signifies the power and will of Allah to create from nothing. *Al-Bāri'* refers to Allah creating in an orderly and systematic manner and signifies that Allah not only creates but also shapes and develops His creations according to His wisdom and design. Finally, *al-Muṣawwir* highlights Allah's ability to give form and attributes to His creations. It indicates that He designs each being with unique characteristics and qualities. When examining the cosmos, nature or even an atom, these names of Allah ought to be reflected on and contemplated.

Like the natural signs and order of nature, these names of Allah can be reflected on and contemplated over regarding nations, societies, and civilisations. Each nation and civilisation comes into existence with its unique identity and culture as part of Allah's grand design. Nations and civilisations also develop and evolve over time as they also undergo changes, adapting to new circumstances and challenges. Finally, nations and civilisations have their own cultures, traditions, and identities. With *Sūrah al-ʿAlaq* in mind, it was not simply mentioning a natural phenomenon about the creation and development of mankind but also a historical sign of this development. *Sūrah al-ʿAlaq* was thus reflecting both of Iqbal's concepts of signs in the Qur'an: Nature and History. With this thought in mind, Muslim historians have always examined the rise and fall and evolution of nations, as well as their unique characteristics within the divine order of things.

For this reason, I stress the importance and need to study history as Muslims. Allah calls on Muslims to not only think about the past in all its forms but to reflect, as it is the reflective and then contemplative person who is the most elevated in a world where most have chosen to switch off and choose to be ignorant, and it is the contemplative person who can attain the heights of wisdom.

History is indeed about the art of reminding so that we do not forget what humanity has achieved. In a world where alternate forms of information are attacking memory, whether that be social media, advertising, or mass media, I hope to encourage Muslims to pursue history as a vocation which has long been part of our tradition, which is deep, intellectual, complicated, truthful, and meaningful. I do not simply make the case as some have, that we should merely read history books, watch TV shows, or listen to lectures. While all these mediums have merit, I request to re-introduce the studying of history as a vocation into our communities that encourages language learning and examination of primary sources, facilitating the critical and creative mind and promising writers of consequential narratives. But additionally, history for me, if written and taught from the perspective of seeing the grand design of nations, societies, and civilisation, their emergence, evolution, and even collapse, can be equally a point of contemplation regarding the *Qudra* (power) of Allah. Thus, it is not just about reminding readers about things that are forgotten but contemplating how societies come into being and how they disappear from human memory.

This is noteworthy as while most academics in the West focus on the influence of Aristotle and Plato upon Muslim thinkers, Iqbal emphasises that the Qur'an and Islam have been central to Ibn Khaldun's ideas of historical criticism and theory. When examining Ibn Khaldun, which I shall do later, one can see how the Qur'anic principles influenced him in his theorising on concepts regarding nations, societies and civilisations when writing his history works. According to Iqbal, the Qur'an is an example and source of moral framework and inspired historians like Ibn Ishaq, at-Tabari, and Masudi.

For Iqbal, the Qur'anic notion of history points to the idea that nations are collectively judged and suffer for their misdeeds. Iqbal stresses that the Qur'an urges the reader to reflect on mankind's past and present experiences. He continues that the Qur'an's interest in history as a source of human knowledge extends further than the mere indication of historical generalisations. The narratives in the Qur'an, thus, are not mere stories but, in fact, narratives that compel the reader to reflect and contemplate, understand, and consider their current predicament, as well as establish imaginations of the future.

This also helps the Muslim historian to conceptualise historical individual agency and its relationship to structural change. It is this idea of establishing an imagination of the future where the distinction ought to be made that Allah presents narratives in the Qur'an and not mere stories, as stories do not intend to provide the reader with the projection of the future. Imām al-Ghazālī is one example of a scholar influenced by this. During his time, he was aware of the challenges of storytelling, and thus, when speaking of his own experiences, he framed it within the emerging tradition of *ḥikāyah* (narrative) tradition. The narratives in the Qur'an are indeed powerful as they do not simply speak to the audience during the time of Revelation but present an archetypal feature where those who are of understanding learn about the actions of previous peoples and the consequences of those actions.

When looking at the Qur'an, while Ibn Khaldun and Iqbal do not clearly specify what it was that they drew their inspiration from, we can assume that it was the *āyāts* that mention the need to reflect and contemplate about the past people, that every people have a set time and that people who have strayed from the good path have ultimately trod the path to their own demise.

The Qur'an points to making such observations of what has come before. Allah says in the Qur'an in *Sūrah Āl ʿImrān*, "*Many were the ways of life that have passed away before you: travel through the earth, and see what was the end of those who rejected the truth*". (TQM Yusuf Ali, *Sūrah Āl ʿImrān* 3:137). Allah makes the point that when we travel, we should observe the signs of previous nations who are no more and think and reflect upon those reasons; in this case, what led to the end of many nations was their rejection of the truth. When thinking about the truth, this was not simply the truth of *tawḥīd* and worship but also of the need to run societies with goodness and justice. Allah once again mentions this point in *Sūrah Yusuf* when He says, "*Nor did We send before thee (as Messengers) any but men, whom We did inspire (men) living in human habitations. Do they not travel through the earth, and see what was the end of those before them? But the home of the hereafter is best, for those who do right. Will you not then understand?*" (TQM Yusuf Ali – 12:109) and then again in *Sūrah Muhammad* when He says, "*Do they not travel through the earth, and see what was the end of those before them (who did evil)? Allah brought utter destruction on them, and similar (fates await) those who reject Allah*". (TMQ Yusuf Ali, *Sūrah Muhammad* 47:10)

The repeated emphasis on the rejection of truth and justice as primary factors leading to the downfall of nations underscores a moral imperative. It suggests that neglecting ethical principles and justice can lead to devastating consequences. By observing the remnants of past civilisations, one is reminded of the importance of upholding truth and righteousness to foster a just society. Moreover, these reflections encourage a proactive approach to governance and community life, urging individuals and nations to prioritise values that promote harmony and justice. Ultimately, the call to reflect on the fate of those who came before serves as both a cautionary tale and an invitation to build a better future grounded in moral integrity that is mentioned in the Qur'an and practised by the Prophet ﷺ.

This leads to the next point, which is that each nation, people or civilisation has an allotted time. Allah says in *Sūrah al-A'rāf*, "*To every people is a term appointed: when their term is reached, not an hour can they cause delay, nor (an hour) can they advance (it in anticipation)*".(TQM Yusuf Ali – *Sūrah al-A'rāf* 7:34) And then again in *Sūrah Yūnus*, "*Say: "I have no power over any harm or profit to myself except as Allah willeth. To every people is a term appointed: when their term is reached, not an hour can they cause delay, nor (an hour) can they advance (it in anticipation).*" (TQM Yusuf Ali – *Sūrah Yūnus* 10:49). These *āyāt* point to the idea that nations have a beginning and an end, just like life itself, and no society or nation will escape this. This is both a Qur'anic concept and an observable rational fact that every nation of the past has ended, whether that be the Romans, the Mongols, or the Ottomans. It must also be remembered that if Muslim societies do not pay attention to this principle, then not only will they not prosper, but they too shall meet the fate of the nations before them who chose to ignore the principles of good governance and cultivating a just society. It should also serve as a reminder to people who are under oppression, that if they are under these types of circumstances, these forms of oppression will also end, as oppression is, in fact, a reflection of injustice, which leads to the decline of a nation.

I would argue that if one pays close attention to the Qur'an and then studies the history of nations one will learn that this will be the fate of nations of today too, and it is worth it for nations and their peoples to pay attention to the fact that if they have not done good in this world, that there will be consequences not simply in this life but also in the next. The Qur'anic teachings should urge contemporary nations to reflect on their moral and ethical standings, as when these nations come to an end, their worldly contributions may be written in history books, but what awaits them in regards to Allah's judgement is far more important. This should serve as a reminder of the transient nature of power and prosperity. If Muslims do not warn the leadership of their nations of their current predicament, they too will be held accountable, as it is better for a people to collectively work towards establishing justice in this world than to create a world of chaos and discord.

If we have not done what Allah has commanded and not made an effort to uphold the principles of Islam, then Allah will indeed hold us accountable in regard to our individual actions, as well as holding us accountable to the nations we were a part of. We can see this point in *Sūrah al-Jāthiyah* when Allah says "*On that Day you shall see every people fallen on their knees. Every people will be summoned to come forth and see its record and will be told: Today you shall be requited for your deeds.*"(TQM Maududi - *Sūrah al-Jāthiyah* 45:28). The *āyah* from *Sūrah al-Jāthiyah* emphasises that on the Day of Judgement, people will be called to account not only for their personal deeds but also in the context of their communities and societies. This collective accountability serves as a reminder that the choices made by a nation—its values, policies, and treatment of its members—have significant implications for all its people. When societies stray from justice and righteousness, the consequences can affect everyone, reinforcing the idea that individuals are part of a larger moral fabric. The imagery of people falling to their knees signifies the gravity of this reckoning, reminding us that no one can escape the impact of their nation's actions. It underscores the importance of striving for good within our communities and advocating for justice and truth. Prophets did not simply come to improve the character and temperament of individuals; they were sent to address nations and communities and uphold justice to leaders.

So according to the Qur'an, what can lead to the end of a nation? As I have mentioned in the previous paragraphs, the end of nations is ultimately down to the fact that they sway from the truth and bring about discord in this world. Allah says in the Qur'an "*If Allah were to punish men according to what they deserve. He would not leave on the back of the (earth) a single living creature: but He gives them respite for a stated term: when their term expires, verily Allah has in His sight all His Servants.*" (TQM Yusuf Ali – *Sūrah Fatir* 35:45). This *āyāt/āyah* emphasises that while Allah is fully aware of human actions and could impose immediate consequences, He grants respite and allows people to navigate their own paths. This mercy allows societies the opportunity to reflect, repent, and reform. I would further argue that Allah has sent His Messenger ﷺ and given us the Qur'an for this reason so that we abide by what is right, as human beings left to their own devices will most certainly fall into disarray. That does not mean Muslims cannot meet the same fate, and the warning to the *ummah* would be to make sure they adhere to the principles of Islam. Allah, in His mercy, has permitted human beings to arrange their own affairs; He has sent them guidance, but when they have turned away from it, as mentioned, it has led to the destruction of a nation, and they have a fixed time for how much bad they can do in this world.

That does not mean all nations collapse due to them moving away from the principles of Islam. Nations may collapse due to a host of reasons; this could be due to the aggression of other nations, or due to the stresses created by natural disasters, or a nation's inability to adjust to a changing world. In the end, all things come to an end, while unjust practices that lead to the collapse of nations in this world are the most abhorrent ways of collapse nonetheless irrespective of how a nation or civilisation collapses, in the end, we will be held to account in regard to our actions and what we did to make a positive change. It is for this reason that upholding truth to tyranny is important, not simply to change the conditions of how a people is treated but also to address the various matters in one's community and society. If a nation comes to an end while upholding justice, then Allah surely will reward them accordingly.

It is this view that has led Muslim thinkers on the cyclical nature of civilisations, drawing on both Qur'anic teachings and historical examples. The idea that every nation has a designated lifespan is a reminder of the impermanence of power and prosperity. A nation may decline due to material matters, but as the Qur'an points to and history shows that, once a society strays from ethical principles and good governance, it often also faces consequences that can lead to its decline. This is echoed in various Islamic principles where the moral integrity of a society is seen as foundational to its longevity.

Additionally, the notion of accountability—both in this life and the next—serves as a moral compass, encouraging individuals and nations to uphold values that promote justice, compassion, and integrity. This concept emphasises that the choices made today will shape the future, not just for the present generation but for those who follow. The Qur'an indicates this need for self-awareness and ethical governance, urging contemporary societies to learn from the past to avoid the pitfalls of corruption and moral decay. It is for this reason that the study of history for Muslims is important, as they ought to examine the nations of the past, be they Muslim or non-Muslim, to learn from these points.

The cyclical theories discussed by Muslim scholars were based on two principles. The first was the Qur'anic evidence as proof of the Divine will and order of things, and the second was a rational examination of nations of the past based on the principles of the natural law of societies. As mentioned, like the rules of nature, the rules of human civilisations also have a natural law that would lead to their end, and once nations go into the final phases of this natural law, it will lead to their demise. While many modern nations only focus on material decline, however, as highlighted in Islam, when nations ignore the principles of justice, compassion, and truth, they also set themselves on a trajectory towards decline. This aligns with the concept of accountability in the Qur'an: when societies become corrupt and prioritise self-interest over the common good, they disrupt the balance that sustains them. The "final phases" that have often been mentioned in many cyclical theories by Muslim thinkers could refer to the stages of moral decay, social discord, and the erosion of trust and justice within a society. History has shown that these conditions often lead to chaos and, ultimately, collapse. The Qur'anic perspective emphasises that this form of downfall is not merely a matter of chance but rather a predictable outcome of the choices made by its people. We see this when Allah says in *Sūrah al-Ḥijr*, "*Whenever We destroyed a town, a definite term had previously been decreed for it. No people can outstrip the term for its destruction nor can it delay it.*" (TQM – Maududi – Sūrah al-Hijr 15:4-5) And in *Sūrah Qāf*, "*How many a nation did We destroy before them that were stronger in prowess than these. They searched about the lands of the world. But could they find a refuge? Verily there is a lesson in this for everyone who has a (sound) heart and who listens with an attentive mind.*" (TQM – Maududi – Sūrah Qāf 50:36-37).

This suggests that this fall is down to human choices, as human beings have a choice to do good in this world, or they can do bad. This brings to the fore the idea of the *Qadr* of Allah regarding the laws of rise and fall, and free will that Allah has granted human beings. Human beings do have an opportunity to make right the mistakes that they have made, but they have to come to realise their plight, accept that they have done wrong, and then work to change it. If not, the Divine order of things will lead to their end. Allah says in the Qur'an in *Sūrah al-Raʿd*, "*There are guardians over everyone, both before him and behind him, who guard him by Allah's command. Verily*

Allah does not change a people's condition unless they change their inner selves. And when Allah decides to make a people suffer punishment, no one can avert it. Nor can any be of help to such a people against Allah." (TQM Maududi – Sūrah ar-Ra'd 13:11).

For societies to improve, they must first recognise their shortcomings, accept responsibility for their actions, and commit to meaningful change. This process of reflection and transformation is essential for addressing the root causes of discord and moral decline. Moreover, the warning that once Allah decides to impose a punishment, it cannot be averted, serving as a reminder of the seriousness of collective actions and the consequences of moral failure. It underscores the urgency for communities to strive for righteousness and justice, as these are key to fostering a thriving society. While Allah is aware of our actions and has guardians over us, the power to change our circumstances ultimately lies within ourselves.

I must, however, stress that just because one is residing in a nation or civilisation that has become morally corrupt does not mean that they will be held accountable for the corruption of the nation so long as they have attempted to do good, warn people of their actions, and attempted to invite people to change course towards justice. As Allah says in *Sūrah al-Mā'idah*, "*O you who believe! You are not responsible apart for yourselves. If you are rightly guided, the error of he who strays will not harm you. To Allah will all of you return; then He will let all of you know what you did.*" (TQM *Sūrah al-Mā'idah* 5:105) and again Allah says in *Sūrah al-An'ām*, "*And it is He Who has made you generations coming after generations, replacing each other on the earth. And He has raised you in ranks, some above others that He may try you in that which He has bestowed on you. Surely, your Lord is Swift in retribution, and certainly He is Oft-Forgiving, Most Merciful.*" (TQM Mubarakpuri-Sūrah al-An'ām 6:165). Allah has made it clear that those who work in the path of Allah will be rewarded. But while one may be rewarded by Allah for their efforts to do what Allah expects from them, it does not mean that they will escape the worldly fate of a nation or civilisation that will come to an end. Allah will reward in the *ākhirah* those who worked to be upright, warned the people of their ways and tested them with hardship during their lives.

Thus, while there is no clear philosophy in the Qur'an about a historical method, the Qur'an does point to concepts and re-occurring themes so that we may learn from the past, whether that is the lives of individuals or a nation. In particular, the fact that the Qur'an makes a point on matters of morality, ethics, enjoining the good and justice makes the case that history writing ought not to simply be about material progress but that key aspects of our humanity are based on our values, principles and worldview, and as historians we need to offer writings related to this. This should make clear the importance that what we learn from the past should also shape us towards goodness. Of course, the Qur'an is not a chronical of history, but it does indeed comment on the moral habits and attitudes of nations, as I have just shown. Those who study history in a contemplative form will recognise that the Qur'an highlights certain principles.

These principles are that firstly, the norms of history are universal for all peoples, for all times, irrespective of their worldly qualities. These norms are not simply exclusive to non-Muslims or Muslims but humanity. Also, they are not restricted to simply nations and peoples of the past but people today. The Qur'an is a book for all times, and it speaks to us today as it will to the people of the future. Secondly, Allah highlights the reasons why nations in the past have failed, suggesting that if nations and peoples sway from Allah's norms this will lead to decline and eventually their destruction. Finally, human beings have free will, and Allah will hold people accountable for their actions both in this life and in the next life. While Allah has permitted human beings to choose how they wish to live, He has warned human beings that if they stray from righteousness, it will lead to their demise and that for Muslims, their objectives as a nation are not simply on worldly achievements, but we are expected to be principled in accordance with Islam. Allah highlights the reason for such a demise but does not put a time frame on it, as each nation shall run through their natural course, suggesting that there is a natural law of life. Human beings do have the ability to change, but they would need to reflect as a collective and then first work to change as well as ask Allah's assistance in improving. Thus, we learn from this that human actions create cause-and-effect situations. Not every nation is the same, of course, but there are indeed tendencies in peoples, and this is what *ʿulamāʾ* have taken from the *āyāt* I have mentioned above. In that sense, Muslims should see themselves as fortunate that Allah has given us His Qur'an to remind us, as without it, we may easily fall into the trap that our existence in this world is for material success only. In that sense, this ought to also be a point for Muslim historians, which is to also add works that remind Muslims of their responsibilities.

After Much Hardship and Struggle the Victory of Allah Indeed Arrives

Sūrah al-Nasr

Bismillāh-ir Rahmān-ir Rahīm

إِذَا جَآءَ نَصْرُ ٱللَّهِ وَٱلْفَتْحُ ❁وَرَأَيْتَ ٱلنَّاسَ يَدْخُلُونَ فِى دِينِ ٱللَّهِ أَفْوَاجًا ❁فَسَبِّحْ بِحَمْدِ رَبِّكَ وَٱسْتَغْفِرْهُ ❁ إِنَّهُۥ كَانَ تَوَّابًا❁

I started the previous section with the first *Sūrah* revealed to the Prophet Muhammad ﷺ *Sūrah al-ʿAlaq* as a way of making the case how the Qur'an evokes the past to encourage us to remember. The *Sūrah* began with the command to "read/recite", highlighting the importance of knowledge, learning, and literacy in Islam. It highlights Allah's role as the creator and reminds humanity of their origins, emphasising that humans were created from a "clinging substance", which underscores the theme of creation. Finally, the *Sūrah* emphasises that all knowledge is ultimately derived from Allah, who teaches humanity what they do not know. *Sūrah al-ʿAlaq* is a profound and a foundational *Sūrah*, as it highlights the importance of knowledge and the relationship between the creator and humanity, but it also highlights what it means to be human. Any attempt to assist the reader in contemplating and reaching the state of *iḥsān* should be based on evoking the memory of

Allah, applying the words of Allah as source and inspiration, and reminding the reader about the Divine order of things and His *Qadr* (Divine Decree). In this manner, the reader will attain the required humility of recognising their place in the order of creation and their purpose and relationship with Allah.

In this section, I want to explore how *Sūrah al-Naṣr* can be understood with regard to recognising some of these themes again regarding humility, the remembrance of Allah, understanding the order of things, and how nations change and evolve in relation to the notion of time, and once again the *Qadr* of Allah (Divine Decree) regarding how Allah gives His victory and how moments in Islamic history can reflect this principle.

There are various interpretations of *Sūrah al-Naṣr*, with *ʿulamāʾ* indicating that the Revelation of this *Sūrah* was the sign that the *din* [Islam] had been completed and that the Prophet's ﷺ life was coming to an end as he ﷺ had achieved his mission. The *Sūrah,* named after the word *naṣr* (victory), does not mean a victory in a particular battle but rather the complete triumph of Islam. An additional agreed-upon interpretation of the *naṣr* of Allah (Victory of Allah) implied the Muslim conquest of Mecca after the Muslims became despondent because of the Treaty of *Ḥudaybiyyah* when the Muslims had to return to Medina after preparing for the pilgrimage to Mecca. However, in the long term, the treaty was a strategic victory for the Muslims, as the opening of Mecca was not possible without it; the *Fatḥ* (Opening) of Mecca was not the victory, but, in fact, the victory was the moment in *Ḥudaybiyyah.* This point is further mentioned in detail in *Sūrah al-Fatḥ* in the Qur'an.

In *Sūrah al-Naṣr,* Allah says, "*Verily when Allah's (naṣr) comes, then comes the (Fatḥ) opening*". Here, *naṣr-Allāh* means the help of Allah and the victory of Allah. It is not for us to determine when Allah's help and victory comes to us, but it is for Allah to choose. Only when Allah decides to give us victory does the opening of hearts and places take place, and people turn to the truth in droves. A reading of this *Sūrah* can be understood in context to linking the situation at *Ḥudaybiyyah*, which paved the way for the *Fatḥ* (Opening) of Mecca. I shall expand on this point below shortly. It also means that throughout the struggle Muslims faced, Allah gave them help and victory. The victory for the Muslims establishes the fact that Allah provides His help even when we may feel otherwise, as Allah is the *al-Hakīm* (All-Wise).

However, I want to stress that while sometimes we expect victory to be close, what Allah sees as victory and what we perceive as victory can be very different. Also, what Allah considers a short time and what we perceive as a short time can once again be different. History shows us that the concept of change may, in fact, be generational. We pass on knowledge generationally, and while doing that, we are also changing the world. We continuously see in human history that while one generation attempts change, it is another generation that finally achieves it. Thus, while Muslims indeed should work to change their immediate conditions, they should also have in mind that their ideas and efforts are part of a larger schema in which they may not see the fruits of their efforts. Instead, they are part of a large generational process, and the next generations may achieve the success of their efforts. This is what I mean by being process-driven. In this sense, Muslims should, of course, work to see change in their lifetime, but by studying history, they should also be aware that they have a duty to pass down knowledge to the future generations. Being process-driven implies that while we work for the intended outcome, the outcome—in this case, victory—is in the hands of Allah when He sees fit.

I want to reiterate that it is essential to recognise that what we perceive as victory may not align with a broader understanding of success. The reason I stress this is to explain how this distinction can offer comfort during challenging times, reminding us that patience and perseverance are often part of a larger plan. The idea that change can be generational is particularly significant as knowledge and experiences are passed down, influencing future generations in ways we might not immediately recognise. There are ample examples of such in the *Sīrah* and throughout Islamic history, as I shall explain shortly.

This process of being generational highlights the importance of continuity and legacy in shaping history and also indicates understanding the laws of history in which everything has its natural order and time, and that change cannot occur until the correct conditions are met. By adopting a mindset which recognises that we are part of a larger process, we can work towards immediate change while also understanding our role in a longer narrative. This perspective encourages the passing down of knowledge and values, ensuring that each generation is equipped to build on the foundations laid by the last. Ultimately, this approach fosters resilience and hope, reinforcing the idea that while immediate results may be elusive, lasting change is often a collective, generational effort.

Hence, the interpretation of *Sūrah al-Naṣr* indicates that when Allah gives us His help and victory, people may turn to Islam in their droves. This timeless *Sūrah* reflects this and presents another essential concept: steadfastness. The *Sūrah* alludes to the idea that help, victory, and opening require the Muslim to be steadfast. The Muslim needs to be steadfast in the immediate test they are facing; they also need to be steadfast as the test can be for the whole community. The *ummah* also has to be steadfast generationally, in which one generation after another has to remain steadfast while passing on the truth of Islam, in which the constellation of truth returns to the Muslim civilisation. During those moments, Muslims are not simply expected to be steadfast but must also be cultivators of knowledge in all works of life and work to change their situation. Muslim scholarship and *ʿilm* production continued during the Crusades, Mongol rule, and even during the colonial period; Muslims have continued to cultivate the civilisation that has been built on the Qur'an and the *Sunnah* of the Messenger of Allah ﷺ. The last century has witnessed much knowledge and identity preservation, and while many Muslims continue to struggle beneath the poverty line, this *ummah* has also attained many material resources.

The *ʿulamāʾ* have agreed that *Sūrah al-Naṣr* was the last *Sūrah* to be revealed. As I mentioned, it refers to the victory of the Muslims against the Quraysh, who had become enemies to the Muslims and the call of Islam. The victory, however, was not simply that the Muslims had opened Mecca and returned it back to *tawḥīd* and rightful *ʿibādah* (worship), but that after that people became Muslim in droves. This became even more significant as the Muslims struggled with a host of trials and tribulations, such as being tortured by the Quraysh, facing boycotts and sieges as well as going on numerous wars. It was for this reason that this *Sūrah* has also been called *Sūrah al-Fatḥ* (The opening or victory).

The main theme of the *Sūrah* is that it reminds the *ummah* of Islam's victory and that the *ummah* should receive victory by being humble and recognising that victory belongs to Allah and comes from Allah, and thus, Allah deserves full praise. There is no victory without Allah's help. The next point is to appreciate that to attain victory, there is going to be hardship, struggle, effort, and, indeed, loss. But ultimately, for those who are steadfast in the path of Allah, not only will truth defeat falsehood, but there will also be great reward from Allah in both this life and the next. The victory for this *ummah*, however, is not merely material victory but is the victory in which people turn to the truth of Islam in their droves. In this sense, there are three main forms of victory. The first is the steadfastness in which a Muslim must overcome their worldly desires and fears; second, the victory of Islam and the defeat of falsehood, as Islam is a *din* of justice, and finally, the victory in people turning to Islam in large numbers.

By being aware of this, being aware of the struggle that came before, and by witnessing people turning to Islam, it is worthy of recognising the greatness of Allah by thanking Him and asking Him for forgiveness in a state of humility. The *naṣr* of Allah thus comes to the believers with *īmān* in their hearts who are determined to achieve what Allah has commanded, to be steadfast in the effort even if they are tested, endure loss and hardship, to trust Allah, to unify as an *ummah* and to thank Allah as true victory cannot be achieved without Him. This point is important as it shows that not only is the Muslim evoking the assistance of Allah but also trusting the plan of Allah.

When examining this *Sūrah* as a Muslim historian, one can attempt to interpret the events of the *Fatḥ* of Mecca in two ways. The first is to view this *Sūrah* within a micro-history context, the second is a macro-history context. The next point for the Muslim historian is to take into account that there is a reoccurring theme regarding the victory of Allah's *din* over falsehood.

It is worth examining this *Sūrah* in the context of the *Sīrah* as this can provide context. Regarding micro-history, when one can see that after the Muslims were forced to leave Mecca, they had gone through a series of hardships enforced upon them due to the disdain the Quraysh held against the Muslims and the call of Islam. When the Prophet ﷺ informed the Muslims that they were to perform the pilgrimage, they became ecstatic with joy and excitement. This was because, firstly, many of the Muslims had left their possessions and their homes in haste to return "home" which was indeed something to be excited about. Secondly, they were to go on the pilgrimage and perform this worship. As the Muslims arrived at *Ḥudaybiyyah* close to Mecca, they were apprehended and refused entry to the city of Mecca. The Quraysh then sent their emissary Suhayl bin Amr to negotiate with the Muslims and place it in a treaty form, which came to be known as the Treaty of *Ḥudaybiyyah*. Both parties came to an agreement where the Treaty of *Ḥudaybiyyah* provided several key provisions:

- Muslims would return to Medina without performing Umrah that year but could return the following year.
- A ten-year truce was established, allowing both sides to live peacefully without conflict.
- Any tribe could join either side, thereby forming alliances.
- If a Meccan converted to Islam and fled to Medina, he would be returned to the Quraysh, but Muslims who sought refuge from Mecca would not be returned.

Upon agreement of these terms, many Muslims were disheartened by the terms, especially the return to Medina without performing the pilgrimage. However, the Prophet Muhammad ﷺ emphasised the treaty as a victory and a divine sign. The Treaty of *Ḥudaybiyyah* ultimately allowed for a period of peace and facilitated the spread of Islam. It led to increased conversions, as Muslims could now freely interact and preach without the threat of conflict.

When the Banu Bakr tribe, who were in alliance with the Quraysh, broke the treaty, it triggered the Muslim response to go to war with the Quraysh. During the moment of truce, the Muslims were able to strengthen their ranks and create alliances, making them stronger than before and more prepared to tackle the Quraysh. Thus, upon the breaking of the treaty, the Muslims declared war on the Quraysh. Upon seeing the large Muslim armies coming towards Mecca, the Quraysh surrendered. The Muslims entered Mecca in peace and restored the Kaaba as the centre of worship, and during that point, many people entered Islam.

In light of *Sūrah al-Naṣr*, when examining these events from a micro-history perspective, one could say that it explains the events that unfolded. We can examine many points of the *Sūrah* where, prior to the *Fatḥ* (opening) of Mecca, many Muslims continued to suffer after the agreement made at the Treaty of *Ḥudaybiyyah*. Muslims had returned disappointed, and yet the treaty created conditions where the Muslims were able to become stronger. It required the Muslims to be patient, steadfast, and trust the Prophet ﷺ and Allah, who knew better than their own judgement. When Mecca was finally opened, this was indeed a victory from Allah—unimaginable for many Muslims at the time. The turnaround from what transpired at *Ḥudaybiyyah* and the opening of Mecca was a short time span. When the Muslims entered Mecca, they thanked Allah for this victory with humility and praised and glorified Him. All the requirements that are spoken of in *Sūrah al-Naṣr* fit the narrative of the opening of Mecca.

When examining this *Sūrah* from a macro-history perspective, we can examine how, from the inception of the Prophetic mission, Muslims went through a host of hardships, struggles and challenges. Muslims had died at *Badr, Uḥud*, and many other battles with the Quraysh. The Muslim had remained steadfast from the early days of the Prophetic mission, but the fact that they continued to ask Allah for help and trust in His victory was an indication of their trust in the Prophetic call. From the start of the *daʿwah* (invitation to Islam) by the Prophet to the increasing number of people becoming Muslim since then, where the Prophet ﷺ was chosen as the leader in Madinah. Thus, after the opening of Mecca, the peninsula was opened up for the call of Islam, and many people within the region turned to Islam after that.

These two readings can show how the Qur'an can be informative in understanding Allah's prescription of what Muslims ought to do and how one can provide perspective when advising Muslims. The fact that *Sūrah al-Naṣr* was the last to be revealed and was an indication that the life mission of the Prophet ﷺ was coming to an end can be considered a reflection of the Prophetic mission as a whole, as *Sūrah al-Naṣr* once again fulfilled all the requirements of such. In that sense, along with the Qur'an, the *Sīrah* becomes instructive for the Muslim historian in understanding key moments or *āyāt* during the life of the Prophet ﷺ, as well as the life of the Prophet ﷺ as an *āyah (*sign*)* as a whole. Whether we are applying micro-historical methods or macro-historical methods, the key for the historian is to attain all the information, study them in context, and try to establish whether the events provide an understanding of the conditions of what Allah has mentioned. This is not simply a method one would use on past events but also present situations as a way of drawing meaning and inspiration from the words of Allah, the Majestic Lord of All the Worlds.

When examining Islamic history, we can once again interpret moments when Muslims represented the themes in the divine command of Allah similar to the condition in the *Sīrah*. In this sense, I want to highlight the idea of reoccurring themes in human history, and thus, *Sūrah al-Naṣr* being a source that can also be relevant for all times. For example, the *Ṣaḥābī* and second *Khalīfah* ʿUmar Ibn al-Khaṭṭāb's (ra) opening of *Bayt al-Maqdis* shows parallels that can be discussed in this light when we examine the contents of the *Sūrah* and the themes from the *Sīrah*, from a micro and macros-history perspective. In the case of ʿUmar Ibn al-Khaṭṭāb (ra), we can see that the Persians and Eastern Romans had laid to waste much of the region, that people were being tortured, and that when the Muslims went to give *daʿwah* to Roman Emperor Heraclius, some of them were tortured, including Abdullah bin Ḥudhāfah (ra). The tensions between the Muslims and the Eastern Roman Empire increased until the Muslims defeated the Romans at Yarmouk. After the victory of Yarmouk, the area became open for Muslim conquest, and thus, when the Muslims gathered their forces for *Bayt al-Maqdis*, the Patriarch surrendered the city only if ʿUmar Ibn al-Khaṭṭāb (ra) would come personally. Upon entering the city in peace, Umar (ra) drew a peace treaty permitting the inhabitants to live in harmony. The Muslims once again praised Allah for victory, as victory comes from Him, and acted in full humility, as was the case in the opening of Mecca. After this, the city was revitalised by the Muslims, and people in the immediate region turned to Islam in their droves. From a micro-history perspective, one could highlight the specific events, struggles and victories that the Muslims went through in opening *Bayt al-Maqdis.* From a macro-history perspective, the scale can be brought out in the way I have done above to make the case that the narrative fits the conditions of the *Sūrah*. When examining the re-opening of *Bayt al-Maqdis* by Ṣalāḥ al-Dīn al-Ayyūbī and Fātiḥ Sultan Mehmet's opening of Constantinople, we can interpret similar parallels once again. From a micro-history perspective, we can examine the case of Ṣalāḥ al-Dīn and his struggle to retake *Bayt al-Maqdis,* from a macro-history perspective, we can examine the conditions from the time of the fall of *Bayt al-Maqdis* in 1099 up until Allah giving victory to the *ummah* via Salahuddin in 1187. Likewise, in the case of Fatih Sultan Mehmet, a micro-history approach can tell us about how Fatih Sultan's men struggled in their attempts to open Constantinople, and then a call to steadfastness, and how Allah finally gave them victory. Or we can place this in a macro-history perspective, showing how the Ottomans endured challenges after being defeated by Timurlane, to the Ottoman interregnum, to the coming to power of Fatih Sultan Mehmet in which victory was finally achieved due to the will of Allah. In this sense, both the Qur'an and the *Sīrah* become informative to the one who pays attention. It must be noted, however, that these realities require interpretive faculties, and mistakes can be made, and thus, one's analysis can be questioned. But the point is that this can provide Muslims with perspective, hope, and a greater spiritual understanding of the principles of their faith as well as the manner in which Allah's Qadr comes into effect.

In essence, when examining the history of Islam, we witness that it was through difficulties, challenges, hardships and tests that Allah gave victory. This indicates three points worth mentioning. Firstly, that Muslims must follow the guidance of Allah as understood from the Qur'an and *Sunnah*, and once all the conditions are met regarding obeying Allah and His Messenger ﷺ, then naturally, the conditions will emerge for victory. Examining the conditions is not easy of course, but this is what Muslim historians ought to try to do. Likewise, when a nation or people flagrantly moves away from the conditions of justice, goodness, and ethical governance and commits oppression, then likewise, the laws of history show that their end is also imminent, and they shall be disgraced. However, for falsehood to be defeated, truth is required to emerge as a counterweight. As the law of history shows that whenever there is tyranny, a restraining power of justice emerges. In this case, we can see in history that Muslims saw themselves as the representation of justice, and this should be highlighted to the *ummah* today. Secondly, it must be emphatically stressed that victory comes from Allah, and He may choose whoever He wants to attain such victory; and for Muslims, even if they do not witness or are not part of the victory, they must remember that they are part of the process, as the Muslim is required to work towards making this world a better place in accordance with the prescriptions found in the Qur'an and *Sunnah*.

Finally, the last point regarding *Sūrah Nasr* is it reminds us that all praise belongs to Allah and that after reciting this *Sūrah*, one should praise Allah in the way we have been asked to praise him by the Prophet ﷺ and ask, "Oh Allah Glory to You and all praise, O Allah I ask you to forgive our sins." — Ameen.

It is Allah in His *Raḥma* who created us, taught us knowledge, and inspired us. It is Allah to whom victory belongs, and all praise belongs to Him and Him alone.

The last century has seen Muslims face extreme violence, which has led to migration, the destruction of Muslim networks and institutions, and dislocation from their past. As a result, the Muslim mind, which is dependent on the knowledge of the past, has become scattered due to having large holes in the collective imagination. The modern world's framework of abandoning the past has detached Muslims from any real meaning of not just Islam but also what it means to be human. As a historian, reclaiming our histories is an attempt to fill those holes so that we do not become disconnected from the community of believers of the past. Not only that, but it is also so that our minds and souls are not disconnected from each other. The study of history is to remind people what they have forgotten; it is to provide meaning to how to remain consistent; it is also about promoting truth, dispelling falsehood, and providing lessons. The Qur'an has made all of these requisites for the Muslim historian through a constant where Muslim historians were involved in writing about their past. Central to the act of history writing is the concept of narrative, which Muslim historians of the past understood. They were diligent in their quest for truth and endeavoured to write about it and be aware of the importance of sources and their weaknesses. However, historians also recognise that simply relaying past events without providing value, meaning, lessons, and imagination for the future in narrative form is not enough. Writing in such a way that the reader can resonate with the narrative and internalise it is a requirement for a good historian. For this reason, I hope that more Muslims write their histories, and that they write them in accordance with the tradition that has served them so well. I hope that we will invest more into history and into the manner in which we write.

The Qur'an Points to The Messenger ﷺ as the Chosen Exemplar Elect – The Sīrah as a Source for the Muslim Historian

"O Prophet! Verily We have sent you forth as a witness, a bearer of good tidings, and a warner."

(TQM – Sūrah al-Ahzab 33:45)

In this section on the Qur'an and history, I have frequently referred to the *Sīrah* (life-story) of the Prophet ﷺ to provide context to the *āyāt* of the Qur'an. It is my belief that a Muslim historian must be well versed in the Qur'an and the *Sīrah*, as well as the tools that one acquires when training to be a historian and dealing with sources, ideologies, and styles of writing. This is because the life-story of the Prophet ﷺ is not only full of events that Muslims can learn from, but his ﷺ life-story as a whole, when reflected and reflected upon, explains the Prophetic mission in totality as one of guidance. When the Qur'an and *Sīrah* are studied together, we learn that the Qur'an actualises the Prophet's ﷺ presence by embedding him within the sacred narrative, reminding believers of his exemplary character and his fulfilment of Allah's commands. While the *Sīrah* gives details of the important episodes in the life of the Prophet, such as the *hijra* (migration) and military campaigns, the Qur'an uses these events to speak of significant moments in the relationship between Allah and His Prophet ﷺ.

When examining the works of Muslim historians like Muḥammad bin Jarīr al-Tabarī, we can see how he synthesised the Qur'an, *ḥadīth*, and *Sīrah* as sources into broader historical accounts, incorporating the Prophet's ﷺ life into the larger narrative of Islamic history. These works not only documented the life of the Prophet ﷺ but also contextualised it within the development of the Muslim community and the expansion of Islam.

Thus, the need to study the *Sīrah* should not come as a surprise, as it concerns the life of the most exemplary human being: the Beloved of Allah, our Master Muḥammad ﷺ. Studying *Sīrah* gives us an understanding of the life of the Prophet ﷺ and the life of the Muslim community and a better understanding of the Qur'an in context. As an Islamic science, the *Sīrah* has shaped the way Muslim historians first approached history writing. Employing it as the discipline of history, chronicles of the Companions, key events, and battles make up the initial *Sīrah* works of the first Muslim historians. Later, as documents were collected and narratively compiled, they documented and elaborated on the lives of notable Muslims after the first three generations, creating a larger corpus of Islamic historical works. Given its seminal place in the Islamic tradition, I argue here that the *Sīrah* should, therefore, not be seen as a standalone biography but rather as a foundational work that can shape how we write history.

The descriptive approach of history writing has dominated the Muslim world since the earlier works on the *Sīrah*. The corpus of *ḥadīth* and *fiqh* works, which dealt with the Prophetic sayings, actions, and silence on certain matters, tended to be written in a more descriptive form, letting the validity of the text provide the core meaning of what needed to be understood. While the approach to provide dates and events in sequence is, of course, needed to allow readers to determine what took place in the past, a prescriptive approach—where the writer actively gives an opinion to confer lessons and values to the reader—is also needed. Needless to say, a balance between them is needed most: while the writing of *Sīrah* did indeed influence earlier history writing in the descriptive sense, I would like to stress that *Sīrah* can also influence the prescriptive approach as well. This way, the scholar engages with both facts and evidence in helping the reader grapple with some of the more complicated questions history can pose.

Thus, I propose that the *Sīrah*, along with the Qur'an, ought also to be seen as a primary source that examines the life of the Prophet ﷺ: to be used as evidence to provide a moral and ethical benchmark by which other nations and people can be examined; as a form of comparison and contextualisation that can provide patterns in leadership, ethics, communal dynamics, politics, and wars; as well as enrich our understanding of Islamic history and global historical narratives when possible. Simply put, it can set a Prophetic standard of how human beings, societies, and nations ought to be analysed. In that sense, I argue that every Muslim historian should deeply study the *Sīrah* so that firstly, the life of the Prophet ﷺ may shape their heart and intellect and secondly, so that events—as *āyāt*—can be analysed as a way of investigating recurring events, themes and moments.

I would stress, however, that internalising the finality of his ﷺ Messengership and the divine nature of his ﷺ ordained mission means this mode of thinking and writing can only come from the intellect and heart of the Muslim historian who has already submitted to the idea of the *Shahādah*—the rational proof that he ﷺ *is* the Prophet. It thus requires a mind whose boundaries are delineated by the framework of the *ʿaqīdah* of Islam; and thus, any interpretive approach is bound by the wakeful fear of Allah as a sign of *īmān*, thereby shaping *how* we ought to be and subsequently, as historians, write. Hence, it goes without saying that this approach can only be done by a Muslim, who accepts that the Prophet ﷺ is an example for all peoples and, in so doing, submits to his ﷺ Prophethood.

Having read countless *Sīrah* books over the years, I notice that where they differ at times, although largely using the same reports and evidence is what an author chooses to include or exclude, or, at times, what points they feel are more worth detailing over others. Some scholars have written the *Sīrah* as the beginning, middle, and end of the life of the Prophet ﷺ, while others have focused on specific parts and written about themes. But all who have written the life of the Beloved of Allah have done so with the main objective of the Prophet's ﷺ life being instructive. As a result, I do not intend to say that one *Sīrah* work is better than another—they *all* add something of value that brings us closer to Allah and His Messenger ﷺ. Instead, I stress that a Muslim historian should attempt to engage in the reading of as many *Sīrah* books as possible so that they can learn something from each human endeavour that has attempted to bring the Muslim closer to Allah via the Prophet ﷺ as the Final Messenger. However, for the sake of this book, I have chosen to mention some scholars who have influenced me into thinking that the *Sīrah* can be a source for Muslim historians to write Islamic history from an *Islamic* perspective.

The Need for Morals and Lessons – Purpose for the Muslim Reader is Required

According to the late Syrian *ʿālim* Shaykh Muḥammad Saʿīd Ramaḍān al-Būṭī, a new *Sīrah* for a new generation was needed to respond to his concerns that secular forms of knowledge were reducing or ignoring the metaphysical aspects and miracles that occurred in the life of the Prophet ﷺ. Al-Būṭī argued that his aim of writing his *Sīrah* was to address Muslims who merely have a cognitive understanding of the truth of Islam, including in matters to do with the life of the Prophet Muḥammad ﷺ, and that this simple truth can be elevated to a degree more profound. For him, the *Sīrah* is to highlight the practical task of helping the reader understand the practical reality of the Prophet Muḥammad ﷺ as a complete whole.

As a result, Shaykh al-Būṭī broke down the five main aims of why, in his mind, the *Sīrah* is important:

1) To characterise an understanding of his ﷺ Prophetic character.

2) To expose the reader to the Prophetic model of exemplary virtue.

3) To enable people to better understand the Qur'an, as events in the Prophet ﷺ's life interacted with the Qur'an.

4) To allow the Muslims to acquire sound, accurate foundation in Islamic knowledge and culture, whether that be the Islamic doctrine or regulations of morals.[7]

5) Finally, to teach Muslim teachers *how* to be a teacher in the image of the Prophet ﷺ.

Shaykh al-Būṭī examined how, throughout Islamic history, Muslims took an interest in the life of the Prophet ﷺ. ʿUrwah Ibn al-Zubayr (d. 92 AH), Abān Ibn ʿUthmān (d. 105 AH), Wahb Ibn Munabbih (d. 110 AH), Shuraḥbīl Ibn Saʿd (d. 123 AH) and Ibn Shihāb al-Zuhrī (d. 124 AH) were the initial Muslim scholars who took an interest in documenting the life of the Prophet ﷺ. However, these works became scattered over the years, though parts of them, according to al-Būṭī, can be found later in the works of Muḥammad bin Jarīr al-Ṭabarī (d. 310 AH). It was not until Muḥammad Ibn Isḥāq (d. 152 AH) that literature on the *Maghāzī* (military campaigns) was comprehensively compiled and then extended out to the life of the Prophet ﷺ. The full compilation has not survived, but segments of its content can be found in the *Sīrah* of both Abū Muḥammad ʿAbd al-Malik Ibn Hishām (d. 218 AH) and al-Ṭabarī. These works on the *Sīrah* were dependent on three main sources:

1) The Qur'an.
2) Books of *ḥadith*, including Imam Malik's *Muwaṭṭā*ʾ and Imam Aḥmad Ibn Ḥanbal's *Musnad*.
3) Narrators interested in the life of the Prophet ﷺ like the Companions (ra).

Shaykh al-Būṭī accepted that the earlier scholars tended to refrain from providing personal analysis and rather preferred the reliability or certainty of a report—this is what al-Būṭī

7 Shaykh al-Būṭī reflects on this point by saying, "His life ﷺ is nothing other than an illumination, a concrete reflection of the entire corpus of Islam's principles and precepts."

deemed an "objective methodology". However, al-Būṭī recognised that contemporary students, both in the West and non-West, who had become accustomed to Western forms of learning required the author to be prescriptive in helping them understand the morals and lessons of each milestone or *āyah* of the life of the Prophet ﷺ. That did not mean Shaykh al-Būṭī was advocating a Western style of writing: al-Būṭī rather argued that the Western method of writing chose to reduce the notion of Prophethood from the Prophet Muḥammad ﷺ. In other words, this style of writing was *emptying* the *Sīrah*, and Islam in general, of the supernatural elements concerning the Prophet ﷺ's life and would simply reduce his ﷺ achievements to mere human achievements. This, for all intents and purposes, would remove the notion of Prophethood as the central theme of the *Sīrah*.

The concern for Shaykh al-Būṭī was that the *Sīrah* attests to *īmān*, which included Paradise, Day of Judgement, Resurrection, and Perdition. The point of the *Sīrah* was that it was the life of the Prophet ﷺ as the Final Messenger—and yet he ﷺ was also the Walking Qur'an; and the Qur'an, after all, was Revelation: the mainstay and source of Islam, the epitome of all miraculous phenomena. It must be stressed that al-Būṭī was concerned regarding the modern interpretative methods used by scholars trained in Western academia. For him, there was a reason why the *ʿulamāʾ* had chosen to adhere to the method of not exercising their own interpretation of things, in case the untrained scholar misunderstood or misinterpreted the Prophetic mission. As a result, while not providing a methodological framework, al-Būṭī nonetheless tried to establish a didactic approach to writing, teaching and studying the *Sīrah*, in which the traditional sources framed the narrative, but he would opine on the evidence as an *ʿālim* who could do *ijtihād* in these matters.

Being Tested is the Natural Order of Things and Learning from Life and the Qur'an

Before the passing of the Sudanese scholar Malik al-Badri, *raḥīmullah* (May Allah have mercy on his soul), I was fortunate enough to be in his company, where he mentioned his interest in the manner the Prophet ﷺ was tested by Allah and how, via character and action, he endured and overcame those tests. In our conversation, I learnt that the Prophet ﷺ was not being tested by Allah *as if* there was a test for him to pass. He ﷺ was chosen by Allah—how can the one chosen by our Lord fail a test put before him? After much thinking, I thought maybe the Prophet ﷺ was being tested so that we Muslims could learn from it—it was an example for us. That would feel like the obvious answer.

But Malik al-Badri made me aware of another point—a rule of history, which is that the Prophet ﷺ was being tested by life itself in order to shape him for the next test.

Years of contemplation in the cave of Ḥirā' had prepared the Prophet ﷺ for Revelation.

He was further tested when he ﷺ gave the first *da'wah.*

He was severely tested by the loss of his ﷺ wife and uncle in what is known as the Year of Sadness.

Each test prepared him ﷺ for the next phase, and each test was witnessed by the Muslims.

Yet through it all, not only did he display exemplary character, patience, and restraint, but he also found solutions. And more importantly: he ﷺ *never* wavered in his relationship with his Lord.

Additionally, I was reminded that not only was the Prophet ﷺ being shaped by the Divine will of Allah via the tests he ﷺ went through, but he was also nurtured by the Qur'an. Allah says in *Sūrah al-A'rāf*, "*[O Prophet!] When you do not produce before them any miracle, they say: 'Why do you not choose for yourself a miracle?' Say to them: 'I follow only what is revealed to me by my Lord. This is nothing but a means of insight into the truth, and guidance and mercy from your Lord to the people who believe.*" (TQM Maududi – 7:203)

After speaking to Malik al-Badri, I sat there reflecting on the life of the Prophet ﷺ. In examining the hardship he ﷺ went through in life, I thought about my own growth as a person. But after speaking to Malik al-Badri, *as a historian*, I also started to examine how the *ummah* responded whenever tested and whether the *Sīrah* could be an example of how the *ummah* had learnt to behave in the same way. To me, this was a *very* different way of examining the life of the Prophet ﷺ.

The Model of Prophetic Justice

This leads me to the Malaysian thinker and scholar Sayyid Muhammad al-Naquib al-Attas. When in Malaysia, I attended a symposium where al-Attas spoke about his ideas. What caught my attention and what is relevant to this section is when al-Attas spoke about the nature of Prophethood and the notion of justice, which is part of the Prophetic missions. Al-Attas mentioned that upon deep reflection and contemplation he came to the conclusion that *adab* is missing among Muslims today.

He was not using the term to mean 'good manners' or 'etiquette' as popularly understood today. Instead, al-Attas stated that he was using the term in the way it was used in order to understand the Divine message—that is, *adab* as the reflection of wisdom, which comes from knowing that true wisdom is knowledge which tells you the proper places of everything. To attain this understanding was to correctly understand reality and the knowledge that Allah has presented to us via the Qur'an and *Sunnah.* While human beings can become wise upon pondering upon the realities of life, true wisdom in understanding *ḥaqq* (truth and reality) is needed in understanding the Prophetic mission, and the notion that Prophethood is the only way one can come to Truth. It is for this reason that all the previous Prophets and the Final Prophet ﷺ were sent, as human beings require knowledge and guidance from Allah. Allah has done that by His Word, the Qur'an, and His chosen Messenger ﷺ. This is because human beings cannot know everything.

Thus, the Prophet ﷺ was the perfect human being, as he represented the perfect message of Islam. Through him ﷺ, we can understand the notion of *'adl* (justice) in the way Allah intended. Al-Attas broke this down as having four main components:

1) *Amr* — that justice requires the act of command, laws and prohibitions.
2) *Ahl* (experts or authorities) — that the implementation of justice requires people who are authorities and capable of enacting justice.
3) *Ḥikmah* (wisdom) — the knowledge that informs you of the proper place of everything. This includes not simply matters of the material but the spirit and hereafter.
4) *Adab* — the conformity of correct action to wisdom. If such is done, then the condition of justice is actualised, which is the condition of things in their proper places.

These qualities, alongside the notion of justice as al-Attas has mentioned, can be found in the Prophetic mission—thus making the key point that studying history from an Islamic lens is to seek notions of justice whenever possible, and highlight to Muslims this requirement that is expected from Allah, and that, when enacted, conforms to a life of tranquillity.

Hence, the Prophetic mission was a mission of justice; al-Attas' explanation is helpful in making a sound case for the Muslim historian to seek this understanding from the *Sīrah* and then examples in Islamic history that conform with the reality of the conditions of justice so that the *ummah* have examples they can aspire to and perhaps attempt to actualise this as a reality.

The Prophetic Model is One of Foundational Ethics

More recently, the Muslim Moroccan philosopher and scholar Taha Abdurrahman has spoken of how the *Sīrah* can provide a methodology regarding the foundations of the Prophetic ethical framework. Abdurrahman explains that there have been two ways in which the *Sīrah* has been traditionally viewed; the first was by the People of Theory (*Ahl al-Naẓar*) and the second by the People of Narration (*Ahl al-Khabr*). This created a framework where thinkers adhered to certain methods of theory and of narration. In particular, for Abdurrahman, these were made up of three types:

1) The methods of the *muḥaddithīn* (scholars of *ḥadīth*)
2) The methods of *mu'arrikhīn* (historians)
3) The methods of the *fuqahā'* (jurists)

Taha Abdurrahman thus argued that while the method of the *muḥaddithīn* had great value as it was based on the correctness of the reports used, its strictness, while important for *ḥadīth* studies, ought not to be as binding method-wise when it comes to the history of the life of the Prophet ﷺ. Keep in mind, however, that he *did not* argue that *aḥadīth* should not be used or incorrectly interpreted—he stressed on including *aḥadīth* in the writing of the *Sīrah*. He also raised the same concerns regarding the need for the juristic approach to be examined as well, as this approach has been reduced mainly to the extraction of rulings.

Abdurrahman's prime concern was *the absence of an interpretative value* on the life of the Prophet ﷺ, which he feels is needed for today's students. Abdurrahman thus pointed to the need for a more "intellectual approach" (*ṭarīqa fikriyya*) that included a balance between the three methods and an accompanying interpretive method. As a result, he proposed that *akhlāq* (ethics) should be added as a branch of study for the *Sìrah*.

When speaking of the interpretive method, Abdurrahman stressed that it has to be restricted to the *ʿaqīdah* of Islam. He writes that the Muslim, after forging the Covenant with Allah via the *Shahādah*, also confirms a trusteeship that is in accordance with the ethical and spiritual meanings of Islam. This method of ethics, when examining the Prophetic biography, has to adhere to the standards of ethics found in the biography of the Prophet ﷺ. Thus, any new writing of the *Sīrah* must include three aspects:

1) *Tafakkur* (Contemplation) — resorting to contemplation rather than mere thinking.

2) *Āyāt* (Signs) — considering the signs within the life of the Prophet ﷺ, with regard to the Prophet ﷺ himself being a sign for humanity, and to reflect upon his life in totality.[8]

3) The Covenant — found in Scripture.

When speaking of the Covenant, Abdurrahman mentions that these two can be broken down further into four:

8 This does not mean to simply examine the life of the Prophet ﷺ in events or moments, but rather holistically. Abdurrahman argues that signs, by their nature, are not hidden—but rather, are there in plain view and require examining, explaining, and understanding.

1) The Covenant of Testimony [*Mīthāq al-Ishhād*]
2) The Covenant of Entrustment [*Mīthaq al-Isti'mān*]
3) The Covenant of Transmission [*Mīthāq al-Irsāl*]
4) The Covenant of Distinguishment [*Mīthāq al-Ikhtiṣāṣ*]

Taha Abdurrahman believes that for there to be an Islamic approach to both studying the life of the Prophet ﷺ and writing about it, the intellect needs to be made subservient to *akhlāq* that the Prophet ﷺ represented—what one would call the 'Prophetic Ethic'. He argues that when the Prophet ﷺ taught and acculturated the Companions, he not only provided an intellectual and spiritual education but also coalesced their intellects with the Prophetic ethic, such that they were not simply satisfied with being *mu'minūn*. Rather, they were further elevated to the stage of *muḥsinūn*, at that level of *Iḥsān* where they see their world and everything they do as apropos of the Prophetic mission. In that sense, Taha Abdurrahman has made a strong case for the *Sīrah* to be studied by Muslim historians in order that they themselves may reflect and also encourage the reader to contemplate, see, and understand the signs and appreciate the Covenant that shapes the Prophetic ethical framework in all matters of life. This is because, for Abdurrahman, Islam is a *din* of *akhlāq*.

I would thus extend that the principles that Taha Abdurrahman is proposing fit well with my point of the *Sīrah* being a foundational text for the Muslim historian alongside the Qur'an. Al-Būṭī was correct in his assertion that the *Sīrah* provides lessons and morals by which other moments in history are measured. Malik al-Badri's point on how the Prophet ﷺ and the Muslims of his time were tested can also be instructive in examining how Muslims have been continually tested throughout history—and how such is the nature of human life. Al-Attas' notion of understanding justice in Islam, which can be understood from the Prophetic mission, is also important in examining when Muslims took this concept as foundational. Finally, Taha Abdurrahman's point on the Prophetic ethic being foundational to the Prophetic mission and the writing of *Sīrah* can extend to the way we write history.

The *Sīrah* is not only important in regard to the Prophet ﷺ, but additionally, we are introduced to the *Ṣahābah* also and see how the Prophet ﷺ shaped them to internalise the Prophetic mission. In doing so, after the death of the Prophet ﷺ, we saw a continuation of the mission of Islam via the *Ṣahābah*, which set in motion the ideals of Islam in a generation where the Prophet ﷺ was no more. This was the first opportunity to examine the ideals examined in Muslims without the Prophet ﷺ. What we see is an endeavour to uphold the Islamic ideals; later, after the death of the *Ṣahābah*, we saw these ideals practised by Muslims up until today. Thus, the *Sīrah* also highlights how a Muslim historian can examine ideals and attempt to examine other moments in Islamic history that can benefit the Muslims.

Thus, I have found benefit in the ideas of these Muslim thinkers regarding how the *Sīrah* has to be instructive in shaping history writing. It is imperative that we are able to show *and* reflect when and how Muslims have been able to emulate the signs and tests that the Prophet ﷺ went through. In doing so, the Muslim reader can see a pattern of consistency that demonstrates how Muslims across the history of Islam have striven to uphold the values and principles found in the *Sīrah*.

When examining this section, I want the Muslim reader and historian to take away these points. The first is that for an Islamically-oriented approach to writing history, it is imperative that the Muslim historian's ideas and works are in conformity with the Islamic *ʿaqīdah*. This means that their ideas and methods must be firmly placed within the confines of the boundaries of the *ʿaqīdah* while also being inspired by it. The next is that the Muslim historian should attempt to exercise the use of the Qur'an and *Sīrah* as sources as a way of guiding the Muslim reader to understand the divine will and divine order of things as have been relayed to us by Allah and His Messenger ﷺ. Muslim historians must study the Qur'an and *Sīrah* so that they can consolidate their own *īmān* and get closer to Allah. But also, that the Qur'an and *Sīrah* should also be introduced in historical works that encourage the reader to reflect and contemplate the divine guidance of Allah as mentioned in the Qur'an, in which they can be seen to be actualised in historical moments so that the reader can look to reach the stage of *iḥsān*. Additionally, the *Sīrah* ought to provide tangible examples that can help the reader understand the *āyāt* of the Qur'an in a practical sense regarding realities and conditions that fit Allah's words. The *Sīrah* itself ought to be examined as the sacred history of the Prophet ﷺ, and thus, in and of itself, a work of inspiration and guidance. Thus, the Qur'an and *Sīrah* should not only guide the heart of the historian but should be used to bring into context the divine word, the sacred Prophetic examples and the lived realities of the *ummah*. This, then, cannot only help Muslims in getting familiar with the Qur'an and *Sīrah* as sources but also provide relatable meaning for Muslims regarding the Qur'an, the life-story of the Prophet, and the *ummah* of the past.

ب

SECTION III

AN ISLAMIC ETHOS TO KNOWLEDGE PRODUCTION

Islam, Īmān and Iḥsān are the Three Pillars of Islamic Knowledge

In this section, I shall explore whether there is a framework that can be applied to producing knowledge in accordance with Islam and, by extension, whether we can use such a framework as historians. At first glance, it may not be deemed necessary to write in an "Islamic manner", as the neutrality of secular writing and knowledge production would lead one to think that this is in conformity with Islam. One would assume that neutral or "objective" forms of knowledge production, while not supportive of the Islamic mission, would not be antagonistic towards it. This would lead one to believe that the suggestion I make is simply the act of writing history covered in a superficial Islamic garb of words, prayers, and invocations. However, I would like to stress the need to recognise that there is no such thing as neutral or objective knowledge production. All forms of intellectual efforts are value-laden, even this work of mine. I make it clear that this work is intended to explain to Muslims the dangers of forms of knowledge that masquerade as neutral and how an approach that is in conformity with the Islamic *ʿaqīdah* can help develop a means of how Muslims should view sources, secondary material, as well as provide solutions as forms of *naṣīḥah* (advice), *ḥikmah* (wisdom), and *daʿwah* (invitation) in accordance with Islam and its message.

While I do not claim to be a person of wisdom or a philosopher inspired by Muslim thinkers, I have taken the famous *ḥadīth* known as the Ḥadīth Jibril as a simple template for the reader of this work to see how an Islamically inspired approach can be actualised. That is not to say that Muslims in the past did not undertake such an approach. But with the newer developments in history writing, I am proposing to find ways where a balance can be made that combines the two methods, from our tradition and the new tradition, in conformity with the Islamic *aqīdah.* There are indeed Muslims in the Muslim world who are working for such ends, and I see the need and benefit of collective effort.

In the *ḥadīth*, there are three key pillars which one could say can act as the foundations of an Islamically-oriented approach, which I find helpful to writing history for the Muslim. I shall explain this in detail below later. These are *Islam*, *īmān,* and *iḥsān*, which are connected and all lead to the varying degrees in which one can write works with Allah in mind. Simply put, the first approach, which is Islam, is to make the case of the Islamic *ʿaqīdah*, in which all knowledge should be in conformity to the *Shahādah* of Islam and the standards that knowledge can be beneficial as an act of worship. The second is *īmān*, in which the writer goes beyond just examining whether knowledge is in conformity with Islam and is driven in a solution-based approach that not only provides worldly solutions but also spiritual ones, in which the reader is inspired to seek solutions from the Qur'an, *Sunnah*, and *Sīrah* but then act upon them too. Finally, the last stage, *iḥsān*, which is the stage where a knowledge producer has attained a level of wisdom in the matters of understanding the world, human nature, and historical patterns, as well as spiritual matters. In this stage, they are people of deep contemplation, and that contemplative approach is found in both their historical analysis and their solutions, drawing the reader to understand the greatness of Allah, His Oneness, and His Divine Will. The solutions provided should inspire the soul to want to act in conformity with the intellect, where it becomes inspired in awe of Allah's majesty and submits to Him with the knowledge that it wants to do acts of devotion to Him even in isolation when no other person can see them. It means reading a work of history, for example, and seeing that a people faced great hardship in the way of Allah and were unable to actualise their efforts, but unknown to them, Allah's plan was something else, and that what Allah had in store for them was far better than what they wanted. It attempts to show a grand schema or inner spiritual depth. For a Muslim to read history like this can bring them closer to Allah, appreciating that nothing happens without the will of Allah and that He knows better than what we know. This type of transformative manner in examining history can then be related to existing realities and encourage people to reflect and then contemplate the greatness of Allah, hence making them people who are always aware of Allah's presence in every walk of life.

Thus, the first approach to knowledge production for the historian is a mere examination of the data and sources, to make sure that the sources are valid, not corrupted, agreeable, and informative. Once that has been achieved, the historian relays this information in an analytical manner, explaining the details of events, their impact and consequences. This is the act of analysis, addressing possible criticisms, and providing vocabulary that explains particular phenomena. Such an approach would be seen as being in conformity with Islam as it is a logical and analytical deduction of events and ideas; it examines the sources and applies them accordingly. One may discover that a source has been misinterpreted, that new information has become available, or that the primary source itself needs testing for validity. One may discover that another historian misinterpreted the primary sources, missed a source, or made mistakes. There may be need for revisions or discovery of new information in order to establish the truth. All these forms are in conformity with Islam, and so one may argue that so long as a Muslim follows this approach, then their work is Islamic. In principle, this approach should be undertaken regarding scholarship. Later, however, I will highlight some of the dangers that have emerged from Western academic-style scholarship, which is often seen as simply following the actions and methods I have just explained. First, I want to explain an *īmān*-centred approach.

An *īmān*-centered approach, however, would suggest that the historian not simply analyse the sources, data, and facts nor simply examine the validity of the author's interpretive findings and narrative but that their work attempts to provide solutions. These solutions, firstly, could be an attempt to examine what the people in the past could have done differently and how we can learn from those examples. Secondly, solutions should be offered to the readership by relating past events to their current lives and offering them ways that they can learn from the past. It may be that they can learn in terms of mistakes they made, or it could be in terms of things they did well that we are no longer applying. Additionally, by attaching the readership to people of the past, it can make them feel like they are part of a larger body, a greater plan—part of humanity, not only in terms of the present but since the time of the Prophet Adam ﷺ. Just as scientists are encouraged to reflect and then contemplate the vastness of the cosmos and the order of things within it, likewise a Muslim historian should examine the vastness of history and our place in it. This leads to humility and recognising the natural order of how things are put in motion, whether in the cosmos or human history. Everything is part of the divine plan and divine order of things. But just as there are complexities in understanding the specifics of the natural world, likewise, there are complexities in examining and explaining the human lived experience. The solution, however, for the Muslim historian is not simply to stop there but to draw from the Qur'an, *Sunnah*, and *Sīrah* as a way of highlighting the divine plan as well as understanding that we have solutions in the tradition of Islam. Thus, *īmān* is the solidified belief and to act in accordance with the prescriptions of Islam, which means to act in accordance with the *Sharīa*, and providing *naṣīḥah*, and *da'wah* from the precepts of Islam is part of an *īmān*-centered approach. Finally, one may understand the deeper meaning of things when studying history, they may be able to join the dots in trying to visualise the grand narrative of Allah's plan, they may seek to take the ethical considerations into account and provide solutions that are not simply practical but are within an ethical and moral framing, and attempt to heighten the spirituality of the reader. *Iḥsān* is the final approach in which both the practical and spiritual dimensions of the reader are taken into consideration when providing solutions—where a deeper and contemplative approach is established as *ihsan* is the ultimate level of *īmān*.

Thus, there are three stages of writing history. The first stage is the analytical approach. The second stage is to provide solutions, both rationally and from the sacred sources. The third stage, the highest form of writing, encourages the reader to exercise their contemplative faculties and to think deeper about their existence. This is the *iḥsān*-oriented approach. Not all forms of writing have to be written in the *iḥsān*-oriented approach, however. At times, a simple analysis would suffice, while at times, the readership may not be at the level to appreciate the deeper meanings of history, and at other times, people may need solutions from the past for practical purposes. However, the point is to suggest that in regards to stages, actions, methods, and works that are in conformity with the Islamic concept of *iḥsān* are of the highest degree, and this is what a Muslim historian should aspire to, as only a Muslim can write in accordance with *iḥsān*, as this requires *īmān*—with certainty in belief in Allah and a deep understanding of the need to act accordingly to what Allah has prescribed.

The Essence of Ḥadīth Jibril ﷺ [9]

The lengthy *ḥadīth* has a few points worthy of interest that I would like to explain, which I think are helpful for Muslim historians to write history from an Islamic perspective before I mention the ideas of Islam, *īmān,* and *iḥsān*. The first

---

9 Full ḥadīth—In the collection of Imam Nawawi's *Ḥadīth al-Qudsi* (40 Ḥadīth), The ḥadīth is narrated by Umar Ibn Khattab (ra), who said: "While we were one day sitting with the Messenger of Allah ﷺ, there appeared a man dressed in extremely white clothes and with very black hair. No traces of journeying were visible on him, and none of us knew him. He sat down close by the Prophet ﷺ, rested his knee against his thighs, and said, "O Muhammad! Inform me about Islam." The Messenger of Allah ﷺ said, "Islam is that you should testify that there is no deity except Allah and Muhammad is His Messenger, that you should perform *Salah*, pay the *Zakāt*, fast during *Ramadan*, and perform *Hajj* to the House (The *Kaaba* in *Mecca*), if you are able to do so." The man said, "You have spoken truly." We were astonished at his questioning him ﷺ and telling him that he was right, but he went on to say, "Inform me about *Iman*." He ﷺ answered, "It is that you believe in Allah and His angels and His books and His Messengers and in the Last Day, and in *Qadar* (destiny), both in its good and in its evil aspects." He said, "You have spoken truly." Then he said, "Inform me about *Ihsan*." He ﷺ answered, "It is that you should serve Allah as though you could see Him, for though you cannot see Him yet (know that) He sees you." He said, "Inform me about the Hour." He ﷺ said, "About that, the one questioned knows no more than the questioner". So he said, "Well, inform me about the signs thereof." He ﷺ said, "They are that the slave-girl will give birth to her mistress, that you will see the barefooted, naked, destitute, the herdsmen of the sheep (competing with each other) in raising lofty buildings." Thereupon the man went off. I waited a while, and then he ﷺ said, "O Umar, do you know who the questioner was?" I replied, "Allah and His Messenger know better." He said, "That was Jibrail ﷺ. He came to teach you your religion."

point is about style and the pedagogy used by both Jibril ﷺ and the Prophet ﷺ, as both were aware of what was taking place. We notice that Jibril ﷺ, upon sitting down respectfully facing the Prophet ﷺ, drew his knees closer to the Prophet's till they touched and then gently placed the palms of his hands on the Prophet's thighs before proceeding to respectfully ask him. We can infer an important lesson of Islamic edification (*tarbiyah*) from this narration. Closing the physical distance was a form of pedagogy between the Messenger of Messengers ﷺ and the beloved of Allah ﷺ. He sat directly in front of the Prophet ﷺ, face to face. In addition, although it was Jibril ﷺ who was asking the questions, to the surprise of ʿUmar Ibn al-Khaṭṭāab (ra), the Prophet ﷺ did not assert a sense of hierarchy, but rather that he ﷺ and Jibril ﷺ were teaching the Muslims together.

What this indicated first was the decorum/etiquette and *iḥtirām* (respectful mannerism) that Jibril ﷺ showed the beloved of Allah ﷺ. He sat before him and asked a series of questions, for which the Prophet ﷺ gave short and concise answers. There is something to be said about how one ought to teach. While Jibril ﷺ asked specific questions, the Prophet ﷺ also answered in a clear and concise manner, explaining the concepts which Jibril ﷺ subsequently reaffirmed. What we first take is that the works of *ʿilm* and their practitioners have a duty of care in the way that they teach, whether in written form or in practice, where a style is followed that presents goodness and respect. We see that it was not simply Jibril ﷺ who used a question-and-answer method when speaking to the Messenger of Allah ﷺ, but the Prophet ﷺ did the same with ʿUmar Ibn al-Khaṭṭāb (ra) as well when he ﷺ asked: "Do you know who the questioner was?" The Prophet ﷺ asked his senior Companion a question as a way of eliciting an answer from him rather than telling him that the man who had questioned him was the Archangel Jibril ﷺ. In doing so, he repeated the question-and-answer style that everyone had witnessed. Asking questions stimulates deeper thought and analysis: it creates an interactive learning environment where knowledge is actively constructed, encourages self-reflection, and helps solidify knowledge. I cannot stress that any teacher or knowledge producer must take into account the importance of their ideas and how they transmit them to the learner. Also, just like in the case of this *ḥadīth*, good knowledge production for a wide audience should be clear and concise in the ideas and points they are trying to make, as there is no need to conflate ideas, which the minds of people might find difficult to grasp.

In order to achieve this level of contemplative thought, it not only requires one to develop a historical mind, but it also requires capable teachers. In the pedagogical tradition of Islam, the teacher is central to the learning process. The teacher not only passes down the knowledge to the student and cultivates the curious mind, but the teacher, as a living example, also shapes the student's character. This process is the way in which the Prophet ﷺ taught the meaning of the Qur'an to his *Ṣaḥābah* (Companions). The development of *Sunnah* was based on the notion that the Qur'an requires detailed interpretation. The Qur'an also pointed to the Prophet ﷺ as the teacher of the Qur'an and his *Sunnah* (Prophetic way/tradition) as an integral form of support for the Qur'an. Imam al-Ghazālī mentions clearly in his works the need for a master-and-disciple relationship between the teacher and the student. This creates affection between teacher and pupil and cultivates a community that is living with references from their teachers. The Muslim communities were most successful when they had teachers as nodes of *ʿilm* in their communities who cultivated the Prophetic tradition of *ʿilm* (knowledge) and *ʿamal* (correct action) into their students. In the West, books are written to be read; in our tradition, books are written to be taught, and the teacher is central to that teaching culture.

Although it is not directly related to the *ḥadīth* in regard to what I hope to address here, I find it essential to point out that in Islam, the atmosphere of *ʿIlm* is one in which goodness is learnt and attained, where the angels are present, and in which the one learning and the one teaching are being rewarded in the eyes of Allah by discussing the most elevated of concepts, which is to get closer to Him. This environment requires respectful behaviour for all those present. *ʿIlm* in Islam is not simply knowledge in the way of just learning information. There is an etiquette of learning, a sense of respect between teacher and student, and an etiquette of love and kindness that needs to be displayed. All those who witnessed this moment learnt from this behaviour, and all those who read this *ḥadīth* are expected to nurture the same. The Prophet ﷺ could have simply told the Muslims at the time what these concepts were, as he ﷺ had done on countless occasions on these subjects. But Allah wanted to show the Companions of the Prophet ﷺ and us, who still engage with this *ḥadīth*, via the medium of His angel, Jibril ؑ, how to make a teaching practice a *sunnah* by Jibril ؑ interacting with the Prophet ﷺ in front of the *ummah*.

Another point about this *ḥadīth* which I would like to mention is that when Jibril ؑ asked the Prophet ﷺ about the last hour and the Prophet ﷺ responded with the answer "that the one questioned knows no more than the questioner," this indicates that the idea of the end of time is something that only Allah knows. The Prophet ﷺ was aware of many signs leading up to the last hour, which he informed us of, but did not tell us when the last hour would be. As a historian, this point is important, that although we know that this world will end we do not know when, just like we do not know when we will die, and when a nation or civilisation will end, and thus, via extension while historians may observe patterns and signs of the demise of a people, nation, or civilisation, we are still not able to give a time, as that is in the hands of Allah; we can try to anticipate these things, but this is an issue that belongs to Allah and Him alone.

Islam, Īmān, and Iḥsān – A Brief Explanation

Islam literally means "submission" or "surrender" to the will of Allah. It refers to the outward practice of the faith, encompassing the actions and rituals that a Muslim performs. It is also etymologically related to the words "*Salāmah*" (safety from danger) and "*silm*" (peace). To understand Islam in a simple sense, as mentioned in the *ḥadīth* that I shall later explain, we first need to define the five pillars that constitute the core ritual practices of Islam. These are:

1) The ***Shahādah***: The declaration of faith, affirming Allah's Oneness and Muhammad's ﷺ Prophethood.
2) **Ṣalāh**: The performance of the five daily prayers.
3) **Zakāt**: The compulsory giving of alms or charity to those in need as a form of worship.
4) **Ṣawm**: Fasting during the month of Ramadan.
5) The **Ḥajj**: The pilgrimage to the holy city of Mecca, which is required once in a lifetime for those who are able.

Īmān means "faith" or "belief." Etymologically, it denotes the profession of the truth of something as opposed to falsehood. Religiously, it refers to the internal conviction and acceptance of the core tenets of Islam. There are **six articles of faith: *Īmān* is articulated through the belief in:**

1) **Allah, and His Oneness.**
2) **Angels,** which are the existence of angels created by Allah.
3) The **Books**: The holy scriptures revealed by Allah, including the Qur'an, the Torah, the Psalms, and the Gospel.
4) The **Prophets**: The belief in the Prophets sent by Allah, including Muhammad ﷺ as the final Prophet.
5) The **Day of Judgement** The belief in the resurrection and accountability after death.
6) The **Divine Decree**: The belief in Allah's predestination and divine will.

Iḥsān means "excellence" or "perfection" in worship and conduct. It represents the highest level of faith and consciousness of Allah. It involves acting with sincerity, integrity, and compassion in all aspects of life. Simply put, **Islam** focuses on the external actions and practices of faith. ***Īmān*** emphasises internal belief and conviction in the core tenets of the faith. ***Iḥsān*** represents striving for excellence and sincerity in all actions, creating a comprehensive and holistic approach to living a life dedicated to Allah.

Fundamentally, this *ḥadīth* is the essence of the *Sunnah* and knowledge production. By examining this *ḥadīth*, which is not simply an example for those in attendance but for Muslims until the end of time, we witness the special relationship between Jibril ﷺ and the beloved of Allah ﷺ, how they interacted with each other to teach the masses, in a style which has now become known as being *Jibrīlī*, and finally, how time as a variable is something which is in the realm of Allah alone, a point which is significant for Muslim historians to recognise. One could argue that the *ḥadīth* also points to the gradients of the Islamic *ʿaqīdah* in which one first submits to Allah (Islam), then one believes in their hearts (*Īmān*), and then one strives to perfect it (*Iḥsān*).

In the Qur'an, in *Sūrah al-Ḥujurāt* (The Dwellings), Allah mentions the difference between those who submit but have not yet fully believed in their hearts when He says, "*The Bedouins say, "We have believed." [O, Prophet] Say, "You have not [yet] believed; but say [instead], 'We have submitted,' for faith has not yet entered your hearts. And if you obey Allah and His Messenger, He will not deprive you from your deeds of anything. Indeed, Allah is All-Forgiving and Most-Merciful.*" (TQM 49:14 Sahih International Translation).

It is clear from this *āyah* that mere belief for the Muslim is not enough, that they must act upon that belief, and that the belief must be in conformity with the tenets of *īmān*. This indicates that a Muslim should not just simply declare their *Shahādah* and think it is sufficient to be Muslim. Instead, it implies that once the *Shahādah* has been taken that a Muslim should follow the prescriptions of the faith. This means performing all acts of worship in the way the Messenger ﷺ has taught us. Additionally, it includes fulfilling the conditions of *īmān* and acting upon them with full knowledge. While a person who does not pray *Salah* five times a day is nominally considered a Muslim, we can diagnose from this that they have not acted in accordance with *īmān*.

Thus, the *Muslim* and the *Mu'min* are clearly identified in the Qur'an and differentiated in gradation. All Muslims should subscribe to being *Mu'mins*, which suggests that a proper understanding of the Islamic *'aqīdah* is not simply testifying to the *Shahādah* but acting upon what it requires.

Allah also speaks of the *Muḥsin (Good-doers)*, and it is worth noting that the *Muḥsin* is continuously mentioned in the Qur'an as the "Good-doer", having an exceptional rank, as the *Muḥsin* is the one with the highest level of *taqwā* (consciousness of Allah). To be a person who has *iḥsān* means that, while all Muslims who act in accordance with Islam have *īmān*, there is a gradient that differentiates between the one who does only the prescribed acts and follows the *Sharīa* and then the one who does this and attempts to perfect themselves by also being cognisant of Allah at all times. This means acts are always done in the knowledge of pleasing Allah, getting close to Him, remembering Him at all times, and submitting oneself in total humility. This can involve doing *dhikr*, perfecting one's character, striving selflessly for Allah, and accepting life's challenges with patience and humility, and recognising Allah's plan.

The *ḥadīth* points to 1) Submission, 2) Belief with conviction, and then 3) Being "Good-doers" for the sake of Allah. I shall describe in detail later in this essay what it means to have *iḥsān*, as I accept that simply describing it as doing good does not do it justice.

The ultimate level of *Islam* must be the one who looks to represent Allah at the highest of levels. While these concepts can be seen as grades, these are also concepts that are connected, as shall be explained in this section. Either way, I argue that *Islam, īmān* and *iḥsān* primarily are about centring Allah, and a historian and knowledge seeker must attempt to adhere to all three as this is the highest-level objective of *ʿilm*, to both be conscious of Allah, and to make the reader equally conscious of Him too.

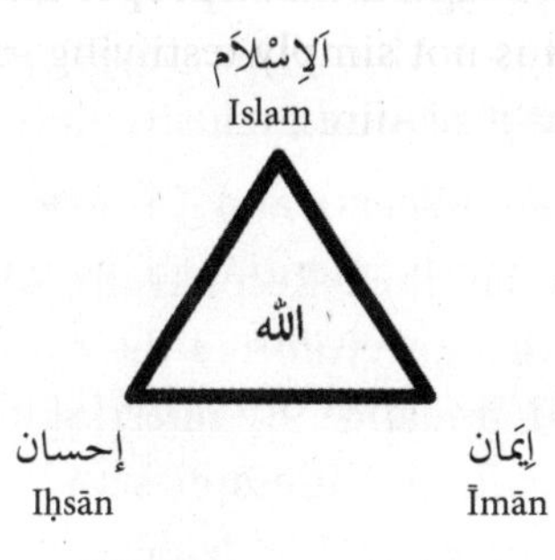

Allah at the centre of Islam, Īmān, and Iḥsān.

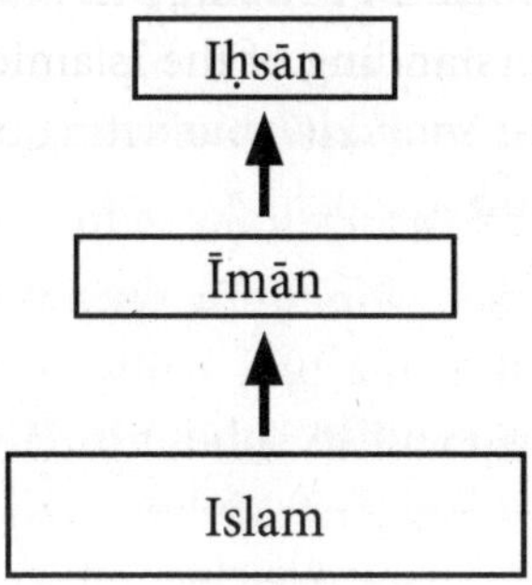

Islam, Īmān, and Iḥsān as levels.

The Case for the Islamic ʿAqīdah – Islam

Allah has made the *Shahādah* the requisite for being Muslim and becoming a member of the *ummah* of Islam, as a result of which, he or she is then commanded to perform the other four pillars of worship, the minimum that Muslims must perform. The *Shahādah* represents the *ʿaqīdah* of Islam, and the other tenets indicate the centrality of worship and the foundations of a worship-oriented life thereupon a life of *ubudiyya*.

In the *Shahādah*, the use of "I testify" highlights the importance of conscious affirmation and understanding. It implies that one must fully grasp the implications of this declaration, underscoring the significance of knowledge (*ʿIlm*) in faith. The phrase "*lā ilāha illā Allāh*" begins with a negation of divinity and worship for other beings, and an affirmation that divinity and worship are exclusively for Allah. This establishes the foundation of monotheism, emphasising exclusive devotion to Allah.

Thus, worship is central to the declaration. Recognising Allah as the only deity worthy of worship reinforces the commitment to submit to His will and guidance. By referring to the Prophet Muhammad ﷺ as "*ʿAbdu-hu*," it emphasises his servitude to Allah, indicating that he ﷺ lived a life dedicated to fulfilling Allah's commands, not his own desires. This sets a model for all Muslims, highlighting that true servitude involves submission to the divine will. The Prophet ﷺ acted as a channel for Allah's message, which means that his teachings and actions are authoritative for Muslims. This reinforces the understanding that Islamic practice and beliefs are defined by divine guidance, not human interpretation. The understanding that the Prophet ﷺ is bound by Allah's will implies that all Muslims, whether scholars or laypeople, must adhere to the same principles. The parameters of Islam are established by Allah, and any deviation from these is not permissible. The *Shahādah* unites Muslims in their recognition of Allah's sovereignty and the Prophethood of Muhammad ﷺ. This collective declaration fosters a sense of community and shared purpose in worshipping Allah and following the path laid out by the Prophet ﷺ. I would like to stress that the *Shahādah* is more than just a declaration; it is a comprehensive statement of faith that encapsulates the essence of Islamic belief. It calls for an understanding that is both intellectual and spiritual, guiding Muslims in their relationship with Allah and their commitment to living according to divine guidance. This foundational declaration serves as a reminder of the responsibilities and principles that shape the lives of all believers.

The second part of the second testimony also indicates that the Prophet Muhammad ﷺ is the Messenger of Allah, meaning that he ﷺ has been sent as an example of how to be a worshipper of Allah, and that he ﷺ has brought a message to mankind, which is the Qur'an and *Sunnah*. In this sense, the Qur'an, as the word of Allah which was communicated through the Prophet ﷺ to humanity, must also offer a Muslim historian a framework. Also, when we learn of a particular action, behaviour or event, the Qur'an should be used to show how Allah has spoken of such matters to remind us of the reoccurring nature of the human lived experience. The *Sunnah*, likewise, also provides plenty of examples, and the

Sunnah too can provide additional information that can be helpful to the Muslim historian.

The *Shahādah* is thus a rational declaration of one's knowledge of Allah, one's purpose regarding their relationship to Him, which is to worship, that all of humanity must worship Him, and that the method to do that is in the manner which the Prophet Muhammad ﷺ brought that message. Belief and knowledge of a creator can be rationally understood and proven; once this is established, we are informed that the Creator's name is Allah. The name Allah, which although can be used to mean God, is a proper noun. Allah is not just the "God of the Muslims", but the God of all creation. As a proper noun, His name is a supplication and an invocation, and therefore, one must say Allah as often as they can.

As our testimony of belief is connected to the idea of worship, how we worship is also an important point, and we can rationally deduce the notion of *Nubuwwah* (Prophethood). Because human beings are informed by Prophets, the idea of *Nubuwwah* is the sensible deduction that human beings require examples in human form of how to worship. As Muslims, we are informed that the name of this Prophet is Muhammad ﷺ, meaning we now worship Allah in the way the Prophet ﷺ has been commanded, and we follow him by extension. This is the comprehensive understanding of the *Shahādah* as it encompasses all of Islam, which includes the Qur'an, *Sunnah, 'ilm*, and the *Sharīa*. This is what it means to submit to Islam.

The *Shahādah* is a comprehensive declaration of what a Muslim internalises in their heart. They vocalise it with their tongues, and they indicate it with their actions and behaviour. This testimony is the ideal that shapes and drives the individual, the *ummah*, and those in authority and power. The question of what Islam is, which includes the other tenets of worship, is intrinsically connected to the *Shahādah*, which is a requisite of faith. These forms of worship, such as *Ṣalāh*, fasting in *Ramaḍān*, *Zakāt*, and *Ḥajj*, are actions for the individual and community. Thus, worship comprises all aspects of a Muslim's life. The worldview of Islam is about worship and is Allah-centred (*tawḥīd*). If the primary purpose of humanity is to submit to and worship Allah, which the worldview of Islam is based on, then it is only natural to suggest that the most elevated forms of knowledge production (*ʿIlm*) must reflect this. It is not an outrageous statement to make when I say that the most elevated form of *ʿilm* ought to be related to Allah, who created and taught *insān* (humanity) *ʿIlm*, and to His Messenger ﷺ and His *din*, which is Islam. There can be no belief without the *Shahādah*, meaning that for any project to be Islamic, it must submit to Islam and adhere to that basic testimony, which includes us as individuals, our works of *ʿilm*, and even our politics.

Knowledge production is not a neutral act, as it is not just a mere statement of abstract fact. Knowledge pertains not just to simply knowing but also to acting, and so both knowledge and action pertain to purpose and objective. When reading works of history, one should recognise that they are part of a larger corpus of knowledge production which is predicated on philosophies, ideologies, power, and perspective. These philosophies, ideologies, and so on emerge from a *ʿaqīdah*. The *ʿaqīdah* shapes them, and it is from the *ʿaqīdah* that thoughts that turn into action come from. These works, which are interpretive, are not simply a reflection of facts but rather belong to specific motivations. These motivations, especially in the academic space, have been determined by the secular *ʿaqīdah*. The secular *ʿaqīdah* refers to a set of beliefs, values, or guiding principles that are not based on any religious faith or spiritual doctrine but rather are grounded in secular (non-religious) ideals. This type of *ʿaqīdah* is built on principles derived from human experience only, where reason is devoid of Allah, and ethics, which are presented as universal, are not guided by the

Divine or by the Prophetic message and character. They present themselves often as a commitment to universal human rights, scientific understanding, and democratic values.

In the case of history, to facilitate the study of history within the secular realm, the processes by which historians examine sources and the emphasis on empirical data point to an attempt to make history writing a secular endeavour, not one that can and ought to be religious. The attempt to use religious methods in the secular tradition is seen as being a subjective faith-based intervention. This means that the secular not only has a view on faith—and in our case, Islam—but it also has a different position on reality.

A secular understanding of reality is typically suggested to be grounded in empirical evidence, rational inquiry, and the scientific method. There is no place for Allah, or the Qur'an and *Sunnah* in such scholarly activity. It seeks to explain and explore the world through observations, experimentation, and reason, while avoiding religious interpretations. However, while suggesting that it is based on rational inquiry and scientific method, it fails in its rationality to accept the centrality of Allah in reality. Thus, the secular *ʿaqīdah* fails to understand reality as it rejects Allah. An understanding of reality that rejects Allah subsequently has no room for His Prophet ﷺ, the human soul, Allah's divine will or plan, or heaven or hell. It not only reduces reality to the confines of a narrow box but subsequently reduces what it means to be human as well. Thus, no human experience can be examined or understood beyond the merely material realm of action. Thus, both reality and the human experience are stripped to simple events without purpose. By removing the possibility of human purpose, life loses meaning and leads to despair, confusion, depression, as well as injustice and oppression.

Without purpose, how can a human being make sense of their reason for being in this world, beyond the act of just living for material reasons? It leads to injustice and oppression because firstly, it incorrectly understands the reality of the world we live in, and thus, disrupts the harmony of life, and secondly, it does not take into account the act of justice from Allah. This leads to humans not feeling accountable for their actions and enacting crimes without consequence.

This can be understood from an authentic *ḥadīth* of the Prophet ﷺ narrated by Abdullāh Ibn ʿAmr [Ibn al-ʿĀṣ]: "Indeed Allah does not seize knowledge by taking it suddenly from people, rather he seizes it [slowly] by taking the scholars [through death] until no scholars will remain. Then the people will take the ignorant as leaders; they will be asked, and they will give verdicts without knowledge. They will be deviated and they will deviate others."[10] This *ḥadīth* regarding knowledge details how Allah does not just swipe knowledge away suddenly, but that people of knowledge gradually die, and knowledge is lost over time to the point that people become unaware. Once people of knowledge and guidance gradually phase out, ignorance will take over.

Regarding Muslim knowledge producers, therefore, we need to think about and attempt to challenge the *secular ʿaqīdah*'s culture of knowledge production, as it is spreading ignorance. It is removing purpose from the lives of humanity, which is linked to the *ākhirah*. As Muslims, we really need to ask ourselves what the value of our efforts in scholarship is. If it is not guiding the *ummah*, and by extension humanity, towards reviving themselves in this *dunyā* by understanding that this is linked to knowledge of their *din*, then what is it for?

This means that when historians are writing from the *secular ʿaqīdah*, they are unable to correctly diagnose a comprehensive view of reality, whether past or present. As a consequence, when examining human experience, especially

10 Bukhari (100) and Muslim (2673)

Muslim experiences, they are prone to misunderstanding intentions, motivations, actions, and beliefs. This imposition not only distorts our understanding of reality and how we should undertake the act of knowledge seeking and production, but it also restricts us in asking questions about matters of the past. The method can explain an aspect of reality and get it correct insofar as simply from an analytical perspective, but it cannot provide solutions, as that requires one to turn to the divine wisdom of the One who created them and sent the Qur'an and the Prophet ﷺ for this purpose. Thus, the issue of the secular *ʿaqīdah* is not simply that it removes Allah in the understanding of the past but also that it lacks the desire to provide a solution for the betterment of humanity regarding both worldly matters and the spirit. This is opposite of the purpose of *ʿilm* in Islam. If it were simply an act of secular knowledge being misleading or restrictive, that is one thing, but western secular academia and its forms of knowledge production have been heavily inspired by ideological trends such as Marxism, liberalism, positivism, nationalism, humanism, feminism, and postcolonialism, to name a few. So deeply ingrained are they in the secular experience of modern knowledge production that to decipher them for the average reader is almost impossible. These secular ideologies have profoundly affected how we understand historical narratives, particularly with an emphasis on human agency, societal structures, and rational analysis. The ideologies thus shape how we gather data, how we take meaning from them and what values we add to the narratives we write. Additionally, these ideologies in totality do not conform with the Islamic *ʿaqīdah*, as they reject the centrality of Allah.

One may say that these ideologies may help historians in modes of analysis, and a Muslim historian should attempt to negotiate with some of these ideas in order to see which ideas are in conformity with Islam and, if they do not contradict the Islamic

ʿaqīdah, how they can help us in understanding a matter in the past. There is no doubt that there is a lot to gain if they are handled with care and examined correctly, recognising where such ideas and methods can be useful. This type of exercise may be practised by the Muslim historian in analysing events and matters of the past. However, I would argue that only a select few can navigate such complicated waters. The Muslim readership requires scholars who can help them understand this.

The point here is not about whether one is Muslim or not, but rather about the framework in which knowledge is permitted to be written. This is why I want to make a distinction between a historian who is Muslim and a Muslim historian. A Muslim historian is driven by Islam and has īmān and produces knowledge in accordance with that. They may choose to engage in the secular method or produce works that are simply analytical, but that too is done with the understanding that whatever they write should not contradict the Islamic *ʿaqīdah*. Thus, even if a Muslim is writing in a secular framework, the work is in conformity with the *ʿaqīdah* inasmuch as the work does not contradict it and provides information and possible insights about matters of the past. But it lacks in that it fails to provide and permit a comprehensive writing about reality, as that can only be done through writing with the lens of the *ʿaqīdah* of Islam. It also lacks the ability to provide correct solutions, which are solutions from Islam, as it would not be permitted.

If a historian is able to write in such a manner, navigating the ideologies, being aware of its dangers and how Islam is viewed, then the argument that this can be seen as writing in conformity with Islam is a position I am willing to accept, even though it reduces the human experience primary to the examination of empirical data only. Secular forms of knowledge production will accept Islam inasmuch as Islam is a religion where Muslims do acts of worship. What it has yet to do is permit a theory of Islam or an *īmān*-based approach, as that would be in direct conflict with it. It is like the example that the UK permitted a Muslim mayor of London and is tolerant towards Muslims and Islam. To that, I respond that the UK will not permit a *mu'min* mayor of London, inasmuch as the *mu'min* is searching to actively change the world in accordance with the understanding of *īmān*. So, while in the secular governmental structure, he may be permitted to pray, he will not be permitted to provide solutions from the Islamic *ʿaqīdah* and sacred texts when dealing with everyday matters.

However, if history is to be written within the *ʿilmī* tradition, it will need to not only conform to the *ʿaqīdah* of Islam but also represent it. One may argue that in Western academia, they could write history that fits the accepted structures of what the academic culture requires and still not contradict the Islamic *ʿaqīdah*. While I acknowledge that this is possible, it is the lowest form of knowledge production, even if sophisticated and intellectual, as it provides nothing but *dunyawī* (worldly) knowledge, and little in the form of a general purpose in life and the hereafter for the person reading. It may enrich their knowledge and awareness of something, but for it to be transformative, it will need to provide a solution. When that type of knowledge production is accumulative, it inadvertently orients the heart of the believer to the *dunyā*, as nothing in the text or in the style of knowledge production brings them closer to Allah. Although the intellect is being stimulated, the soul is being neglected. Over a prolonged time, this type of knowledge production dislocates not only the soul of the reader but, more dangerously, the soul of the knowledge producer.

Knowledge that is primarily focused on *dunyawī* (worldly) matters may lack the spiritual depth that is essential for holistic understanding. This understanding is one about both this life and the next. While it may be sophisticated and intellectually rigorous, it often fails to address fundamental questions about purpose and the *ākhirah* (afterlife). When a knowledge producer or reader is primarily dealing with or producing works that reduce this balance, it can have an impact on the spiritual aspect of a person, in which they may assume that matters to do with spirituality are only for worship or religious knowledge. This leads to the erroneous assumption that while works of *fiqh*, *taṣṣawuf*, and *kalām* have a spiritual dimension, works of history sit primarily in the secular space.

However, in order to produce knowledge in full conformity with the Islamic ʿ*aqīdah*, the work has to be one that is based on *īmān*, where the full reality is accepted. This reality is the centrality of Allah to reality and the Islamic understanding of what it means to be human, as well as adhering to the principles in producing knowledge that not only adheres to but promotes the Islamic mission. Rejecting Allah and His Messenger ﷺ is both a rejection of *the* truth and an obfuscation of reality. This is why I want to repeat here again when Allah says, "*The Bedouins say, "We have believed." [O, Prophet] Say, "You have not [yet] believed; but say [instead], 'We have submitted,' for faith has not yet entered your hearts. And if you obey Allah and His Messenger, He will not deprive you from your deeds of anything. Indeed, Allah is All-Forgiving and Most-Merciful.*" (TQM 49:14 Sahih International Translation).

The Fundamental Tenets of Īmān

Regarding *Īmān*, in accordance with the Ḥadīth of Jibril ﷺ, we believe in the tenets of *Īmān*, which are called "*Arkān al-Īmān*". The first is belief in **Allah**, which has already been discussed. We also believe in **Angels**, and via extension, other metaphysical entities and concepts, such as the *jinn*, *Shayṭān* (the devil), *karāmāt* (miracles), and the essence of *Waḥy* (Divine Revelation). These are all parts of our world that are not simply material. In Islam, we have a host of accounts of the Prophet ﷺ meeting the Angel Jibril ﷺ; we have accounts mentioned in the Qur'an of Allah sending angels during the famous Battle of Badr. While in the case of the Prophet ﷺ, we have the Qur'an and *Sunnah* as sources that indicate the existence and interactions with angels and *jinn* alike, contemporary Muslims may argue that it is harder to empirically prove anything more than this, and that we take matters to do with the metaphysical in a historical work on trust. When we write about such matters, we must be aware that these are tenets of belief and should be written in accordance with them. There should be no embarrassment on matters of belief, just as in the case of the Prophet ﷺ who went on the *Isrā* and *Miʿrāj* to meet Allah. This happened, and it has been attested in both the Qur'an and *Sunnah*. A Muslim writing about this history need not feel uncomfortable about what secular academia may say about it. Even at the time of the Prophet ﷺ, the Arabs questioned this, but the Muslims attested to the *Isrā* and *Miʿrāj* as a matter of belief.

The next is the belief in the **books** and **Messengers**. The Muslim must believe in the Qur'an, and believe that previous Prophets were sent with the message of *tawḥīd* that the Qur'an points to and that the previous Prophets were callers to the same message of *tawḥīd* as the Prophet Muhammad ﷺ. The earlier books and Prophets were practitioners of Islam and *Īmān*, but the laws in them have since been abrogated by the Qur'an and the Prophet Muhammad ﷺ. The Muslim historian is compelled to adhere to the principles of the **Qur'an** (Book of Allah) and ***Sunnah*** (The Prophet Muhammad ﷺ) as these are the holistic means of communication and manuals that Allah has gifted humanity. In doing so, one takes inspiration from the Qur'an in order to understand the plight of a given people, nation, or Prophet.

The Qur'an and *Sunnah* are filled with evidence that helps us understand the nature of the world we live in. If Muslim historians are to provide moral advice to Muslim readers, naturally, this points to the notion that Allah has sent down a framework for us. The absence of any moral analysis is to the detriment of the Muslim community. Once again, while academic works, due to the notion of "objectivity", may choose to abstain from giving the reader moral advice, for the Muslim historian, writing from the perspective of Islam's morals and ethics is important in helping Muslims take meaning and learning from the past. Simply leaving this for the reader or student to discover without any intervention or support from the historian is alien to the culture in which Islam has been taught, which is that the teacher is central to the learning process. While modern books may be written with the idea of not having a teacher in mind, in Islam, books are always written with lessons and with the understanding that they ought to be taught, maintaining a relationship between the one acquiring knowledge and the one passing it on. As a result, it is imperative that the Muslim historian is solution-driven according to the way of the Qur'an and *Sunnah*, and that their intellectual endeavour is in conformity with them. Whenever we are producing works of history, if we are writing from the perspective of Islam, a key matter is to help Muslims be aware of causality and how historical events and change always reveal something about the divine order of our universe. In some ways, one could argue that there is a Sharīa of the cosmos, which everything submits to, and then there is the Sharīa that Allah has sent in the way of Islam that ought to be implemented in order to give harmony for humans in this life and the next.

Finally, there is the belief in the **Day of Judgement** "*al-īmān bi al-yawm al-ākhir*" and ***al-Qadr*** (the Divine will and decree of Allah). It is important for the Muslim historian to appreciate that, as Muslims, we have a different conception of time, and while it is important to examine human agency when writing history, it must be remembered that Allah has the ultimate agency. This is something which is often omitted from writing, which leaves Muslims lost and hopeless.

Muslims were aware of the temporal nature of this world and that they were part of a larger process. They were also aware of their fallibility, not simply in matters of life and death, but regarding a culture of accountability and that they were to be held to account by Allah. The Last Day reflects this idea, as it indicates that Muslims of the past, while they may have committed mistakes and crimes, were still part of a worldview that had, collectively as a civilisation, internalised that there was an ultimate authority to which humanity was accountable. When understanding this, one can often see how Muslims kept holding themselves to a standard that was *ākhirah*-oriented. They were aware that this world was temporary and that there was a next life.

Being aware of a Day of Judgement compels the Muslim historian to make the reader aware of the notion of accountability, and that actions have consequences not only for this life but also for the next. The writer themselves must also be aware that they must not write falsehood as they too will be held accountable on the Day of Judgement. This is especially important as we are writing about people from the past who can no longer defend themselves. The idea of slander in one's work is not simply an act of intellectual integrity but also a matter of accountability in the eyes of the One who will judge us.

Additionally, understanding that there is a Last Day means that there was a beginning, and this is consistent with the natural law of what Allah has created. Just as we have a beginning and an end, nations likewise have a beginning and an end, and all life has a beginning and an end. It should, therefore, come as no surprise that many Muslim thinkers wrote about cyclical theories of time, as all signs point to this understanding.

Finally, by attesting to the Divine will of Allah (*al-Qadr*), Muslims are aware that there are things beyond their capability and control, and it is important for the Muslim historian to understand the ideas of time and agency in this way. When writing about Muslims in the past, one should afford them some leeway, understanding that this world is a test and even the best of us, who may adhere to every requirement of Islam, may be tested in ways that are unimaginable. But a Muslim historian, once they have known an outcome, may help the reader appreciate the idea of the *Qadr* of Allah and how Muslims may learn from this. Muslim historians should entertain the idea of helping the reader and student appreciate the notion of accountability and Allah's ultimate agency when advising them about the past, which is something lacking in academia. Not only this, while we as historians may see patterns in the past, we also notice what are called contingency points that draw us closer to Allah by recognising that the causality of events, either due to the patterns or contingencies, point to the Divine order of the universe. Allah has set in motion the order of things. Allah is in full control, and we humans are at the mercy of His intervention. Allah says in the Qur'an, "*They plan, and Allah plans, and Allah is the best of all planners*". (*Sūrah al-Anfal* 3:54 TQM)

One would assume that the notion of the end of times does not exist in academic works. But if a student is to pay attention carefully to the narrative of modernity, the ideas lead to theories of inevitability, in which human beings have no will apart from the will of the secular narrative of modernity itself. It is not that *Qadr* does not exist in the sum of works produced within the academic space; it is, in fact, that Allah is replaced by another ideology. In doing so, academic works articulate how the notion of Western "progress" is to be considered the natural consequence of the collective human experience spearheaded by the West, in which the past is simply a stepping stone for a predetermined future. This predetermined future is the secularisation of humanity to the point where religion will have no place in the world we live in, beyond simply a functional position in people's cultures and traditions. But this is simply an ideological narrative construction that will have us believe that the future can be controlled to fit the secular narrative, which there will be no way of reversing, or that human agency is predetermined to facilitate the victory of the secular world over the religious. Yet, just as Allah has mentioned that each nation has a specified time within which they shall not go beyond, even for an hour, so too there is a specified time for ideas and ideologies.

The Need for Īmān (Belief) in Knowledge Output

Once submission (Islam) has been established, then naturally one must produce *'ilm* (knowledge) with belief (*Īmān*). *'Ilm* in Islam is often seen as the form of knowledge that is grounded in spiritual understanding and wisdom. It includes knowledge gained through the Qur'an, *ḥadīth*, and the insights provided by the *'ulamā'*. *'Ilm* is considered beneficial knowledge that guides one toward righteousness and shapes one's character and actions (*a'māl*). Thus, *'ilm* has a practical and transformative approach to shaping human beings and ultimately bringing them closer to Allah. Muslims can write history that bears the general features of *'ilm* that have just been described.

History as a vocation is an *'aqlī* (Rational) vocation in secular academia, so writing history without an *Īmān*-based lens is relatively easy to do. History writing is also unique as it deals with human beings and how they create communities, and how people have achieved and failed at so many other things. It is a universal vocation that is found in all peoples, cultures, and civilisations, and all cultures have different ways of writing about history. In Islam, contrary to the secular tradition, we have a different understanding of what it means to be human. Thus, when speaking of human relations and civilisations, the focus of our investigation is not simply on what transpired, but also on spiritual and ethical dynamics as a way of seeking betterment in ourselves. This approach recognises the need to examine both material and spiritual matters, and then provide solutions, lessons, and insights that are in accordance with the teachings we find in the Islamic *ʿilm* tradition. The intention is to help the Muslim spiritually grow, get closer to Allah, and make beneficial and tangible changes in their lives for their betterment.

An *īmān*-based approach is not simply about diagnosing conditions. It is about giving meaningful lessons from the *ʿaqīdah* of Islam, linking it to Allah and His Majesty, reminding people about the notions of Islamic justice as seen in the Qur'an and *Sunnah*, encouraging Muslims to do good and to abstain from doing bad, and encouraging Muslims to strive to seek the pleasure of Allah, for example. All of these are matters to do with *īmān*. An *īmān*-based approach to history can be done in various ways so long as the Muslim historian is motivated by such an endeavour. Primarily, the Muslim historian must take it upon themselves to want to teach history in this type of method. Simply put, an *īmān*-based approach to writing history is an intervention from the Muslim historian on behalf of the *ummah*. This intervention is an act to encourage Muslims as individuals and a community to deepen their understanding, renew their commitment, and adhere more closely to the teachings of Islam. The Muslim historian is thus inviting the *ummah* to *tazkiyah* (purification) and *iṣlāḥ* (rectification). This requires the *ummah* to recognise that our current condition needs changing, making the *niyyah* (intention) to change, and then making the effort to learn and become motivated to change its current condition. The field of history, which is an intellectual one, is just one of many areas where *ʿilm* can be taught to the *ummah* to better themselves. Encouraging fellow Muslims to increase their *īmān* through learning, worship, and good deeds is important, and writing works to support personal and spiritual growth is needed. A Muslim historian who is concerned for the *ummah* also needs to write works that remind people of *tawbah* (repentance) and remind them to do *dhikr* (remembrance of Allah). It reflects the Islamic teaching that true peace, strength, and guidance come from a heart that is spiritually alive and aligned with divine guidance.

The work of the Muslim historian ought to be seen as an intellectual and spiritual endeavour, to not only purify their own heart and mind but also to support the *ummah*. That requires the historian not to only improve their skills regarding history writing but also to continuously engage with the Qur'an, *Sunnah*, and *Sīrah* as a way of trying to attain the highest form of intellect and wisdom by continually reflecting, observing the past, and finding meaning in the timeless Qur'an. By attempting to do so, they can then help guide the *ummah* by drawing from the religious texts, their own lived experiences, historical research, and deep reflection and contemplation.

An *īmān*-based approach looks to confront the secular tradition of writing, which has become dominant. The historian should not falter when being criticised for doing so. The Qur'an and *Sunnah* are two major sources that help us understand the human condition. Who else knows human beings better than the One who created them? This endeavour should also be considered as an act of *daʿwah* to non-Muslims. The Muslim historian should be able to examine history and show comprehensively how historical matters are connected to the Noble Qur'an and the truth. It should also be able to show non-Muslims the schema of history, as well as helping them appreciate that an *īmān*-based approach to writing history is a more comprehensive approach to reality and truth. By gradually producing this style of literature, Muslims can provide a new space for history readers, which returns to an approach of trying to find meaning in life, to providing solutions from the faith, to attempting to write in a way that takes both the intellect and soul into account. At this time, it is not just the Muslim heart that needs reviving.

Taking an *īmān*-based approach to writing history does not mean simply to remind people of Allah, but to also love, fear, and trust Allah, as these are all parts of *īmān*. Muslim historians should consider that they are writing with evidence to inspire Muslims to love Allah, as this is also part of *īmān*. The idea of writing so that people remember Allah from reading works of *ʿilm* can be likened to evoking emotions in them to want to love Allah. It is not only the love of Allah that one should work to evoke but also the love of the Messenger of Allah ﷺ, as our *īmān* prescribes that both Allah and His Messenger ﷺ are to be loved. Evoking this love can be done by investigating historical works where Muslims were steadfast, where they envisaged Allah's support, and where they were striving to please Him. It can be investigated when Muslims were motivated to transform due to their love for the Prophet ﷺ, as we can see regarding the *Ṣaḥābah*. Islamic history is full of examples of such love. To love Allah and the Prophet ﷺ is cited in the *ḥadīth* narrated by Anas Ibn Malik (ra) when he says that the Prophet ﷺ said:

"When three [characteristics] exist in an individual, he will acquire the sweetness of *īmān*; [the first is] that Allah and His Messenger ﷺ are more beloved to him than anything else; [the second is] that he loves a person only for the sake of Allah; [and the third is] that he dislikes to return to disbelief [after Allah has rescued him from it] just like he dislikes that a fire is kindled for him and he is thrown therein."

Thus, the *muʾmin* does not simply strive to please Allah; they are motivated to love Allah, they look to seek His pleasure, they love the Messenger of Allah ﷺ, and are committed wholeheartedly regarding the struggles of life, knowing that they will be tested. Those who reject Allah or reject the Prophet ﷺ should upset the believer, as this is what it means to have *īmān* in one's heart. Thus, knowledge production regarding the human experience without linking it to Allah or His Messenger ﷺ should agitate the Muslim who is *īmān*-centred.

Furthermore, the concept of *īmān* pertaining to Allah is not simply the love of Allah but also that one must fear Allah as He should be feared, as this is also part of *īmān*, and there is no contradiction in this statement. Allah says in *Sūrah Āl ʿImrān*, "*Do not fear them, but fear Me, if you are true believers.*" [3:175] and in *Sūrah al-Māʾidah* "*Do not fear people, fear Me.*" [5:44]. There are countless occasions in the Qur'an where Allah has made it clear that, as Muslims, we need to be brave and fear Him alone. This means that a Muslim historian can examine and show how Muslims were brave in moments of adversity, how they stood up to tyranny, how a Muslim may have suffered by imprisonment, but they adhered to this principle and how at the end they were vindicated or elevated, or how their acts inspired people to turn to Islam. The opposite can also be studied, such as in situations in which Muslims chose not to fear Allah or abandoned the idea of Allah as the one who ought to be feared over people, which led to corruption and loss.

The need to understand the Islamic *ʿaqīdah* and *īmān* is vital. No amount of history learning can shape the *ʿaqīdah*, but the *ʿaqīdah* must first be established, and only then can a Muslim write about history from the framework of Islam. History is not needed for one's *ʿaqīdah*, as *ʿaqīdah* matters are not speculative or interpretive but rather deal with certainty; instead, history ought to conform to its objectives and supplement other forms of knowledge in order to strengthen it. The best form of history writing for the Muslim ought to be one that reminds Muslims of Allah, their purpose in life, and the morals by which humanity is to live.

As Muslims, we have a purpose of producing *ʿilm*, which is part of *īmān*. Not only is seeking *ʿilm* part of *īmān*, but producing *ʿilm* also, and so history written from an *īmān*-based approach is the act of bringing the vocation of history in the tradition of Islam into the realm of the *ʿilmī* tradition. The purpose of *ʿIlm* is to increase, strengthen, and remind the Muslim of *īmān*, and Islamic history writing must attempt to do that. This is encapsulated in this comprehensive *ḥadīth* by the Prophet ﷺ narrated by Abū Hurayrah (ra):

> "Whoever relieves a believer of a worry from the worries of the world, Allah will relieve him of a worry from the worries of the Day of Judgement. Whoever brings ease upon one in financial difficulty, Allah will give him ease in the world and the Hereafter. Whoever conceals the faults of a Muslim, Allah will conceal his faults in the world and in the Hereafter. Allah will assist His servant as long as he assists his brother. Whoever treads a path in order to seek knowledge, Allah will make his path towards the Garden easy because of it. No group of people gather in a house from the houses of Allah reciting the book of Allah and studying it amongst themselves except that tranquillity descends upon them, the Angels surround them, mercy engulfs them, and Allah mentions them to whoever is near Him. Whoever is delayed [to get to the Garden] because of his efforts, his lineage will not make him go any further."[11]

The *ḥadīth* refers to *ʿilm* and *ʿilm*-producers as part of *īmān* and explains the need to support the Muslims, and help provide ease for them, regarding knowledge, wealth, and assisting them and advising them. A point worth mentioning is that the Prophet ﷺ explains that we should be careful in concealing faults in other Muslims. But furthermore, a Muslim knowledge producer must be aware of the relaxed approach that can become manifested in our communities regarding

11 Muslim (2699)

the knowledge they are engaging with, and make sure that the primary objective of *ʿilm* is not neglected or left to only matters of rulings and rituals of worship. An intellectual approach is required, where the *ummah*'s *īmān* is safeguarded and elevated. A Muslim historian ought to take on the task mentioned in the *ḥadīth* to give ease to this *ummah* and assist them in understanding their *din* and connecting them with the history of the *ummah*.

History works can also provide intellectual and spiritual meaning. As a result, accumulating knowledge that does not incorporate spiritual dimensions can lead to an orientation towards the material world that can have long-lasting effects. If it becomes deeply rooted, this shift can distract individuals and the *ummah* from their ultimate purpose and responsibilities as believers. While stimulating the intellect is valuable, neglecting the soul can have detrimental effects. The Muslim thinker should not think that the *ummah* cannot become contaminated by secular knowledge to the point that reviving them becomes a difficult task for the next generation of Muslims. Instead, we can attempt to intervene right now, rather than leave the *ummah* to their own devices.

Knowledge should ideally elevate both the mind and the heart, fostering a comprehensive understanding of existence that aligns with one's faith. The disconnection from spiritual truths can be particularly harmful to knowledge producers, who may become more entrenched in secular paradigms. This can lead to a sense of emptiness or disillusionment, as their work lacks the transcendent purpose that can provide fulfilment. A more integrated approach to knowledge production would incorporate both intellectual rigour and spiritual awareness. This means engaging with historical, social, and scientific knowledge while also recognising and articulating its implications for faith, morality, and Allah. In Islam, the pursuit of *ʿilm* is not just an academic exercise; it is a means to understand Allah's creation, to fulfil one's responsibilities, and to cultivate a deeper connection with Him.

This implication is more apparent in today's world, where Allah is not sought, and sometimes He is not believed in. If it is assumed that Allah does not exist in our daily lives, and that He does not have relevance in the lives of Muslims before us, the notion of Allah's relevance to human beings can become minimised. Seeking ways to weave Islamic teachings and to include writing about Allah might involve using the Qur'an, *Sunnah*, and *Sīrah* as examples when analysing certain events, human failures, successes, and so on.

The Qur'an is full of examples that can help a historian analyse the human condition. It could also involve exploring how historical events and figures were influenced by their faith, or how Islamic values shaped societal structures and interactions. When one is giving solutions to elevate the *ummah*'s station, works from history can also provide examples of solutions from the Islamic tradition for today's challenges.

By explicitly connecting historical events to Islamic teachings, scholars can challenge the implication that Allah is absent from modern life or from the experiences of previous generations. This connection serves as a reminder of the continuity of faith throughout history. Just as Allah and the tenets of *īmān* have been excluded in the writing style of secular history works, the Muslim historian ought to try to think of how the remembrance of Allah can be part of the writing process. I believe that acknowledging Allah's role in history provides a more comprehensive view of the lived experiences of Muslims, both past and present. It allows for a richer narrative that respects the complexity of human existence, integrating the spiritual and material aspects of life. By doing so, Muslim historians can help restore the significance of faith in public discourse and inspire individuals to recognise the relevance of Allah in all aspects of life. This approach not only enriches the field of history but also reaffirms the centrality of faith in shaping human experience and understanding.

A ḥadīth of the Prophet ﷺ found in the Forty Ḥadīth of Imam Nawawi narrated by Abū Sa'īd al-Khudrī (ra) comes to mind when he ﷺ said, "*He who sees an evil, let them first change it with their hand, and if he is unable to do so, [then let him change it] with his tongue, and if he is not able to do so, then let him hate it in his heart, and that is the weakest of īmān*".

Works of *'ilm* must inspire action; and there must be an act of intellectual bravery in which the writer is not simply criticising ideas but is a person of action that is willing and capable of being action-oriented and inspiring people to take the right action based on the ideas the scholar produces. This means that scholars today will need to not simply produce literature but also take the lead to galvanise the *ummah* in their everyday lives.

One may feel that producing scholarly literature is sufficient. Still, I would argue that in today's day and age, scholars will need to lead by example during moments of crisis. The Prophet ﷺ in his teachings was not simply a man of *'ilm*, but a man of *da'wah*, he led by example, which made the *'ilm* he gave resonate into action. For example, when making a call to action, politics or history can be used to provide the current understanding of things. When providing solutions, they must seek to come from the *Sharīa*. Writing with *Īmān* in mind is not simply an end in the field of history but, rather, can be multi-disciplinary. For example, a historian may be working on a policy paper in which they are using historical analysis, and they find solutions for political problems by using their insight, research, and *īmān*-based knowledge to provide an Islamic solution.

While it might feel brave to criticise orientalism, modernity, and coloniality, as well as forms of intellectual ideologies that are anti-Islam, especially after the decolonial turn which many

Muslims are embracing, alternatives still need to be offered. I assert that what is needed is a transformative approach to scholarship that integrates divine agency into the analysis and interpretation of human experience. A framework for such an approach must be written to pave the way for future generations of scholars to explore and articulate the relevance of faith in their research, fostering a deeper understanding of the interconnectedness of faith, history, and society. This not only enriches academic discourse but also reaffirms the relevance of faith in understanding the complexities of life. By doing so, scholars can contribute to a more nuanced and spiritually informed body of knowledge that reflects the true essence of the Islamic worldview, which not only informs the reader but leads them to activism and politics that are more in line with Islamic principles rather than secular ones. That means that the scholar may also need to reflect this in their own action as a model for others to follow.

I must stress that in the *ḥadīth* above, the Prophet ﷺ was aware that people and conditions may not always permit people to be action-oriented. As a result, he provided them with a way out by encouraging them to do their best. But the *ḥadīth* does not permit the Muslim to abandon the act of confronting disbelief and falsehood. Rather, it refers to a permitted respite until their conditions change. It must not be forgotten that the standard is not to simply go from accepting to hating something in the heart either. The first standard is to be action-oriented, and if this is not possible, then the next standard becomes possible, which is to say something with your tongue and then the next. In the case of knowledge production, there is no reason why Muslims should feel that they cannot create a space for themselves that can foster actions that are rooted in the Islamic tradition and experience, and they do not need to feel that their ideas and works are only valued if published in an international journal or presented at a conference.

The value of their *ʿilm* is what Allah values it as, and this has to be the standard, and then it should become *ʿamal* (action) for both the scholar and those who read the scholar's works.

It is part of *īmān* to trust in Allah, and Islamic history is full of moments where Muslims have done that. It is also part of *īmān* to have hope, and Muslim historians need to teach and encourage Muslims to have trust in Allah and to have hope in Allah's promise to the *ummah,* His support, and His divine plan, as Muslims have in the past. With the secular tradition omitting Allah from the knowledge, learning, and writing process, I suggest that we put mention of Him back on the pages of our works. Our works should include invocations, supplications, Qur'anic references, and explaining His divine will. This is not a superficial act, but rather an act of placing history writing within our *ʿilm* tradition. One may feel this is excessive, but I do not propose this for secular knowledge production; I propose this to Muslim historians who are trained with the tools of the academy. They have a duty towards their community, which means either taking on the responsibility to write for our ummah in a way that is *īmān*-based or supporting members of the *ʿulamāʾ* who want to take on this effort. The *ummah* wants to feel connected to Allah, their Messenger ﷺ and the *ummah* of the past. They also want to engage with history according to a language they understand: Islam.

While secular knowledge production does not seem like a blatant form of antagonism towards Islam and may look similar to the treaty of *Ḥudaybiyyah* for instance, when the Quraysh had the name *Rasūl Allāh* ﷺ meaning the "Prophet/Messenger of Allah" omitted, the *Ṣaḥābah* at the time understood that this so-called act of neutrality from the Quraysh was an act of aggression. It also agitated them because of their love for the Prophet ﷺ, as this was a matter of *īmān*. Likewise, Muslim historians need to wrestle the vocation of history writing away from the secular tradition and place it back within the

Islamic tradition of *ʿilm* production. The current aim ought to be to establish Muslim centres, spaces, and literature that are orientated for the salvation of Muslims, which is called *tazkiya*. In the long term, the aim ought to be to extend this out to humanity, which is what we call *daʿwah*. While access to technology has given us new spaces, new ideas, and new ways of collecting data, in the long term, there must be an attempt to facilitate our own culture of telling our narratives. Suppose there can be Marxist, liberal, nationalist, and feminist historians who write history from those ideological perspectives. There can be no reason why we cannot have Muslim historians who are committed to an *īmān*-centred approach that is reflective of their personal belief in Islam and shapes their knowledge output and intellectual culture.

Īmān requires Taqwā – The Act of Trusting Allah

Before going on to the third tenet, which is *Iḥsān*, I feel it is worth extending the discussion of *Īmān* and the notion of *taqwā*, which links *Īmān* and *iḥsān* together. *Taqwā* is to be conscious of Allah at all times. If one attains the highest level of *taqwā*, they have become a *muḥsin*, meaning one who acts with *Iḥsān*. In all the instances that Allah mentions the *muḥsin* or *muḥsinīn* (plural) in the Qur'an, it is framed in doing the highest level of good, as if the person who does good is doing it while witnessing Allah before him. It is a given that any scholar who produces *'ilm* must reflect both in attitude and their work *akhlāq* (ethics) and *tarbiyah* (good upbringing) inspired by Islam, which indicates *taqwā*. With these, and a mechanism of controlling one's ego, one's work, judgement, and use of morality towards the people of the past help in writing in a way that can help the writer shape the reader to also be a person of *taqwā*. Most history is writing about people who are dead, a past that we were not witness to. In that sense, the manners (*akhlāq*) with which the historian behaves are important, especially in the way they write and speak of the past. Although we intend to learn from the past, there is indeed a thin line between learning and making a judgement which may not be true. Once, I was in an academic conference where an academic quipped that we are lucky that the people we write about are dead and cannot hold us to account. I responded that in actuality, we need to be fearful of Allah, because the people we write about can hold us to account on the Day of Judgement.

As historians know more about the past, they will naturally grow, mature, and improve in *tarbiyah*. Writing about people of the past should not only make you humble in recognising the vastness of the collective human experience but should also make you humble in the eyes of Allah as you become conscious of His greatness. Once a historian attains this historical consciousness, it leads to maturity. This is because, as historians, we are invested in how people and events in the past continue to shape us today, how our memories still require the need to evoke the past, and how our cultures and politics are validated by the way we perceive history. In that sense, history should impact us, make us ask what we may have done in those situations, and examine the fallibility and vulnerability of human beings and their choices. Ultimately, we should try to relate the past to ourselves, to learn from it and provide moral value to the current predicament we are in.

It is for this reason that *taqwā* becomes an essential component of *īmān*. The Muslim historian does not simply exercise belief in Allah; *īmān* is a principle built on *yaqīn* (Certainty). This certainty leads to *taqwā*, of being conscious of Allah, which leads to being upright and pious, and fundamentally creates a consciousness of *īmān* over a secular consciousness. In that sense, *taqwā* must be manifest in the historian, because although history may be seen as an *ʿaqlī* (Rational) vocation in accordance with Western academic standards, it can also be combined with a *naqlī* (Doctrinal) approach for the Muslim historian, in the sense that it can be inspired by Qur'an and *Sunnah*.

Just as secular historians can shape and compound a secular consciousness within their work that can impact the reader,

Muslim historians must do the opposite. As the historian can look over a long span of time, they could feel empowered within themselves. This feeling has permitted many to falsely think they have the right to make judgements on the people of the past in a way that only Allah can. In actuality, a true historian learns two main things when studying the past. The first is that they have the tools, skills, and knowledge which create the historical consciousness that makes them experts in teaching about the past in a way that others cannot. Even though many speakers, *Imāms, khaṭībs*, politicians and journalists dabble in the past, the good historian knows that mastery of the subject belongs to them. The recognition of this mastery is not a sign of arrogance, but rather an acknowledgement of one's expertise. The second is that the Muslim historian learns to exercise humility, as they strive to be conscious of Allah and the vastness of the collective human experience, and that they are just another person in the history of humanity who will be held to account on the Last Day. Muslim historians ought to reflect on what the Qur'an suggests about the human experience, as Allah makes it clear how great nations of the past have perished, and that we are not exceptions to this rule. This humility should be infused in their character, from how they behave towards their work, the people of the past, and the audience to whom they are relaying their information. This humility in recognising Allah's will and His *Qudrah*, as well as heeding His warnings, and the mastery of the vocation by understanding the human condition and its weakness and dependency on Allah, reflects the idea of *taqwā* in the Muslim historian.

Thus, historians who aim to have a high level of *taqwā* should aim to display certain characteristics. The historian must be:

(1) **Sincere.**

(2) They must be **knowledgeable.**

(3) They must seek and present the **truth.**

(4) Be intellectually **brave** in this endeavour.

(5) **Trust in Allah** (*Tawakkul*).

When I say sincerity, I primarily mean sincerity to Allah, as He is the Master of everything. Knowing that Allah is the All-Knowing should mean that any knowledge produced should be for Him and to further His *din* and support the *ummah*. In that sense, being sincere to Allah naturally makes one sincere to *'ilm*, the people of the past, and the target audience of the work produced. Sincerity is a disposition of both heart and mind, because if a historian is sincere, then the reader can ascertain that the work is an honest approach to attain the truth. If sincere, the historian would also be averse to manipulating the target readership and, instead, try to elevate them. This is something I have seen an absence of in the space of Western academia in my experience.

The next point is that the historian must be knowledgeable. Of course, this should be a given, and not much explanation is needed here. But it must be stressed that knowledge without sincerity, especially sincerity to Allah, must be questioned as to whether it is *'ilmī*. Throughout my time teaching Islamic history, Ottoman history in particular, I have found many amateurs teaching Islamic history without the knowledge required from their vocation to make a difference. Most often, amateur historians will make mistakes, reinforce errors, or teach history as a storyteller would.

The point of any knowledge, especially history, is to seek the truth and present it to the best of one's ability. If speaking, writing, and seeking the truth is not part of the endeavour of the historian, then what is the point of their effort? Truth seekers must be knowledgeable and sincere. Can one even speak the truth without knowledge? The purpose of knowledge is to recognise the truth, and so the more knowledge one learns, the closer one becomes to the truth, or so it should be.

We are not simply trying to establish the truth of a certain event, or rebuttal of falsehood, but we are also interested in supporting the ultimate truth of Islam.

When speaking the truth, historians must accept that they may face a host of challenges from people within the field of history, non-Muslim society, and their communities. Speaking and writing the truth is a challenging feat, as the truth has a disruptive quality to it. Knowledge is the opposite of ignorance and truth is the opposite of falsehood, and very rarely do emotive people who are ignorant accept the truth.

The truth requires knowledge, but it also requires the historian to be brave with that truth, as many ideas, impressions, and understandings can be deeply ingrained in a group of people, and speaking the truth requires courage to challenge it. Therefore, a brave speaker of truth should have *tawakkul* in Allah and trust His plan. They should constantly seek Allah's protection and mercy and produce work for the sake of Allah. The Muslim should supplicate to Allah, remain sincere to Him and trust that if all the conditions mentioned above are fulfilled, then irrespective of whether they are tested or celebrated, they have fulfilled their duty in a way pleasing to Allah. They should realise that all praises belong to the One who created them, and all inspiration comes from Him.

If the historian is sincere, strives to seek knowledge, endeavours to establish the truth, and is brave in the face of adversity, they must put their trust in Allah, which is the highest form of *taqwā*, then that should suffice. This is why *taqwā* is needed after *īmān*. These two concepts are two sides of the same coin. *Īmān* is the cup with the solid foundations, and *taqwā* is the purity of the water that is put in the cup, which may fluctuate.

Iḥsān – Seeing Allah as if He is in Front of You.

The last point of Ḥadīth Jibril ﷺ is *Iḥsān*. When the Prophet ﷺ was asked about *Iḥsān*, he ﷺ responded that it means one should serve Allah as if they see Him, and that even though they do not see Him, to know He sees them.

While this concept may seem simple, in fact, this is probably the stage that is the most complex in regard to getting close to Allah. While most would speak of *iḥsān* as acts of goodness, those who have a deep awareness of Allah, to be called a *muḥsin*, are those who have become elevated in a way where their heart has become purified to the point that they are always contemplative and aware of Allah. To be continuously conscious of Allah, when one becomes selfless in their pursuit to please Allah in accordance with the Prophetic mission, is achieved by a few. To achieve this, Imam al-Ghazālī explained *Iḥsān* encouraged Muslims to practice *murāqabah*, or constant mindfulness of Allah's presence. Al-Ghazālī believed that this state could be cultivated through regular reflection, remembrance (*dhikr*), and self-awareness in one's actions and thoughts.

The notions of reflection and contemplation are not just mere thoughts. The act of reflection and contemplation is a long process in which a person thinks about reality in a comprehensive and wholistic way. In this state, while reflection is when one is thinking deeply about ideas, experience, or attempting to gain some personal insight, contemplation becomes both an intellectual and spiritual endeavour. In this process, the Muslim seeks to attain intellectual clarity and spiritual purity. Producing works of such nature that attempt to push the Muslim into a contemplative state means that they are not simply works of history, but also philosophical and spiritual.

These works produced attempts to be transformative to the point that they address the disposition in the reader's heart and mind and try to bring the reader into a contemplative state. Such works should be for a particular learned class, where they are taught, not simply read. This would also require some connection between the teacher and student in order to understand the work properly. These works can then operate as manuals for contemplative thought, to shape Muslims into action for the challenges that lay ahead in the path of *da'wah*. It is inconceivable that such works can be secular in nature, as they are comprehensively attempting to revive the *ummah* in accordance with the precepts of Islam. In this sense, a Muslim historian may produce such enlightened work that makes the reader contemplate the axioms about the laws of history and human beings and link them to Allah. This is done in order to transform the person both spiritually and intellectually, where the idea of Allah's presence is a reflection of one having inner awareness. This awareness leads to insight that is acted upon because of the harmony between intellect and soul. These works thus require contemplation that may take years, may involve personal experiences, and accessing many sources to produce.

The Prophet Muhammad ﷺ would retreat to the Cave of Ḥirāʾ on Mount Nūr (*Jabal al-Nūr*) outside Mecca, where he would spend days in deep contemplation. This habit of retreating to the cave continued for many years before he received the first Revelation. It is important to understand that it was after such contemplation that he was spiritually and intellectually prepared to receive Revelation. His ﷺ contemplation was in conformity with the words of *Sūrah al-ʿAlaq*, which he received. It is difficult to grasp the depth of contemplation of the Prophet ﷺ, as he was indeed a special person chosen by Allah whose heart was specially prepared to receive *waḥy* (Revelation) directly. However, what is worth noting is that after receiving the first Revelation, the Prophet ﷺ did not return to the cave, as he was now ready for the Prophetic mission and the new phase of bringing people to Islam.

The Moroccan scholar Taha Abdurrahman explains that the Prophet ﷺ cultured the *Ṣaḥābah*, such as Abū Bakr al-Ṣiddīq, ʿUmar Ibn al-Khaṭṭāb, Salmān al-Fārisī, and Imam ʿAli(may Allah be pleased with them all), in a manner in which they would be prepared to contemplate, so that they could internalise the mission and its ethical foundations in accordance with their intellect and heart. Their hearts became tied to the ethical component of the Prophetic mission in all aspects of their actions, which were in conformity with the highest degree of *īmān*. The Prophet ﷺ taught the *Ṣaḥābah* the Qur'an and its meaning; they memorised it, internalised it, and acted upon it. They observed the Prophet ﷺ and followed him ﷺ in all matters. They loved him ﷺ and aspired to emulate him ﷺ to the best of their abilities, and were inspired by him ﷺ, which created a unique experience where they were shaped for the Prophetic mission after his ﷺ passing. They understood the mission in totality. They were living exemplars after the Prophet ﷺ of *ʿilm* that was transformative on a deep and contemplative level.

Other examples of exemplars whose lives were transformed include al-Ghazālī who left Baghdad and travelled to Syria for a decade to contemplate and write his magnum opus *Iḥyāʾ ʿulūm al-Dīn* (The Revival of the Religious Sciences), which combined Islamic law, theology, and Sufi practices, aiming to integrate both the outward and inward dimensions of Islam.

Ibn Khaldun engaged deeply in contemplation, particularly on human societies, historical cycles, and the forces driving the rise and fall of civilisations. His contemplative approach is evident in his magnum opus, the *Muqaddimah* (or *Prolegomena*), a groundbreaking work where he introduced an analytical framework to study history, sociology, economics, and political theory.

Mustafa Sabri Efendi, a prominent Ottoman *'ālim* and one of *the* last official Ottoman Shaykh al-Islāms, was deeply contemplative, especially about the spiritual and intellectual challenges facing the Muslim world in the early twentieth century. His contemplations were largely focused on the crisis of faith, secularism, and the philosophical underpinnings that were influencing the Muslim world's relationship with the West. Through his writings, particularly in his seminal work *Mawqif al-'aql wa al-'ilm wa al-'ālam min Rabb al-'ālamīn wa 'ibādihi al-mursalīn* (The Stance of Reason, Science, and Knowledge vis-à-vis the Lord of the Worlds and His Servants, the Prophets), Sabri Efendi delved into deep issues that went beyond political concerns to touch on the core of Islamic spirituality and theology.

Muhammad Iqbal, a renowned Muslim philosopher and poet, often regarded as one of the most significant figures in Urdu literature and Islamic thought in the modern era, also went on a contemplative journey. His works were deeply intertwined with his exploration of identity, spirituality, and the revival of Islamic thought in the face of colonialism and modernity. His works advocate for self-discovery and the revitalisation of the Muslim community, emphasising the importance of inner reflection, and his major philosophical work, *The Reconstruction of Religious Thought in Islam*, discussed the need for Muslims to reinterpret Islamic teachings in the context of modernity and contemporary challenges.

There is no doubting that the works I have mentioned are *īmān*-oriented and fit all the requirements of the previous section. However, these works, which are efforts of a wide range of disciplines and years of contemplative experiences, were not written in one go. It first requires the need to encourage Muslims amongst us to be of a contemplative nature, and to inspire first an *īmān*-oriented approach, and then go on their own intellectual and spiritual journey to transform themselves and the *ummah*. To produce inspiring thinkers who want to achieve such should be an aim, but first we must work on shaping the honest *mu'min* in our *ummah* who is prepared to reach such a level. This should be a collective effort from all in our communities, and this should extend across all disciplines, not just history, which are then used to cultivate a new generation of Muslim intellectuals of the calibre of the people I have cited above. Works like those mentioned above are what the Muslim thinkers need to produce for the *ummah* going forward. This means that the thinker will have to be contemplative and attempt to produce impactful works that are not only transformative for themselves but also transform the *ummah*. A historian may be able to produce such works, as we can see in the case of Ibn Khaldun, but such works are in reality multi-disciplinary and require real contemplative effort that can shape an intellectual class within the Muslim community. In that sense, this is not simply an undertaking of studying history, but becomes an undertaking where history becomes part of the *'ilm* tradition, in conformity with the Islamic *'aqīdah*, that is *īmān*-oriented.

ب

SECTION IV

PATTERNS AND PARADIGMS

Does History Rhyme?

As the saying goes, history tends to repeat itself, or as the American humourist Mark Twain suggested, history does not repeat itself, but it rhymes. Historic recurrence is not new; many thinkers have pointed to the idea that lessons can be learned from the past. Of course, time moves forward, the world evolves and changes, and the idea that humans are destined to repeat the actions of the past requires thorough investigation.

That said, it would not be an outrageous claim to suggest that human beings do indeed follow certain patterns. This is where the Qur'an speaks to the intrinsic nature of human beings, offering timeless advice. Since human nature remains constant, the Qur'an acknowledges our tendencies—such as fighting, going to war, stealing, cheating, doing good, and forming communities—because these are actions we share with people from earlier generations. Allah, who created human beings, knows us better than anyone else and understands that we are often prone to repeating the behaviours of those who came before us.

This recurring nature of human behaviour can be observed in many aspects of life. One way to examine this repetition is through the rise and fall of states, the inevitable end of power, and the cyclical patterns of tyranny that ultimately come to a close. Additionally, archetypal figures emerge, reflecting particular traits that help guide or salvage groups of people. Given these patterns, it should come as no surprise that the Qur'an addresses matters that tend to repeat themselves, such as the dynamic between truth and falsehood, a topic I will explore further below.

Muslim historians have often been deeply concerned with the moral fabric of politics, leadership, and society, seeing these as integral to the well-being and stability of the community. The Qur'an, as a foundational text, has frequently served as a guide for the themes and issues these Muslims chose to address in their writings. Its teachings on justice, governance, and ethical conduct have influenced how historians interpret the actions of rulers and the societal structures they shape. By drawing on Qur'anic principles, these historians have explored the moral responsibilities of leaders, the importance of fair and just governance, and the role of society in upholding ethical values, providing a framework through which to critique and understand the political realities of their time.

An illustrative example of this approach is found in the perspective of the Egyptian-Syrian pre-modern historian Taqī al-Dīn al-Maqrīzī, a student of Ibn Khaldun. In his work *Mawaiz wa al-'i'tibar bi dhikr al-khitat wa al-'athar* (Admonitions and Reflections on the Mention of Plans and Historical Accounts), al-Maqrīzī underscores how the lessons of the past can guide and inform the present. His writings serve as a moral appeal, addressing the challenges faced by the Muslim community during his time and drawing inspiration from the Qur'an. Al-Maqrīzī believed that a Muslim historian's role extended beyond simply recounting events; it was essential to actively engage the reader, encouraging them to extract moral and practical lessons from history. He emphasised the need for readers to deeply reflect on the collective human experience, fostering improvement both on an individual level and within the broader community.

For al-Maqrīzī, history was not merely a collection of past events but a repository of moral lessons that could shape the ethics and behaviour of Muslims. He viewed history writing as an aspect of *ilm* central to the responsibility of the *'ulamā*. More than a mere chronicle, al-Maqrīzī believed that the Islamic purpose of writing history was inherently ethical, rooted in the guidance of the Qur'an and the *Sīrah* of the Prophet ﷺ. History, in his view, was not only a record but also a form of *nasiha* (advice), particularly aimed at those in power. Al-Maqrīzī saw history as a powerful tool for reminding rulers and the public of Allah's warnings, urging them to adhere to righteousness and avoid the pitfalls of injustice.

One of al-Maqrīzī's major concerns was the ruination of dynasties and societies, particularly how power structures and communities repeatedly strayed from justice. Although he did not develop a formal cyclical theory of history, there were elements within his writings that hinted at recurring patterns of rise and fall, especially in his analysis of the decline of Muslim empires and states. He identified the causes of societal collapse and the impact of misrule, framing these observations as moral lessons rather than as part of a deterministic cyclical model. Thus, for al-Maqrīzī, history writing from an Islamic perspective was deeply connected to the reminder of Muslims' ultimate purpose in this world and the Hereafter. Al-Maqrīzī stressed the ideas of when a people rejected a divine message or were unjust and suggested that the point of the *Qisas* (stories/narrative) in the Qur'an was to provide a moral lesson, something that Muslim historians should consider. This focus placed a strong emphasis on justice and highlighted the consequences of deviating from it.

Thus, many narratives in the Qur'an are present for that very reason. An example is *Sūrah al-Qaṣaṣ*, where Allah says, "*Ta-Sin-Mim, these are the āyāts of the book [Qur'an] that make things clear. We [Allah] narrate to you truthfully some of the story of Mūsā ﷺ and Pharaoh for the benefit of those who believe.*" (TQM: 28:1-3). The name of *Sūrah*, the word "*qaṣaṣ*", often translated as "*a story*", actually means to relate events in proper sequence. In this *Sūrah*, Allah mentions additional information about the life of Mūsā ﷺ, which is also mentioned in *Sūrah al-Shu'arā*, and *Sūrah al-Naml* Allah mentions how Mūsā ﷺ ended up in the house of the Pharaoh and was raised in that environment, ultimately becoming the catalyst to bring the Pharaoh down.

The Qur'an mentions how Mūsā ﷺ was made to leave the house of Pharaoh and then returned many years later with the support of Hārūn ﷺ. Mūsā ﷺ would consistently deconstruct the lies of the Pharaoh, in which the Pharaoh created the perception that he was the ultimate power in the land. Each miracle that Mūsā ﷺ displayed exposed the Pharaoh. The Pharaoh and his people accused Mūsā ﷺ of magic, but in reality, Mūsā ﷺ, with the help of Allah, was exposing the framework of falsehood that the Pharaoh's authority rested on. Although the Pharaoh was in a worldly sense more powerful than Mūsā ﷺ, having more resources, an army, and weapons, Mūsā ﷺ was able to defeat him not because of military strength, money, or power, but because Mūsā ﷺ had Allah's support and represented the truth. He was steadfast, was brave and had the will to make the change. Allah's support came in two forms. The first was the miracles Allah sent to support Mūsā ﷺ to show that he ﷺ was a Prophet chosen by Allah. The second was the truth itself, which Mūsā ﷺ represented. Mūsā ﷺ represented not only the truth to dispel the Pharaoh's falsehoods but also strived to show that Allah is the only truth. The followers of *tawḥīd* turned away from the Pharaoh and towards Mūsā ﷺ. As the Pharaoh increased his violence towards society as a way of instilling fear, in the end, once Mūsā ﷺ shattered the aura of the Pharaoh and his reign, people came in support of Mūsā

ؑ. In the end, the fear of the Pharaoh and the perception of his power dissipated.

There are many lessons one can take from this narrative in the Qur'an. Mūsā ؑ faced many hardships, starting with being separated from his biological mother. During his childhood, he ؑ was, from birth, a victim of the policies of the Pharaoh. However, Allah raised him ؑ in the Pharaoh's home. Mūsā ؑ grew up in the heart of power; he ؑ was aware of the Pharaoh's culture, ideas, and strength. Mūsā, thus, was aware of who he was dealing with, aware of the falsehoods of the Pharaoh, and the limits of his power. But Mūsā was unaware of his Prophethood, and when he was chosen, it was an intimate and awe-inspiring experience. Mūsā then ؑ sought help from Allah, his brother Hārūn ؑ, and his followers, having their support. He did not destroy the Pharaoh's kingdom alone. Together, after much hardship and effort, they ended the Pharaoh's world. That is because the Pharaoh's world was based on deception, and the propaganda of his authority was as dangerous as the other things he had done. As such, the key for Mūsā ؑ was not his staff—that was simply an instrument. Mūsā's ؑ miracles were sent to expose the Pharaoh's lies systematically.

When this *Sūrah* was revealed to Muslims, it was relatable to the Prophet ﷺ and his ﷺ followers and was a warning to the disbelievers who were listening that this was not the first time a Prophet of Allah had come as a caller to the truth and destroyed the aggressor. As a child, the Prophet Muhammad ﷺ was raised in the household of the Quraysh, very much in the way Mūsā ؑ was in the household of the Pharaoh. He ﷺ grew up in the heart of power; he ﷺ was aware of the Quraysh's culture, ideas, and strength. The Prophet Muhammad ﷺ was aware, like Mūsā ؑ, of who he was dealing with, the falsehood of the Quraysh, and the limits of their power. Like Mūsā ؑ in the valley, the Prophet Muhammad ﷺ

received the word of Allah in a cave; he ﷺ was unaware of his becoming a Prophet, and it was an intimate and awe-inspiring experience. Like Mūsā ﷷ, the Prophet ﷺ sought assistance from Allah and support from his *Ṣaḥābah* (companions), and the people of *tawḥīd*, the *ummah,* who abandoned the falsehood of the Quraysh. Just like the Pharaoh, the authority of Quraysh was based on deception, and with the Qur'an, his dedication to the mission and support of the *Ṣaḥābah*, the Prophet Muhammad ﷺ dispelled all their falsehoods. In the case of Mūsā ﷷ, Allah mentions how the followers of Pharaoh had seen Mūsā's ﷷ miracles with their eyes and yet still rejected the truth, and thus, were destroyed. In the Qur'an, Allah warns the people of Mecca of a similar fate. However, while the Prophet Muhammad ﷺ did show some miracles as proof to the Quraysh, the Quraysh still chose to reject them as the people of the Pharaoh did. The Prophet Muhammad ﷺ also had the miracle of the Qur'an, the word of Allah, which was a book of guidance, but the Quraysh, like the people of the Pharaoh, suggested that the Prophet ﷺ was a magician. For the people of Mecca, the Qur'an was their timeless miracle, not for their eyes but for their ears to hear. When examining this *Sūrah*, one can see that while the story of Mūsā ﷷ is not entirely the same as the Prophet Muhammad ﷺ, some themes and patterns are similar and can resonate with our struggles today. After all, the Qur'an is a timeless guidance book addressing the perpetual mistakes human beings make.

I mentioned the archetypal nature of the Qur'an and how Muslims must view this as a way of reminding them not only of the pitfalls of people of the past but also of areas where solace in hardship can be taken. An archetype is a character type that continues to appear; it can be a human experience or events that reoccur. Archetypal narrative telling is an emotional engagement with the story. It does not require spelling out why the reader ought to relate to an episode of the past, but simply that the inherent human experience can identify with the theme of the past, as these are recognisable themes either due to our own experience, or because they belong to a corpus of knowledge that is familiar to us. But that does not mean that one's intellect is not addressed. As I mentioned, Allah says, "*Ta-Sin-Mim, these are the āyāts of the book [Qur'an] that make things clear. We [Allah] narrate to you truthfully some of the story of Mūsā ﷺ and Pharaoh for the benefit of those who believe.*" (TQM: 28:1-3).

What meaning do we take from this? We see how the archetypal narrative has a way of reoccurring, and that the narratives can also become embedded as layers. We learn not only from the case of Mūsā ﷺ but also from the case of the Prophet Muhammad ﷺ regarding this recurring theme. The history of the life of the Prophet Muhammad ﷺ re-enforces the narrative of Mūsā's life ﷺ. Just like in the case of the Pharaoh, the power and legitimacy of the Quraysh were built on a perception created by deception. As Muslims, we must dispel those lies, the lies that oppose that Allah is the truth, and the falsehoods upon which their world is built. We need to support each other and have a leadership that is honest and steadfast.

The Qur'an is indeed a book of inspiration, and this is my advice for any Muslim historian who wants to write from an Islamic perspective. I repeat what Allah says, "*For every community, there is a fixed time, and when the end of their term approaches, they cannot delay it by a single moment.*" (TQM 7:34). As a result, just like in *Sūrah al-Qaṣaṣ*, the Muslim needs to be steadfast, they need to turn to the Qur'an for hope, they need to know that tyranny built upon falsehood cannot last and shall come to an end in the way it had with the Pharaoh and the Quraysh. The power of the truth is penetrative, even if it takes time and generations, perhaps.

There will be an end to tyranny, and then there will come a period of prosperity for a fixed time. Then, there will also be an end to prosperity, which is the nature of life in this world. I make the point how rational contemplation leads to emotional and spiritual tranquillity, and this is a significant point of *taf-fakur* (contemplation) for a Muslim, as Allah says in *Sūrah al-Fāṭir*, "*Those who truly fear Allah among His servants, are those who have knowledge.*" (TQM, 35:28 Translation my own). What is worth noting in this *āyah* is that those who are in awe of Allah and truly fear Him are the people who have knowledge of Him. For Muslims today, it is important for them to remember that they need not worry about when Allah's support will come. Just know that it will, as Allah is always with us, and He will inspire change when He sees fit, as Allah's help is near. But we must do the hard work and put the effort in and put our full trust in the outcome that Allah chooses for us. In a globalised world today, the Muslim has been raised in the heart of tyranny and falsehood, and both Muslims and non-Muslims alike are victims of oppression. While we may not have the same material power as the oppressors, we have Allah, His book—the Qur'an—His chosen example and beloved, the Prophet ﷺ.

The History of Nations can be Cyclical or Spiral

Like Ibn Khaldun, I have concluded that history can serve as an example of putting our lives into perspective. In his cyclical theory of the rise and fall of states, Ibn Khaldun mentions that there were six stages to the rise and fall of the nomadic states that he was examining at the time. These six stages were:

Stage 1) *ʿAṣabiyyah* (Social Cohesion) — *ʿAṣabiyyah* refers to the social bonds and group solidarity that unite a community or tribe. This can be based on kinship, shared identity, or common interests. Strong *ʿaṣabiyyah* is crucial for the establishment and initial success of a society. It fosters cooperation and collective action against external threats.

Stage 2) *ʿAṣabiyyah* leads to the emergence of a new ruling group or dynasty. This phase often features strong leadership and a sense of purpose. The new dynasty typically expands its territory and influence, establishing a solid governance structure and promoting economic growth.

Stage 3) The dynasty consolidates its power, develops institutions, and experiences economic prosperity. This is a period of cultural flourishing and military expansion. A strong central authority arises, and societal norms and values are shaped. People begin to enjoy a higher quality of life and security.

Stage 4) Over time, the initial social cohesion starts to weaken. Factors such as luxury, complacency, and internal divisions can diminish *ʿaṣabiyyah.* As the bond among people weakens, the effectiveness of governance declines. Corruption and inefficiency may increase, leading to societal strife.

Stage 5) Societies enter a phase of moral and cultural decline. The ruling elite may become detached from the needs of the populace, leading to dissatisfaction and unrest. The economic structure may also falter, resulting in increased taxation and exploitation of lower classes. This can lead to social unrest and conflict.

Stage 6) The weakened dynasty faces external threats and internal revolts. Eventually, it collapses, paving the way for the rise of a new group with stronger *ʿaṣabiyyah.* This new group emerges, often from a marginalised or discontented segment of society, and the cycle begins anew.

Taking the Qur'an as an example, Ibn Khaldun underlines that the main objective of the Muslim historian is to attain the inner meaning of understanding the human condition. For Khaldun, if humans are to take meaning from peoples of the past, their endeavour must involve speculation and a desire to attain the truth. The historian must establish subtle explanations of causes and present a deep knowledge of how and why things happened. The archetypal nature of historical narratives in the Qur'an heavily influenced Ibn Khaldun's theory of human history.

Inspired by this, Ibn Khaldun discussed his cyclical theory of how all nations emerge, develop and then lose their sovereignty to other nations. His Rise and Fall theory was based on two notions of Qur'anic ideas as well as his own observations. As I mentioned, the first was the notion of archetypal narratives in the Qur'an that provide instances where nations, peoples and powers had risen and fallen. In *Sūrah al-Aʿrāf*, Allah says,

"*For every community, there is a fixed time, and when the end of their term approaches, they cannot delay it by a single moment.*" (TQM 7:34). The second is that for Ibn Khaldun, like in the Qur'an, time was not a linear process. The Qur'anic conception of time is not simply restricted to this world; it is instead cyclical in the sense that "*from Allah we came, and to Him, we shall return*". Allah is the only one who is *al-Awwal* (the First) who has no beginning nor end, and Allah is *al-Akhir* (The Endless) who will be here after everything has ended. Time in Islam is *ākhirah*-oriented (next-life-oriented), meaning we had a life before this earthly abode and shall return to it.

The Qur'an itself is not linear; it has no beginning, middle or end. Instead, it is a series of *Sūrahs* collected in book form, and the reader may choose to read the Qur'an from wherever they deem fit. The first *Sūrah* in the Qur'an is known as *al-Fātiḥah* (The Opening), but it was not the first *Sūrah* revealed. The Qur'an does not need to be read linearly. As a result, Ibn Khaldun established his theory of rise and fall as a series of archetypes that functioned circularly.

However, this was one of many inspirations he took. In his *Muqadimmah* (Prolegomena), Ibn Khaldun starts his work by discussing the importance of history to Muslims. He wanted to make clear how history ought to be written and taught. He says the first is the *ẓāhir* (surface) manner, a descriptive approach to providing information about events. Ibn Khaldun suggests that this style of history writing is focused on a tradition of 'what' happened. Critical of this approach, Ibn Khaldun argues that historians who strayed from the truth exercised little critical thought, as it required many skills of interpretation. In addition, many historians were concerned with preserving information rather than giving it meaning. As a result, Ibn Khaldun accepted that while the *ẓāhir* manner of writing history does have some merit, he pointed to a second way of history production, which he called the *bāṭin* (inner) aspect of history, in which there is an attempt to understand 'how' and 'why' things happened. However, this meant that historians require the knowledge and the disposition to interpret human behaviour and history. Ibn Khaldun emphasises that this is the most comprehensive manner in which a historian can establish the truth of the past and remove falsehoods. He continues that a historian must move beyond mere reporting, and that a good historian and scholar requires critical insight to attain the hidden truth; it takes knowledge to lay the truth bare and polish it so that critical insight may be applied. Ibn Khaldun ends by suggesting that a good historian requires a command of numerous sources and an excellent speculative mind.

Ibn Khaldun was not the only one who made the case of cycles in history, as it is a fact of life that all things created will have an end, from human life to the cosmos. Al-Ghazālī had made this case regarding human life, from the point of formation in the womb of the mother, to the death of a person. This was a full cycle, but like all of us, al-Ghazālī did not know how long each person would live, as that is knowledge only Allah knows. While the average person may go through such a cycle, not everybody does, of course. Many people die young, some due to sickness or many other reasons. In that sense, the cycle was a general paradigm used to make sense of things, not a hard and fast rule. With his cyclical theory, Ibn Khaldun, who was alive during the conflict between the Ottoman Sultan Beyazid I and Timurlane, was pretty accurate in his examination of the rise and fall of states. While he recognised that time is a variable which is difficult to quantify, Ibn Khaldun made the case that the longevity of each state would be approximately 120 years. While he was not correct regarding all of the states he mentioned, it was a close estimate for many.

How, then, does one reconcile Ibn Khaldun's ideas when anomalies seem to challenge his theory? A key moment to consider is the conflict between the Ottomans and Timur. After Timur defeated Sultan Bayezid I and took him captive, it might appear that the Ottomans had fallen into the cycle predicted by Khaldun, with the collapse of their state seemingly imminent. However, what Khaldun's theory failed to predict was that, first, the Ottomans not only survived the interregnum period but went on to become one of the largest and most enduring empires, dominating the region for another four centuries. Several factors could explain this unexpected outcome. One reason could be that the collapse of the Ottoman state was short-sighted. While Timur had defeated Sultan Bayezid, he did not dismantle the intricate Ottoman networks and institutions that had fostered strong loyalty among various segments of the empire. Another possibility is that, while Bayezid was removed from power, it was the Sultan, not the Ottoman state itself, that was overthrown, leading to internal struggles among his sons. Furthermore, there was no viable power to replace the Ottomans at the time, allowing the empire to regain its footing. Finally, Khaldun's theory primarily examined dynastical authority, focusing on the leadership rather than the broader civilisational aspects that allowed the Ottomans to persist. This oversight highlights that Khaldun's theory, while insightful and profound, is not an absolute law but a guideline that helps in understanding cyclical patterns in history. In the case of the Ottomans, it was the resilience of their institutions and the absence of a clear rival power that allowed them to defy the conventional limits of Khaldunian theory.

One way to explain the Ottoman Empire using Ibn Khaldun's theory is to say that the Ottomans kept reinventing themselves every hundred years. This means they still followed the rise-and-fall pattern that Khaldun described, but no other power was strong enough to replace them. Another idea is that the Ottomans learned from past mistakes and slowed down their decline. Or maybe Khaldun's theory just wasn't entirely right.

It's also possible that while his theory works well for older empires, it doesn't fully apply to more modern ones like the Ottomans, which had new ways of running their government, army, economy, and society. A common belief among many Muslims is that the Ottomans slowly declined after the 1500s. Even though many modern scholars disagree with this view, it's still widely accepted in Muslim communities. Interestingly, the Ottomans were aware of Khaldun's ideas and even developed their own similar theories.

The seventeenth-century Ottoman scribe and historian Katib Çelebi was also concerned about Ottoman decline and made the argument that according to Allah's custom, and as it is the nature of sedentary communities and human societies, there appeared signs of agitation in the character of the Exalted State (the Ottoman state) and evidence of discord in its powers. He then placed this moment within a theory similar to Ibn Khaldun's. After quoting Khaldun, Çelebi would compare Ottoman society to the human body. He would make the case that as human beings go through three stages—adolescence, adulthood, and old age—so too do states. He also conceded that some states survive longer, even if they are in the last stage, because they have a stronger disposition. Later, Naima Efendi, an early eighteenth-century historian, also developed such cyclical theories with his own five-stage formula. He said that the first was the nomadic form, the second was tribal solidarity, the third was dynastic, the fourth was disorder and corruption, and the fifth was the exacerbation of the last stage that led to collapse. Like Çelebi, he too viewed these cycles as part of Allah's custom.

In the Ottoman world, Muslim historians continued to find a balance between providing values and lessons to highlight the cyclical approach that was inspired by Islamic teachings and the more source-based approach which was popular in Western Europe. That is, a balance between modes of historiography that are instructive and analytical. By the eighteenth century, Muslim thinkers were examining ideas of *tajdīd* (Renewal) and *iṣlāḥ* (Reform), with Sultan Selim III and Sultan Abdulhamid II being called the *Mujaddid* (Renewer). This thought process emerged from the *ḥadīth* of the Prophet ﷺ narrated by Abū Hurayra (ra), "*At the beginning of every century, Allah will send to this ummah someone who will renew its religious understanding*". Muslims have varying opinions on whether the notion of *Mujaddid* means an individual or a group of people. For the Ottomans, they were aware that the Muslims would go through phases in which a renewal would be needed. The idea of renewal is a reminder to uphold Islam, or to subscribe to its foundational unchanging tenets and adapt to the new conditions of the time. Throughout the eighteenth and nineteenth century, the Muslim world would produce works that examined phases of transition to understand better at the state of the *ummah*, and whether absolute points or milestones in human history can be moments where the condition of people can be reversed, or whether that moment serves as a reflection of the state of people and their condition was irreversible.

It was not simply the Ottoman world that was examining ideas of renewal. The eighteenth-century Indian Muslim scholar Shāh Walīullāh Dihlawī also examined some of the challenges that Muslims were facing in India at the time. Shāh Walīullāh noticed the decline of the Mughal Dynasty, due to the extended reign of Aurangzeb and the emergence of the Marathas, who took advantage of the political vacuum left behind. These were not the only issues that Shāh Walīullāh witnessed; with inter-Muslim contestations and the emergence of the British as a colonial force, Shāh Walīullāh attempted to examine a host of conditions in order to safeguard the Muslim presence in the region. As a result, Shāh Walīullāh stressed the need for intellectual revival, educational reform and socio-economic reformation. Shāh Walīullāh wrote about the socio-economic stages of change, from a primitive village setting to a larger community, a concept which he called *al-Irtifāqāt* (The stages of economic development). He constructed four stages to form a comprehensive theory. The stages were as follows:

1) *Al-Irtifāq al-bahāʾimī* (Elevation from the primitive state:Rudimentary life), which he attributed to village folk.

2) The formation of townships, communities and the city-state. As a result of this, five types of *ḥikma* (wisdom) became necessary: 1- *Al-Ḥikmah al-Maʿāshiyyah* (wisdom pertaining to good manners of living), 2- *Al-Ḥikmah al-Manziliyyah* (the wisdom of a good family life), 3- *Al-Ḥikmah al-Iktisābiyyah* (the wisdom of earning a livelihood, such as the division of labour, specialisation, diversity of occupation, and the use of money), 4- *Al-Ḥikmah al-Taʿāmuliyyah* (the wisdom of mutual dealings), 5- *Al-Ḥikmah al-Taʿāwuniyyah* (the wisdom of cooperation).

3) The formation of the government of the city-state. This stage requires an *Imam* and five institutions emerge: 1) *Al-Qadāʾ* (the judiciary), 2) *Al-Shahryāriyyah* (the executive), 3) *Al-Jihād* (the police and military forces), 4) *Al-Tawallī wa al-Niqābah* (welfare and public works), and 5) *Al-Mawʿiẓah wa al-tazkiyah* (religious and moral business).

4) Internationalism. In this stage, a "meta" government (*Khalīfat al-Khulafāʾ*) emerges. It is a government that regulates all other governments.

All of Shāh Walīullāh's ideas on the development of socio-economic change are seen within this patterned framework. While Shāh Walīullāh has his critics, and his ideas of reforms were unable to restore Muslim power in the way he imagined, his ideas on *al-Irtifāqāt* are reflective of a trend that has existed in Muslim intellectual writings.

In the Ottoman world, the Justice Minister under Sultan Abdulhamid II and *ʿālim* Ahmet Cevdet attempted to understand the Ottoman experience of renewal. He was appointed as the state historian, during which time he wrote his major work, *Tārīh-i Cevdet*, in which he documented Ottoman history from 1187/1774, when the Russians defeated the Ottomans at Kaynarca in the Crimea, up until the abolishment of the Janissary Corps in 1241/1826 by Sultan Mahmud II.

Cevdet, who had also translated Ibn Khaldun's *Muqaddimah* into Ottoman Turkish, also observed patterns and attempted to provide his readership with lessons that needed to be learnt from the past. The influence of Ibn Khaldun on Cevdet led to him finding ways of maintaining harmony between Ottoman-Muslim tradition with the changing times, suggesting that Cevdet felt that a more balanced approach regarding Islam and the changing world was needed. Cevdet believed that the Ottomans could learn how the Western European states had stolen a march on the Ottomans, but also believed that the Ottomans must learn from their history and the history of Muslims of the past.

Cevdet was not the only one who embraced this style of history writing; the Ottoman polymath Namik Kemal followed a similar tradition when writing his history of the Ottoman Empire titled *Osmanli Tārīhī* (Ottoman History). Another thinker at the time was the Arabic-speaking Tunisian bey, Khayruddīn al-Tūnisī, who was also the Grand Vizier to Sultan Abdulhamid II for a short time between 1295–1296/1878–1879. Khayruddīn al-Tūnisī became renowned for his own *Muqaddimah*, entitled *Aqwam al-Masālik fī Maʿrifat Aḥwāl al-Mamālik* (The Surest Path to Knowledge regarding the Condition of Countries), in which he stressed the need for Muslims to study history. He explained how Western European states evolved, and how the Muslim world can learn from this, but still maintain their traditions. Khayruddīn believed that the Muslim world needed to reform during the nineteenth century, and one of the methods he used was to write a historical narrative, from which Muslims could take lessons.

In the Ottoman Empire, historians in that period attempted to balance, on the one hand, how the medium of history writing in the West was changing towards a more academic approach to that was based on covering specific topics, such as the history of the peasantry class, the history of the United Kingdom, or histories of the nation-state. On the other hand, Muslim historians were still trying to provide lessons and show patterns from which the Muslim community could take lessons. From the nineteenth century onwards, the explosion of steam technology and the print press cultivated a new culture that coincided with the emergence of the nation-state model, which meant that the discipline of history writing in Western Europe focused more on source-based history writing.

It must be stressed that it was not simply Muslims who wrote about cyclical theories. The Western European world was full of works on this theme. During the eighteenth and nineteenth centuries, thinkers in Western Europe and the Ottoman Empire examined Ibn Khaldun's ideas to establish where and how nations tend to repeat themselves, and where lessons can be learned. For example, the Scottish eighteenth-century historian Alexander Fraser Tytler claimed that democracies follow a predictable cyclical pattern. He believed that democracies evolved from having virtuous intentions to becoming corrupted, and later declining. He argued that leadership eventually stops acting in the interest of those who elected them. While people vote for the candidate who provides the best commodities for them, in the end, it leads to authoritarian tendencies as societies give up their political agency to the political class so as to meet their material needs. While there is no direct proof of Ibn Khaldun's influence on Tytler, Ibn Khaldun's cyclical theory of the rise and collapse of Muslim dynasties reads similarly.

This type of thought process did not stop here, of course. The nineteenth and twentieth centuries saw the emergence of another genre of writing, this time, civilisational thought. Muslim scholars, in an attempt to counter the colonial West's narrative that they were a civilisational force, started writing works about Islam also being civilisational. The words *tamaddun* and *mediniyet* (civilisation) emerged from this period, showing primarily that Islam was indeed civilisational. Works on Islamic civilisation coincided at the time when ideas of *Ittiḥād-i Islām* (Islamic Unity/Muslim Unity) were becoming popular in response to the colonial encroachment. As a consequence of this, the British, in particular, would also give a name to this phenomenon, calling it Pan-Islamism. The term was then used to suggest a difference between Islam, the religion, and the instrumentalisation of Islam as a political tool. At the time, many Muslims criticised this conceptualisation, and made the case that Islam was as equally political as it was religious from its inception, and that it was civilisational. This led to a host of Muslim writers writing about Islam as a civilisation, with an all-encompassing worldview.

By the twentieth century, the Algerian intellectual Malik Bennabi embraced the ideas of Ibn Khaldun and the Qur'an and wrote about the rise and fall of civilisations in a cyclical format. Bennabi, who had witnessed Algeria attain its freedom from the colonial yoke of France, was still concerned about what he called the "colonisable" Muslim mind and soul. Whether Bennabi had internalised an Orientalist trope from the French, or that he was influenced by Ibn Khaldun, is still up for debate on this point. Ibn Khaldun had said that when a people are defeated, their "soul" starts to emulate the victors. I guess for Ibn Khaldun it is the defeat that leads to emulation as the point of emphasis, whereas for Bennabi it is the point where a society has already permitted one to be "colonisable" thus the emulation begins first, then the defeat as he has put it, which is the critical juncture. Bennabi felt that in order for Muslims to be able to compete with the colonial forces, they would have to become a civilisational force again. He made the case that the first phase—the spiritual phase of a civilisation—was its most concrete, and once we move on to the next phase, the rational stage, it is one of intellectual advancement, and then finally the instinctive/primitive phase shows the spiritual bonds that hold civilisations start to wither and as a result lead to decline. Bennabi makes no secret of his belief in the cyclical theory; he mentions it explicitly in his work. What is worth noting is that Bennabi recognises that each civilisation has its own living identity, but nonetheless still follows a course and a pattern. The main difference between Bennabi and Ibn Khaldun was that Bennabi suggested that civilisations emerged and manifested over a longer period of time and could be passed on from one group to another. For Bennabi, civilisations were far more complicated than an idea-state.

So why are the thinkers so different in their analysis? One reason could be that they are examining different aspects of human societies. In the case of Ibn Khaldun, it was the rise and fall of dynasties, for Shāh Walīullāh, the socio-economic conditions of a society, and for Bennabi, it was the rise and fall of civilisations. As a result, these thinkers were examining different historical milestones to make sense of the patterns within their cyclical theories.

But how do we see these cyclical theories, how can we visualise them? Every state or civilisation will go through these stages. But one of the points we forget is that just like individual human life, not all states and civilisations go through all the stages, and some states and civilisations go through the stages faster than others. In that sense, it might be worth examining these cyclical theories visually as a spiral moving forward in time. Below, I have drawn an image to show how the cycle could look as time is moving forward, and how states go through cycles or spirals. The first image shows the cycle in a fixed sense of time, while I argue that if we adjust our thinking and look at a cycle where time is different for each state, we will see that the cycle is actually an uneven spiral. It's crucial to emphasise that historians rely on evidence when examining cycles within civilisations. Each milestone in a cycle should be contextualised and supported by thorough analysis, rather than viewed in isolation.

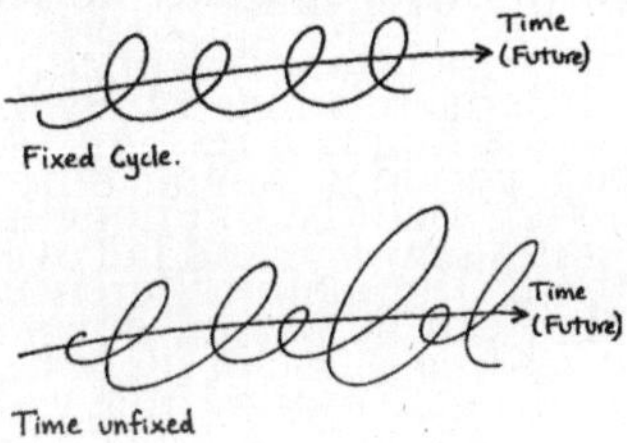

Additionally, acknowledging that not every nation follows a linear path through these cycles is vital. Some may face sudden disruptions—akin to a "car crash"—due to external factors, while others might experience accelerated progress. This variability highlights the complexity of historical development and the need for a nuanced understanding of each unique situation. Overall, cyclical theories can provide valuable insights, but they must be applied carefully and with attention to specific historical contexts. Examining nations side by side can shed light on how the rise of one nation often impacts others, creating shifts in power, trade, and cultural exchange. For example, the rise of a dominant power might inspire neighbouring nations to adapt or innovate in response, while its decline could lead to opportunities for others to assert themselves.

This comparative analysis helps us understand the broader dynamics at play, illustrating that history is not just a series of isolated events but a complex interplay of influences. By studying these relationships, we can gain deeper insights into the cyclical nature of civilisations and how interconnected their fates truly are. This comparative approach allows for a richer understanding of how historical processes unfold in a global context, revealing patterns of influence and response among nations. It underscores the idea that history is often a web of interactions, where the fortunes of one nation are closely tied to those of others. Such analysis can provide deeper insights into the complex interplay of forces that shape civilisations over time.

If we were to add Bennabi's idea of civilisations rising and falling over a long period (Longue durée), then what we would get is that states may rise and fall over a shorter period, but civilisations that can be passed down from one state to another, such as in the case of the Umayyads to the Abbasids, or the British to the Americans, that they may rise and fall in a different type of cycle that whilst still being connected, can still be independent. (See image 2 below)

Another point is that if the universe will end, then time in and of itself ought not to be seen as a straight line but rather a whole cycle. This should not be surprising for the Muslim, as *"from Allah we came and to Him we shall return."* (See image 3 below). Muslims are well in tune with the idea that time is not a flat line, as nothing in the cosmos points to this, whether it is the spinning of an individual atom, the planets circumambulating around the sun, which is also moving in a similar fashion within the galaxy, or people circumambulating around the Kaaba. The idea of cycles and everything having a beginning and an end has been a rather logical way in which people of the past thought. I would add that it was only during the advent of modernity that we saw time in a linear fashion, a constant incline due to progress, but with no future or end in sight (See image 4 below). And yet, death, collapse, and the end are part of what gives the believer a purpose, in recognising there is an *ākhirah*. In that sense, the *ḥadīth* of Jibril

ؑ once again should come to mind. Muslims have also then seen whether we can see such cycles in the past. They may examine the life of the Prophet ﷺ as a cycle, the period of the *Khulafāʾ al-Rāshidūn* as a cycle, the period of the Umayyads as another cycle, and so on.

In the case of the Prophet ﷺ, one could view his role within the context of a cyclical pattern in two distinct ways. The first perspective is to consider him ﷺ as the pinnacle of humanity's journey on Earth. In this view, the human story begins with Adam ؑ, and the arrival of the Beloved of Allah ﷺ marks the highest point in human existence. This moment, when Allah sent His final Revelation through the Prophet ﷺ, signifies the culmination of humanity's potential. From this peak, humanity is seen to gradually decline until the Day of Judgement. The Prophet ﷺ, in this model, becomes the zenith of human virtue, and his advent represents the closing of one era, from which the world begins its inevitable downward trajectory.

The second perspective focuses on examining the Prophet ﷺ through the lens of his life-story, or *Sīrah*, as a series of distinct phases, each offering valuable lessons for contemporary Muslims striving to revive the ummah. By studying the Prophet's ﷺ life in this way, one can identify stages of growth, challenges, and victories that can guide efforts to rebuild and strengthen the Muslim community today. This approach provides a microcosmic history of Islam, where the development of the early Muslim community—its struggles, triumphs, and eventual rise to power—can be seen as a model for modern revival. This perspective also aligns with the theories of scholars like Ibn Khaldun and Malik Bennabi, who focused on the cyclical rise and fall of civilisations. Their concepts of community formation and the emergence of power can be mapped onto the early Islamic community's progression from a small group of believers to a formidable force, demonstrating how the Prophet's ﷺ life serves not only as a spiritual guide but as a historical template for revitalising the Muslim *ummah*.

Another point worth examining is how to view multiple states and civilisations at the same time. While one state is ending, another is rising, and another state may be in a static phase for a prolonged period of time. Some of these states directly impact one another, whereas other states are emerging in a part of the world because they are not in direct competition with other major states.

For example, while Great Britain was consolidating its status as a world power in the eighteenth century, it lost the USA by 1776. The Ottomans, who were coming out of a period of relative peace, would also face a moment of loss in 1774, after being defeated by the Russians at Kaynarca and losing the Khanate of Crimea. In 1739, the Mughal Empire in India was no longer unified, while Japan was still in a position of isolationism during the middle period of the Edo era, which brought it relative stability. By the nineteenth century, the Japanese experienced the Meiji Restoration, dismantling 250 years of Edo rule; the Ottomans, after a civil war between Mahmud II and Mehmed Ali Pasha, entered a period of state reform known as the *Tanzimat*; Britain took control of India, establishing the British Raj; and the Americans were gradually rising as a global power, while the Russians and French were emerging from the taxing Napoleonic wars. None of these developments could have been anticipated a century ago, yet many now take them for granted, assuming such events were inevitable. This overlooks the fact that the world was filled with shifting dynamics, each requiring careful analysis, both from internal and external perspectives.

This complexity, however, has often been oversimplified in historical narratives, particularly when discussing the so-called "decline" of the Ottomans and other Muslim states. The

Industrial Revolution has often been positioned as the key factor in the rise of the West and the perceived fall of the Muslim world due to their alleged rejection of new technologies. However, the Industrial Revolution itself is more a linguistic construct than a singular, easily defined event. It does not offer much insight into how the Ottomans might have revived themselves amidst the global shifts of the time but rather places the Ottomans under a narrative that requires little scrutiny—the narrative of the Industrial Revolution. What it does reveal is the dual nature of historical change—what nations can control and what they cannot. This is why studying the histories of multiple nations simultaneously, as global historians often do, can provide a deeper understanding of the interwoven complexities that shaped the world.

image 2:

image 3:

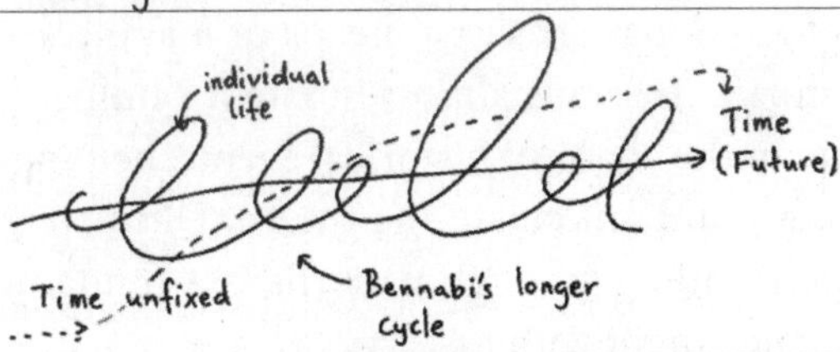

image 4:

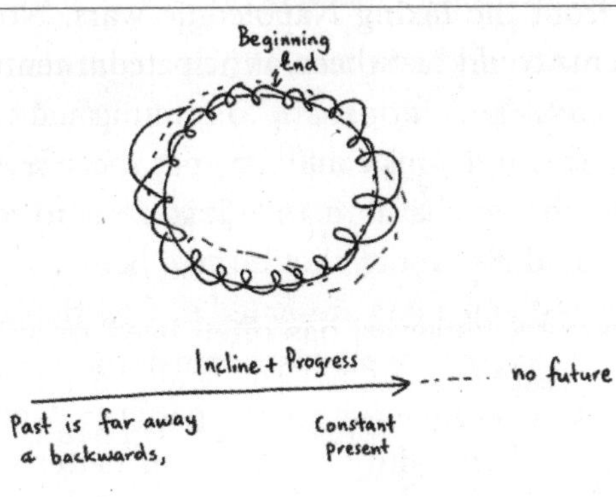

Critics of these cyclical theories will suggest that these historians tend to look for patterns in the past. Some, such as post-colonial thinkers, may argue that irrespective of the sources, what historians do is simply tie together the information they have acquired after much study of the sources available to them. According to these thinkers, historians may see continual patterns and, as a result, join the dots to provide a narrative that fits their framing. If we were to move beyond the cyclical theory, we would see that historians use periodisation, discourse, paradigms, and schemas, all of which have their own frameworks and patterns. In that sense, even the exercise of finding patterns, whether cyclical or linear, is, after all, an interpretive endeavour.

As historians, our task goes beyond identifying patterns in the past; it involves analysing the information available to us and discerning how these patterns inform our understanding of human behaviour and societal change. Each interpretation is shaped by the evidence we gather, and our theories inevitably reflect our historical outlook. This interconnectedness can lead us to seek patterns as a means of making sense of complex histories. It seems almost innate for humans to look for structure in the chaos of historical events, helping us navigate the present and anticipate the future. Ultimately, this quest for understanding through patterns is a fundamental aspect of our engagement with history.

This leads me to my last point. When examining the Qur'an, it is clear that Allah's words are communicated with the idea of patterns in mind. This could mean that history does have a reoccurring theme, that human beings do tend to repeat and rhyme. It could also mean that human beings make sense of knowledge best when it is presented in a particular form. Patterns, themes, and cycles are just some of the ways human beings make sense of themselves. The patterns need not always be exact, as the main aim of a theory or pattern is simply to translate a complex set of ideas in a way that is easily digestible. Or it could be that both are applicable and that there is no contradiction between the cyclical nature of people, that just like in nature, human beings are indeed part of the laws of the cosmos and will repeat patterns, and that part of human learning is that we need patterns to understand. This does not mean that cyclical theories cannot be wrong, as these are simply human endeavours, and we are, after all, fallible, but what is innate, however, is that we continue to think in ways where cyclical theories matter.

Contingency versus Patterns/Cycles

The challenge for many historians is not the patterns but what I will term "contingency moments". Both Ibn Khaldun and Bennabi made the case that there are moments in human history that are beyond the norm that can impact a nation and the course it takes. These contingency moments can, at times, expedite the end of a nation or end it directly. Sometimes, when there is a contingency moment, it can lead to the rapid decline of one group of people while liberating another at the same time. For example, if there is a major natural disaster, it may impact one nation to its detriment but may awaken another nation to reflect and improve itself. Furthermore, if there is a war between two nations, at times, weaker nations may come out on top, changing the course for both the victors and the losers.

In that sense, contingencies are anomalies that occur that do not show any signs of patterns. The notion of contingency is important, as it shows that humans do have free will and that not everything can be anticipated. It is also important for the historian to understand whether a particular moment in history is a contingency moment or not. I will use the example of WWI as a case in point, as never before in recorded human history has there been a war of such magnitude before this. There were many wars and conflicts between the Ottomans and the Russians and Western European powers. But nothing could have prepared these nations for WWI, and while the Ottoman Empire was militarily weaker than these states, there was no telling at the time what the outcome of the war would be.

Those who see WWI as a contingency moment will say that while the Ottoman Empire had problems and reflected signs of weakness, predicting its end due to WWI would have been impossible, as it requires the ability to know the motivations of too many actors both inside and outside. In fact, we see that the Austria-Habsburg Empire collapsed, the Bolshevik Revolution took place in Russia, while Britain was at its zenith point in regard to the amount of land it had grabbed in WWI. By the end of WWII, two decades later, the British Empire had collapsed and lost India, as well as its foothold in the post-Ottoman world, and was being replaced by the USA. Supporters of the Ottoman Empire argue that the Empire may have continued to survive and even transform and reinvent itself, as it had done in the past, had it not been for the anomaly of WWI. As I said, these are points that are up for debate, and this is what I stressed earlier when I said that history is interpretative. But historians need to be aware of these things, as what they do is not simply detailing "facts". These debates are matters that historians continue to discuss. I shall mention, in more detail, the point of contingency in the next section, but I want to point out here how historians operate as a way of making sense of connecting points in history.

In this sense, we can examine the ideas of the American historian John Lewis Gaddis, who mentions three key aspects of time and space which the historian uses to write history in his book *The Landscape of History: How Historians Map the Past*. Gaddis makes the case that it is impossible for the historian to cover every detail of a particular period, event, or moment. Human beings are just not able to encompass everything; only Allah can. Also, being overly detailed makes it difficult for readers to appreciate what is being conveyed, as people tend to prefer pattern-based ways of learning. As a result, Gaddis argues that historians exercise their own agency and write with *selectivity*, *simultaneity*, and *scale*.

Selectivity is straightforward, as every writer is selective in the way they write, and, as I have just mentioned, there is no way of covering everything. But the idea of selectivity is about what the historian thinks is important. As Mazharuddin Siddiqui has mentioned in his *Qur'anic Concept of History* that, in the Qur'an, Allah selectively provides us with information about Prophets, people of past civilisations, in order to provide us with examples of actions that are morally right or wrong. The act of selectivity is self-evident. But Gaddis expands on this by explaining the degree to which a historian should be selective. Gaddis suggests that by remaining in the present as the historian explains the past, they retain initiative, in the sense that they choose who to accredit and discredit. They choose what to focus on, what institutions, people, and subjects to mention. In that sense, this level of selectivity is powerful, as a thoughtful historian can make the difference in shaping people by bringing to light knowledge that can be beneficial to the *ummah*, whether that be in dispelling falsehood, providing new information, or joining dots to show a pattern and trend. In this sense, being thoughtful of what Islam requires Muslims to learn from the past can help the Muslim historian in knowing what points to select as a way of providing meaning to allow Muslims to reflect on the real nature of how the world operates. The point of selectivity is not to be disingenuous and pick and choose, but rather to highlight a valuable piece of information during the writing process.

Gaddis continues by mentioning **simultaneity**, meaning that history can be written about more than one place at the same time. For example, if we examine WWI, I could write about the battles at Jerusalem, Baghdad, Istanbul, and Kosovo at the same time, showing you what was happening on these fronts simultaneously. Clearly, at the time, the soldiers on the battlefield were unaware of each other's plight, but here a historian can show all of these places at the same time, taking a step back and analysing challenges that people at the time could never have seen. In that sense, the historian is not simply trying to tell you what happened, but is also making links so that you can see the bigger picture, something that many storytellers clearly lack. Simultaneity demonstrates how the historian is able to see all the different moving parts and recognise the complexities that people at the time would not have been able to. As Gaddis stresses, a good understanding implies comparisons to comprehend something in relation to others.

Finally, Gaddis points to the idea of **scale**, and how historians can shift the scale from macroscopic to microscopic and then back again. For Gaddis, this is the ultimate tool of narrative. Gaddis argues that anytime a historian uses a particular episode in history to make a point, the act of scale shifting is taking place in the sense that 'the small' can describe the large. For example, one may use a simple event to describe a larger phenomenon, and analogies and examples are used all the time by the historian. Gaddis argues that historians have no choice but to manipulate time and space this way, as the historians' evidence is always incomplete, their perspective limited, and an infinite number of facts and true statements can be discovered. As a result, historians do their best, but guesswork and imagination are required. With this in mind, I shall show how these points can be used to teach the Muslim reader lessons.

From Badr to Uḥud, a Recurring Theme of Contingency Moments

Recently, I have been explaining how studying the past can be meaningful in understanding how Islamic civilisation has continuously gone through challenges and successes. These challenges can be seen as contingency moments or epoch moments in history. Often these involve wars, natural disasters, epidemics, pandemics, unthinkable moments in history, and of course, *nubuwwa*, which is a special case of direct divine intervention. "Contingency moments" could be interpreted as those unforeseen events that disrupt the expected course of history, serving to highlight the underlying divine influence. These breaks in patterns can serve as reminders of the unpredictable nature of life and the presence of a higher power guiding events in ways that may not always be immediately apparent. This view encourages a deeper exploration of how divine will and human action intersect, suggesting that moments of crisis or transformation may carry profound significance, reflecting a larger, often inscrutable plan. It invites reflection on the ways in which faith and historical processes intertwine, offering insights into the human experience of the divine. Recognising "contingency moments" or epoch-defining events allows for a deeper understanding of how these challenges have shaped the course of history. Thus, wars, natural disasters, epidemics, and pandemics often serve as catalysts for change, prompting responses that can redefine societies. For instance, major conflicts may lead to shifts in power dynamics, while pandemics can impact social structures and economic systems.

Additionally, wars and natural disasters can also be seen as subcategories within the framing of contingency moments in history. Wars often lead to changes in power structures, territorial boundaries, and societal norms. They can provoke shifts in ideologies and create new alliances or enmities, leading to long-lasting consequences. For example, conflicts within Islamic civilisation, such as the Crusades or internal strife like the *fitnas*, not only altered political landscapes but also influenced cultural and religious identities. Whereas natural disasters, on the other hand, can expose vulnerabilities within societies, prompting changes in governance, infrastructure, and community resilience. Events like earthquakes, floods, or famines can catalyse social movements, trigger migrations, or even lead to shifts in religious practices as communities seek meaning in their suffering. Both wars and natural disasters reflect a Divine plan, but in different ways. When one is tested by war, it involves human decisions, conflicts, and moral struggles. They can be seen as tests of faith, resilience, and the consequences of human actions, reflecting the complexity of free will and responsibility. Being tested by natural disasters, on the other hand, can challenge individuals and communities to respond with faith, compassion, and resilience. They may inspire acts of kindness, solidarity, and a deeper connection to spirituality, prompting reflection on life's transient nature.

As for *Nubuwwa* (Prophethood) it represents a significant divine intervention that can also shape historical trajectories. The teachings and actions of Prophets provide moral and ethical frameworks that guide communities through times of turmoil and transformation. Prophets sent to human beings are a direct intervention by Allah. They cannot be predicted without Allah providing clues in scripture or from previous

Prophets, and they indicate Allah's agency and intervention directly. While the outcome of wars or natural disasters is also part of the natural order, as everything comes from Allah, it is difficult empirically to observe that these contingency points are direct intervention. The way that historians have spoken of them in the past is that natural disasters are the natural order of nature, whereas wars reflect the natural order of nations and how they rise and fall. Nonetheless, all these contingency moments are important in order to reflect on Allah's *Qudra* (power), as things can change in an instant.

For this section, I have chosen the battles in Islamic history to make this point, as the outcomes of war are never known at the time but still involve human agency. Due to this, war is a unique contingency moment during the time it occurs, as one may be able to examine a trajectory of historical events that lead to this contingency moment between two nations. Like the outcomes of wars, natural disasters are also matters where only Allah knows the outcome. But in these matters, very little to no human agency is involved. Regarding wars, however, we can see how human free will and *al-Qadr* operate.

Using the Qur'an as an inspiration, I will try to explain how Muslims throughout their history have gone through what the Prophet ﷺ and his companions in the *Sīrah* experienced, terming these *Badr* and *Uḥud* moments. Why *Badr* and *Uḥud*? It is not simply because these were two wars that had different results during the life of the Prophet ﷺ, but because these two moments can be seen as metaphors. The Battle of *Badr* was a moment when the Muslims were few, only 313 men against 1000 Quraysh. At *Badr*, the Muslims adhered to the principles of *tawḥīd*, trusted Allah, and through their dedication, religiosity, and obedience to the Prophet ﷺ, they were victorious. In this sense, *Badr* is similar to the account of Dāwūd (David ﵇) and Jālūt (Goliath), in which the simpler army against all the odds was victorious.

Regarding *Badr*, Allah says in the Qur'an, "*You have already come across an instructive sign in the two hosts that encountered each other in battle (at Badr): one host fighting in the way of Allah, and the other that of unbelievers. They saw with their own eyes that one host was twice the number of the other. But (the result of the battle has proved that) Allah succours with His victory whomsoever He wills. In this there is surely a lesson for all who have eyes to see.*" (TQM Maududi – *Sūrah Āl 'Imrān* 3:13)

Uḥud, on the other hand, represented the opposite; the Muslim armies were larger, but they disobeyed Allah and His Messenger ﷺ and became disunited, and as a result, lost that battle. Islamic history has continuously pointed to the presence of *īmān* and *taqwā* in the Battle of *Badr*, and the disobedience and derision in the Battle of *Uḥud*. However, while Muslims can experience a Uḥud moment, Allah has reminded them that they can once again taste victory, so long as they return to what made them successful at *Badr* which was *taqwā*. Allah says "*For sure Allah helped you at Badr when you were utterly weak. Beware, then, of Allah; perhaps you will be thankful.*" (TQM Maududi – *Sūrah Āl 'Imrān* 3:123). In this sense, when I mention *Badr* and *Uḥud* moments, I am not equivocating exact patterns of frameworks but rather using a rhetorical use of these moments that are part of the Muslim imagination and vocabulary to help explain wars in Islamic history that may lead to a contingency moment.

The *Ummah* has gone through many *Badr* and *Uḥud* moments throughout their history, and if the *Sīrah* is to be instructive for the Muslim, then trying to examine some parallels may be helpful. For example, in 463/1071, known as the Battle of Malazgirt (Manzikert), the Seljuk forces under Alp Arslan, the second Sultan of the Great Seljuk Empire, were victorious in defeating the Eastern Romans, also known as the Byzantines, on mainland Anatolia, today's Türkiye.

One could say that 463/1071 was a Badr moment for the Muslims, a moment which created a shift in the region in favour of Islam. However, as soon as the Seljuk forces defeated the Eastern Roman Empire in 492/1099, the Crusaders marched into the Arab world, defeated the Muslim armies and captured *Bayt al-Maqdis*, today's Palestine. This can be roughly understood as a *Uḥud* moment. While the Muslim outrage was great at the time, as the Crusaders slaughtered thousands of Muslims, Christians, and Jews, it was not until eighty-eight years later that Salahuddin's forces would defeat the Crusaders and then reclaim *Bayt al-Madqis* from the Crusaders in 583/1187, which was another *Badr* moment. Muslim success would remain for another seventy-one years; but by 656/1258, the Mongols would sack Baghdad and bring the region under the sphere of Mongol influence—once again, a *Uḥud* moment. As time went by and the Mongols gradually became immersed in the world of Islam by 763/1362, the Ottomans emerged from the ruins of the Seljuk and Mongol world. Murat Hudavandigar, the third Sultan of the Ottoman state, would establish Muslim influence in Rumelia, known as the Balkans. This was again a *Badr* moment. However, as the Ottomans expanded quickly, the forces of Timurlane defeated Sultan Beyazid Yildirim at the Battle of Ankara in 804/1402, bringing Ottoman influence to a sudden halt, and bringing in the period of the Ottoman interregnum, as the two great Muslim armies going to war facilitated the destabilisation of the region. Timur would disband the Ottoman domains and leave it to the sons of Beyazid to fight over their Ottoman estate. One could say this was a *Uḥud* moment. The *fitna* created by the two Muslim sides, which were warring with each other, was problematic for both sides. While the situation looked bleak, in 875/1453 Mehmed II (Fatih) would conquer Constantinople, and for the first time in history, the Muslims defeated a centre of Christendom—a *Badr* moment. While the Ottomans were centralising their state in West Asia, in 883/1478, the Spanish Inquisition began in Spain, ending 600 years of Muslim presence—a *Uḥud* moment. But while Muslims and Jews were being forced out of Spain and making their way into the Ottoman domains, Khayruddīn Barbarossa, the famous Ottoman-Albanian Naval commander in 923/1516, defeated the Spanish expedition that landed at Algiers, restricting Spanish influence on North Africa—a *Badr* moment. All these moments can be seen as contingency moments.

So how was this possible? While the above reflects significant battles in Islamic history, hence the title *Badr* to *Uḥud*, it also should point to how Muslim dynasties, peoples, and communities can recover from exceptional losses. The simple answer is that the civilisational Muslim mindset did not come to an end, and Muslims continued to cultivate knowledge, culture, science, and technology. I am aware that many historians will take exception to this type of history writing, as it suggests that there is a formula and that the nuances of each moment in history are reduced to a pattern. Others will argue that I am simply turning back to the methods of history writing prior to the nineteenth century. But I argue that this type of history has a place.

Meta-narrative writing can highlight that Muslims have been through extreme moments of success, and then extreme moments of failure. Meta-narratives emerged in the West in a different garb, but they still exist. Marxist, feminist, and environmentalist histories tend to produce meta-narratives through their focus on gender dynamics, class clashes, and human-nature relationships. Hence, Islamically-minded history writing can be established methodologically by choosing to focus on particular themes or human dynamics apart from the state/dynasty, for instance, and instead examine themes that are a part of our Islamic tradition and culture.

What I want to highlight in this framing here is that the Muslim community continued to survive irrespective of success or failure. This is a constant. Both *Badr* and *Uḥud* moments, should serve as important lessons for Muslims. The Muslims have always gone through a period of turmoil, and as mentioned in the Qur'an, they are reminded of *Badr*, not as a one-off event, but rather that success shall return. However, Muslims need to go through a series of steps and they need to remain steadfast and patient. This patience is not simply about the moment, but a generational patience. Any real change in any given society takes time; it needs to develop and build over a period of time. The *Badr* moments, as I call them, were predicated upon generational steadfastness and maintenance of the traditions of Islam that bore fruit once society was ripe. Just as positive change takes time, sometimes society does not need to gradually decline, but can be caught unawares by a unique moment in history. This can happen from within or from the outside. Such trends are difficult to predict because change occurs over a long duration, and passing down generational memories of societal evolution is difficult. But as time passes, people can look back in history, and, at times, at their own history, and re-examine how they have reached a certain point.

While I have spoken of major milestones as a way of showing the Muslim reader that history is full of ups and downs, and that shifts in civilisational cosmology happen gradually, it is also worth noting that a series of gradual events can be signs of the coming change, to those who pay attention. The other point worth noting is that while Muslims faced many *Uḥud* moments, the *ummah* continued to develop their societies, educational models, learning modes, as well as their culture and tradition. For example, during the emergence of the Seljuks, they were able to amalgamate Ghaznavid administrative techniques with traditions that existed in the Abbasid world and fashion a culture of unprecedented educational advancement. A sophisticated madrassa system was created under

Nizam ul-Mulk, the prominent Muslim scholar, statesman, and vizier during the Seljuk Empire in the eleventh century. He is best known for his significant role in shaping the political and administrative systems of the Seljuk Empire, as well as for his contributions to Islamic governance and political theory. Under Nizam ul-Mulk, the famous *'ulamā'* al-Juwaynī and al-Ghazālī emerged. The Seljuk state and society were able to benefit from the atmosphere created during their reign due to the intellectual and religious environment that was fostered. When the Crusaders advanced towards *Bayt al-Maqdis,* while the earlier Seljuks were either unable or preoccupied with other matters to be able to deal with the Crusader advance, figures who were under the influence of Seljuk civilisational culture and traditions were able to repel the Crusaders. Once the Seljuks had dealt with more internal issues and immediate concerns, they were able to extend their influence in the region, which was both political and intellectual.

A careful examination of the educational system that emerged in the Seljuk world created the conditions for future generations to raise not only upright and steadfast people who were civilisational, but who could also address the Crusader's presence in the future. In that sense, Salahaddin's success in defeating the Crusaders in 583/1187 was due to the Seljuk victory of 463/1071, which permitted a cultural renaissance of the Sunni imagination. This took a hit in 492/1099 with the Crusader capture of *Bayt al-Maqdis* but was able to facilitate a Muslim victory a century later. 492/1099 had come too early to examine Seljuk cultivation. Not only that, Ṣalāḥuddin's success was due to 'Imād al-Dīn Zangī's success in Urfa in 538/1144, which disrupted the Crusader hold over Urfa, Antakya, and Jerusalem as connected cities. Then in 542/1148, 'Imād al-Dīn's son Nūr al-Dīn Zangī defeated the Crusaders in what was known as the Siege of Damascus. The Zangīs were Atabegs of the Seljuk dynasty. Atabegs typically referred to a noble or military leader who acted as a governor or regent for a young prince or ruler, often in a principality or a smaller state. The term is most commonly associated with the Seljuk Empire, where Atabegs were appointed to oversee regions and ensure the effective governance and military defence of their territories. The role of an Atabeg was crucial during periods of fragmentation and civil strife, as they were responsible for maintaining order and loyalty among their subjects.

Through the inroads made by the Zangīs and the culture of the Seljuk domains, we see the emergence of Salahuddin. In a strange way, one could argue that the Muslims were going through a decline and revival moment simultaneously. Decline in the sense of a military and social decline, but revival in the sense of a spiritual and intellectual one. Once again, it comes down to the milestones we use. When we examine the Qur'an, we see that historical change does not happen suddenly. There is, in fact, a gradual accumulation of milestones or causes which subsequently result in a significant change after a substantial period of time. It is thus important to pay attention to this historical process, as this is the law of Allah regarding this *dunyā* (World), and to ascertain when Allah has offered His support.

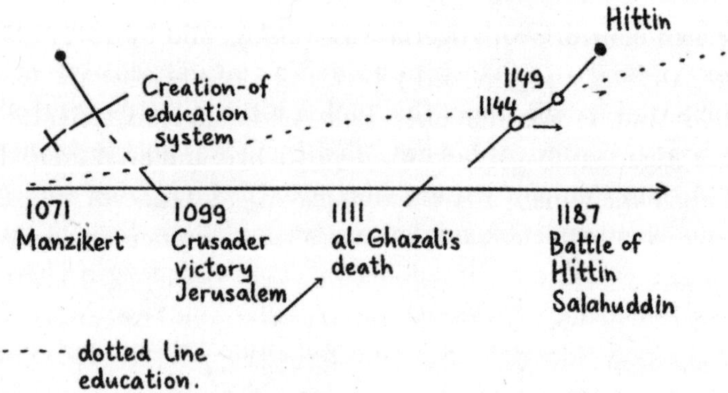

In that sense, a good historian would examine the broader picture and use historical moments as lessons. A good historian would explore details to show that societal transitions lead to peaks and troughs. However, a great historian can both tell the meta-narratives and provide complex details. So, is there anything for Muslims to learn today regarding this style of narrative teaching? My answer is yes. One could argue that the collapse of the Ottomans in 1340/1922, and then the abolishment of the Caliphate in 1342/1924, was another *Uḥud* moment. In the 100 years since the Ottoman collapse, Muslims have witnessed the Western colonisation of Muslim lands, the creation of the state of Israel and the subjugation of the people of Palestine. However, in the last 100 years, British and French colonial rule has also been removed. Muslims are once again reflecting modes of great education, and the next century could be a period of intellectual revival. Some may argue, however, that modern Muslim states simply left the colonial structure behind but were replaced by another imperial Western power. Still, nonetheless, a change is indeed taking place, and examining the fruits of a culture of resistance requires more intellectual treatment.

In 1245/1830, the French colonised Algeria and stripped it away from the Ottoman Empire. During the French occupation, millions of Algerians were killed. By World War II, French control over Algeria was waning, and by 1373/1954, the Algerians had moved to remove French presence from their land. It was not until eight years later, in 1381/1962, that Algeria fully gained its independence, and even then, the French killed many more before leaving. But indeed, they did leave eventually. If 1245/1830 was a *Uḥud* moment for the Algerians, then 1373/1962 may be a *Badr* moment for them. I may say, perhaps, that in Algeria, political and military independence is not the end, such as the case in Hittin when Salahuddin defeated the Crusaders, but independence could be akin to ʿImād al-Dīn's victory at Urfa. While some may argue that Algerian success can be seen as a moment of decolonisation, others will say that the Algerian nation-state replicated the very traditions it fought against. Ultimately, judging our existing realities requires intelligent minds.

The point of the above example is to highlight how change takes time and show that success is not a simple affair. It also shows that even when victory is achieved, the world is still a complicated and messy place, and a moment of victory does not mean that the world has become a perfect. I say this to highlight how to make sense of events regarding Palestine and Western Asia. So far, the Israeli occupation has consisted of seventy-five years of brutality, but just as in the case of the Crusaders and Algeria, eventually, the outside forces will have to leave. In the case of the Crusades, it was eighty-eight years, and in the case of Algeria, it was 132. The point to stress once again is how we understand change and what our understanding of time is. As I have mentioned earlier, the modern mind has become myopic, or we can say time has collapsed for us, where we can rarely make sense of how change takes place. Being stuck in a perpetual present means we sometimes cannot see how things are changing, as change happens gradually. This is why meta-narratives of history become essential, as they can be helpful for us to learn lessons.

Many people ask me if there is room for hope for Muslims today, as many students I talk as times feel a sense of despair due to our current predicament in comparison to an Islamic history that is often presented within nostalgic framings. My simple answer is yes, there is room for hope. Firstly, because as I started with this book, Allah has made it clear in the Qur'an that every nation has its time, and every phase, including hardship, shall pass. Secondly, the constellation of the Muslim world has continuously evolved and changed, much like the shifting currents of a river, constantly reshaping its course and boundaries. Muslim presence in Spain lasted for 600 years, and the Ottoman presence in the Balkans was about the same. Muslims have been subject to the Spanish Inquisition, the Trans-Atlantic slave trade, the Crusaders, the Mongol invasion, and colonialism. In modern history, the Muslim world has witnessed the collapse of the Ottoman Empire, the partition of India during which millions died, and the creation of the state of Israel. Whether in the West or Far-East Asia, Muslims continue to be subjugated to hardship as individuals, communities, and an *ummah*. But there is resilience in this *ummah* which is unprecedented compared to any other community. The longevity of the *ummah* is based on the fact that Islam has a civilisational worldview that cultivates. It produces a culture and tradition of knowledge production that resonates with all peoples, and so even though throughout the history of this *ummah*, we have faced moments of extremity, nonetheless we are still here and will continue to be. Islam is the only ideological worldview committed to the truth of Allah, the truth of His *din*, and to manifesting that truth in all walks of life. For that reason, while Muslims may face stiff challenges today, an investigation into our history will show why we continue to exist as a civilisation and why, even during periods of extended struggle and discord, we continue to offer this *ummah* and humanity at large an alternative vision for both this life and the next.

As a result, it is not simply that Muslims need to study history to understand themselves better, to learn from the past, or to place themselves in the timeline of human history. Instead, Muslims need to recognise that they deserve to be here, in this world, and that they are a part of this long tradition and that it is for them to remain positive, not fatalistic, stay optimistic, and attempt to establish the truth in their world. While humans have become conditioned to want instant results, gratification, and change, one lesson we can learn from our past is that change takes time. The Muslim is not "progress" driven in the way the modern man is, rejecting the past as a decadent moment in the timeline of human history. The Muslim is "process" driven, in which that past is important, and the future is still shaped by the tradition, thus we recognise that the past is a repository and that results are in the hands of Allah. Thinking this way can provide us with a better understanding of the future of this *ummah* and allow us to recognise whether our collective immediate future will get better or worse, but that we will nonetheless continue to work to make the world a better place for the present and future.

ب

SECTION V

STUDYING ISLAMIC HISTORY FROM A CIVILISATIONAL APPROACH

The Need to Examine the Bigger Picture

In this section, I shall examine why studying Islamic history as the history of a civilisation can help the Muslim reader attain a better view of the consistencies of Islam not only as a practised religion but a *din* that influenced and cultivated ethical and moral governance, expressions of art and architecture that reminded people of Allah, and advances in the field of science and technology. When studied this way, Islamic history need not simply be a set of dates or events, but rather can introduce the reader to good Muslim behaviour, the Muslim path to administer justice, the consistencies of an ethical and moral framework in relation to governance, the cultivation of societies, and the spread of Islam.

This will not only inform the Muslim reader of the vastness and richness of the influence of Islam over the large tapestry of the Muslim world throughout time and space, but it should also provide confidence in the Muslim regarding many of the misconceptions that have often been written about Islamic history. In addition to understanding the Islamic civilisation, I would also encourage the study of other civilisations, as Muslims in the past did. This should help explain to the Muslim reader the constancy of the Islamic call undertaken by the *ummah* throughout history and how Islam and the Muslims interacted with various peoples, religions and civilisations by adhering to the values and principles of Islam. This should also help them understand their place in regard to belonging to the greater *ummah* that goes beyond time and space, and also provide examples of how they too can practice the Islamic call in our current reality as a civilisational *ummah* which belongs to a rich and vibrant tradition that continues to be practised since the time of the Prophet Muhammad ﷺ. Thus, this can help them understand that the Islamic call is not simply to reach out to individuals but to communities, societies, nations, and humanity as a whole.

The Emergence of a Civilisational Discourse

In response to the colonial encroachment and subsequent collapse of the Ottoman Empire, Muslim thinkers started to posit the question of Islam being a civilisational influence for good. This had already begun by the time the British had colonised India, but by the twentieth century, Muslim thinkers started to express how the *ummah* and Islamic civilisation could be revived again. When studying Islam, and only seeing it from the actions of rulers, one may lose sight of how Islam, through structural, political, and institutional frameworks, was able to provide a lived experience in harmony with both this world and the next. That also meant that in Islam, nature was also seen to be something to work with, not control, as has been the case with modernity. This harmony did not simply have to do with people and power, but with the world in which they lived.

I have become quite surprised at how often Muslim scholars, when reading Islamic history, will point to how Islamic history is full of leaders who were "butchers and tyrants". This type of reductive language of expressing the ills of politics, in actuality, does not reflect how Islam sees politics, and how Islamic politics have been practised. Contrary to belief that has been popularised that political power is corrupting and the *ʿulamāʾ* abstained from being involved, in fact, a more generous reading of Islamic history would point to political power being seen as a practical necessity, as it is simply a responsibility of managing the affairs of society. The fact that the Prophet ﷺ was a political leader points to this fact, as he was neither corruptible nor corrupting. The challenges that many Muslim leaders have faced throughout Islamic history are no different from those any person has faced in any position of authority, whether that be religious authority or political authority, as human beings will always find ways of differing and competing with each other. I also place this caveat that I am aware that people have committed crimes, mischief, and acted in a misguided manner throughout our history. I do not intend to provide a utopian or nostalgic reading of our past. But even these moments are moments we can learn from.

As a result, I would like to include the ideas of the sociologist of Islam, Armando Salvatore who in his book *The Sociology of Islam* makes the following convincing case: if Islam is understood as a religion, civilisation, and a matrix of social and institutional arrangement within which a culture of civility is reflected, then we can start to move away from the simplifications that I mentioned in the previous paragraph. The culture of civility refers to the practices, values, and behaviours that promote respectful and constructive interactions among individuals and communities. It encompasses the idea of engaging with others in a way that acknowledges their dignity and fosters understanding, even in the face of disagreement or conflict. For Salvatore, Islam has historically provided an *idiom of civility*—a framework for civil interaction—across vast time periods and expanding geographic regions, helping to bridge cultural, linguistic, and religious divides. His choice of the word *idiom* is significant: it implies that civility in Islam is not just one element, but a range of expressions through which Islam is holistically lived and embodied, forming a civilisational world rooted in a culture of civility. Notably, Salvatore avoids the term *civil society* when discussing Muslims. Instead, he speaks of *civility* as a lived practice of knowledge and power derived from Islam itself—highlighting what makes the Islamic tradition distinct. He continues that Islam facilitates shared experiences that are understood by the people who interact with it and practice Islam. This is not simply provided by Islamic jurisprudence but also customs and civil practices, which, while different, still find a way of being part of a whole.

Furthermore, drawing on Ibn Khaldun, civility is an act or practice that emerges from the tradition of knowledge and is actualised by politics, and then formalised in society. In this sense, the civility of Islam is a language that is spoken by the *ʿulamāʾ*, implemented by those in authority, and practised by all who belong to the *ummah*, and by extension, all those who live in the Muslim lands, including non-Muslims. In this sense, the idea of *ʿilm, siyāsa*, and *ʿumrān*, which is always developing, applies here.

What Salvatore refers to as 'civility' is alluded to in what Sayyid al-Naquib al-Attas calls *adab*. In his *Prolegomena to the Metaphysics of Islam*, al-Attas covers the notion of *adab*, which he says is the "right action that springs from self-discipline founded upon knowledge whose source is wisdom". It's a reflection of something that's been internalised in *insān*, which Al-Attas describes as the "recognition of the proper places of things". The ability to come to this recognition means that the person has the right knowledge about the nature of reality, and the ensuing acknowledgement involves acting rightly because the person knows where to place himself in due relation and accordance with the proper places of everything. The just order emerging from this implies an underlying system, which al-Attas explains is revealed by the Qur'an as the hierarchy of being and existence, where Allah is at the very top. Keeping in mind his definition of the worldview of Islam as "the Islamic vision of reality and truth," *adab* thereby paints the picture of the man governing his entire being with true knowledge and carrying his entire self with reverence so that Allah gifts him *ma ʿrifah* of the true nature of existence [*wujūd* = *al-Ḥaqq*] and his own being; and in so doing wakes up to how he exists at all times within that larger hierarchy.

However, I need to stress that there is a difference between the two concepts in case people assume that 'civility' is a translation of al-Attas' idea of *adab*. In the case of Salvatore, he has found a term that best describes to a secular mind what al-Attas is explaining to a Muslim reader or a person who is seeking the truth. For Salvatore, in regard to the knowledge structure he is writing in, he is simply diagnosing what was inherent in the Islamic civilisation regarding Muslim practice, there is no attempt to provide a solution, or seek change. That is not the intention of his academic endeavour. However, it is a pertinent articulation of understanding the impact of the Islamic worldview on the Islamic civilisation. Whereas al-Attas is trying to activate the Muslim to properly understand a key concept that was inherent in Muslim societies as a way of reviving them and taking them out of their declined state. Simply put, al-Attas as a Muslim thinker is providing solutions from Islam to improve Muslims and humanity—he is giving *da ʿwah* and is interested in changing the state of the *ummah*. Thus, he is not only providing a explanation of Islam as a *din* and civilisation but is also speaking as a member who continues to belong to it. This is the difference between a secular orientation of knowledge and an Islamic one. Hence, Salvatore's notion of civility should be understood in light of al-Attas' more comprehensive explanation of *adab* as a *mode* reflective of the condition of justice (*ʿadl*) infusing society. Society would be in ruin because the individuals have been thoroughly secularised, i.e. seeing the universe only on the empirical level and believing that there's no underlying moral governance and judgement rooted in Allah's Divine Names. Al-Attas describes the development of a religious society based on how religion (*al-Dīn*) would remind the believer of the debt of existence they have incurred (*al-dayn*), so the whole *Sharīa* is premised on the demonstration of how they could "pay back/express" their indebtedness, in so doing, formulating a *madīnah* and then *tamaddun*.

If *'ilm* is knowledge, then with *adab* it becomes *ḥikmah* (wisdom) in which the knowledge is applied correctly in the way it was intended. According to al-Attas, wisdom is a kind of knowledge bestowed by Allah to those who deserve it according to His Will. It has two aspects corresponding to the two dimensions of existence, the spiritual and the physical. Wisdom flows through the faculties of the rational soul and the practical soul; both the cognitive, theoretical reason, and the active, practical reason. Practical reason acts in agreement with the rules and principles of theoretical reason. When rightly disposed, practical reason actualises the state of the soul by which it perceives truth and falsity, and distinguishes the true (*ḥaqq*) from the false (*bāṭil*). If theoretical reason is not trained and developed in the understanding of true knowledge and the exercise of sound reasoning, then practical reason will not be able to distinguish between true and false in actuality, in statements and in beliefs, and good and bad actions. Thus, if the requirements of theoretical reason are left in abeyance, aberrations become manifest in the soul, causing it to vacillate between states of excess and defect, and to perpetrate acts of injustice to itself and others.

This is not simply a superficial actualising of the knowledge, but rather a deep internalising of it, in which goodness can be actualised across all levels. While this is important for the individual to learn, al-Attas' main point is the disintegration of *adab* on a societal level, which leads to the decline of a society. But al-Attas' explanation is not simply an intellectual endeavour; al-Attas explains from both the Islamic texts and Islamic history that these ideas are rooted in the Islamic message and were practised by Muslims in the past.

If I were to combine the idea of al-Attas regarding *adab* with Salvatore's idea of 'civility' as an interpretation of that, then they both point to the idea that society, with its hierarchies of power in submission to Islam, facilitates goodness as a cultural norm and lived experience.

This notion of *adab* thus combines the Islamic concept of justice, which has an ethical and moral component to it. In the Qur'an, Allah says in *Sūrah an-Naḥl*, *"Surely Allah enjoins justice (al-ʿadl), kindness (iḥsān) and the doing of good to kith and kin, and forbids all that is shameful, evil and oppressive. He exhorts you so that you may be mindful."* (TQM *Sūrah an-Nahl* 16:90). This is the famous *āyah* that is recited in every Friday *khuṭba* (sermon) reminding and instilling in the hearts and minds of the congregations of two key principles regarding the Islamic message: justice and goodness.

In this *āyah*, Allah addresses three things which are worth mentioning about what is justice and good. These are: 1) To do justice, 2) To be good, 3) To give relatives (their due). Then, He forbids three things. These are: 1) Shameful acts, 2) Evil deeds, 3) Transgression.

Thus, this *āyah* makes the case regarding justice that one ought to be just to oneself, to find balance in life and to be fair between two parties when administering justice. Justice is also related to *iḥsān*, and it should come as no surprise that the application of justice requires the highest form of goodness, in which one is actively conscious of Allah. This means that at the heart of justice is a moral and ethical principle of goodness.

Hence, along with the meaning of *iḥsān* in the *ḥadīth* of Jibril ﷺ, *iḥsān* in the context of justice applies to the ethical and moral standard that justice in Islam implies. One can say, in accordance with the idea of *adab* which al-Attas mentions, that it captures the essence of this *āyah*, regarding Islam.

When al-Attas mentions the absence of *adab* he is thus making the case that Islamic history has ample examples when it was practised. But more importantly, al-Attas is making the case that the current world we live in has lost its sense of justice, which is a value required for social cohesion, and more importantly the balance between the spiritual and material aspects of humanity. The current decline in humanity, including the *ummah*, is down to this loss, consequently permitting a world of injustice in every matter. Thus, whether it is the notion of *adab* from al-Attas, or the notion of *akhlāq* as in the case of Taha Abdurrahman, what is clear is that justice in Islam has a core value which promotes what we can call an ethical core. The Prophet ﷺ was a reflection of justice and ethics; these were the ideals that he ﷺ trained into his *Saḥābah* and what Muslims practised historically. I would argue that when studying Islamic history, there are numerous examples of this in practice, and a Muslim historian ought to be able to express this for Muslim readers.

Additionally, the above *āyah* explicitly forbids wrongdoing and transgression, which are the opposites of *ʿadl* (justice), with *ẓulm* (oppression or injustice) being the primary manifestation of such transgressions. When examining Islamic history from a civilisational perspective, it is crucial to explore the concepts of justice and *ẓulm* in depth. Throughout the Qur'an, Allah frequently attributes the downfall of nations to their transgressions and oppression, emphasising the catastrophic consequences of *ẓulm*. This concern has been so significant that, throughout Islamic history, Muslim scholars have consistently advocated for the pursuit of justice and warned against the dangers of becoming an oppressive society. Many scholars have written extensively on the importance of upholding justice and have either petitioned rulers or called for reform, urging the rulers and the people to steer clear of *ẓulm* and adopt justice as a central tenet of governance.

This focus on justice is not merely a moral or ethical stance, but a critical foundation for the prosperity and stability of any society, ensuring the protection of rights and the well-being of all members of the community.

For example, in the nineteenth century, the Tunisian *ʿālim* and historian Aḥmad Ibn Abū al-Ḍiyāf in his *Itḥāf ahl al-zamān bi akhbār mulūk Tūnis wa ʿahd al-āmān* (Presenting Contemporaries the History of the Rulers of Tunis and the Fundamental Pact) argued against the notion of oppression and the importance of justice in Islam. His book, which was a work of history and political treatises, had a strong thesis regarding how Islam viewed good governance, justice, and oppression. He explained this by using many *āyāt* from the Qur'an and a host of examples from Islamic history, including from the second *Khalīfah* and *Saḥābī* Umar Ibn Khattab (ra), the Abbasid *Khilafah* and the Ottoman Sultan Sulaymān al-Kānūnī, citing that Islam was against oppression and was a civilisation administered by justice as mentioned in the Qur'an. He argues that via the example of the Prophet ﷺ, Islamic civilisation was one that prospered in this life and facilitated harmony and felicity. For Ibn Abī al-Ḍiyāf, Islamic history had ample examples of when Muslims adhered to the principles of justice, which had an ethical framework of governance.

Such ideas in society are actualised and manifested by Muslim networks, which create human links with each other. They create institutional consistencies, which create a dynamic Muslim world that is plural and different yet connected. From the manner in which people trade with one another, to the acts of generosity and giving in the way of Allah, acts of collective worship, and the kindness shown to one's kin, the Islamic tradition is full of acts that are predicated on the virtuous ethics which create a just society. In particular, I would like to point to this quality as a foundation found in the character of the Prophet ﷺ, which we should all attempt to emulate. In the Qur'an, Allah says, "*It was thanks to Allah's mercy that you were gentle to them. Had you been rough, hard-hearted, they would surely have scattered away from you. So pardon them, and pray for their forgiveness, and take counsel from them in matters of importance. And when you are resolved on a course of action place your trust in Allah; surely Allah loves those who put their trust (in Him).*" (Maududi *Sūrah Āl ʿImrān* 3:159)

The *āyah* emphasises Allah's mercy and guidance towards the Prophet Muhammad ﷺ. Allah highlights the importance of softness in heart and speech, as these qualities foster compassion and understanding within the community. This reminder serves to strengthen the bond between the Messenger and the believers, encouraging them to adhere to his teachings and live in a way that reflects mercy and kindness. By emphasising these virtues, Allah reassures the believers of His support and guidance, reminding them that true strength lies in compassion and adherence to divine commandments. This approach not only nurtures a strong community but also helps individuals grow spiritually and morally. The *āyah* also mentions the call to consult, with others which also underscores the value of collective decision-making and humility in seeking guidance. It encapsulates a key principle in Islamic leadership: leading with mercy, inclusivity, and trust in Allah.

Today many people may find such ideas hard to grasp, as it requires a representation of it in reality, but we have ample examples in Islamic history. In order to appreciate the ideas of al-Attas or Salvatore, one needs to be able to conceptualise power vis-à-vis *ʿilm*, *din*, and *siyāsa*. Once this is understood, only then can one understand the art, science, architecture, and institutions of Islam that came from it. The need to teach about authority, leadership, and good governance is important so that we can foster strong thought leaders who can be responsible for the *ummah*, provide solutions for them in accordance with Islam and the changing realities of the world, and can present Islam and its teaching as a civilisational alternative in contrast to the moral decay that has become manifest in our world. By showing the Prophetic example a new generation of upright, brave thought producers who are sound in their religion and steadfast during moments of adversity and yet responsible for representing the *ummah* can be produced. In addition to that, examples of such traits need to be shown throughout the history of Islam so that Muslims can see that such requirements can be found throughout the history of Islam, as the correct implementation of the *Sharīa* and manifestation of the principles of Islam in the Muslim culture naturally facilitates such outcomes. Islam has been the most instrumental religion, as Salvatore states, in cultivating diverse civilisational constellations. As a result, the study of Islamic history is not simply an exercise in a better understanding of ourselves as a *ummah* but also what is lacking in Western modernity itself.

Nubuwwa, Khilafah, ʿUlamāʾ, Ummah, and the Muslim World

As I have mentioned at the start of this book, the history of Islam is a history of those who have submitted to Islam. Muslim historians were historically in no doubt regarding the connection between Islam and authorities, whether that be earlier Prophets ﷺ, the Prophet Muhammad ﷺ, the *Sahabah*, the *Khulafah*, *ʿulamāʾ*, military men, Sufi sheikhs, or guilds. Much of the chronicle of Islamic history writing has centred around the writing of power.

Today, more than ever, there is a need to understand how Islam—and particularly how the Prophet ﷺ—embodied and exercised power. The Prophet ﷺ unified various dimensions of life in his person: religious, social, legal, and political. After his death, these dimensions, once concentrated in him, evolved into distinct institutions as Islam continued to unfold across different times and places. If the Prophet ﷺ represented both the ideal and the method of Islam, then post-Prophetic Muslim governance can be seen as a continuation of that ideal—what might be called "idea-governments." These were states built on ideological foundations, much like the Ottomans, who adopted the concept of *Din-ü-Devlet* (Religion and State) to integrate faith with governance. Similarly, one could argue that the United States functions as an idea-state today, or that the USSR was one in the past—each shaped by a foundational ideology, just as the Ottomans were.

It is important that we can examine how Islam's morals and values influenced and shaped its power, and how politics under Islam was organised. It is equally important to write about the challenges the various authorities in the Islamic world faced, and why Muslims were aware of the dangers of being a minority without being in power. It was under the civilisational authority of Islam that *Sharīa, Fiqh*, *ulum al-Dīn*, the madrassas, art, architecture, and science flourished. The inability to understand Islam in these terms renders us to imagine Islam as a "religion" only for the individual. The history of Islam and power does not start solely with the Prophet ﷺ but with all the Prophets, as human beings by nature are political agents, they formulate complex groups and societies which require governing. Human beings from the time of Adam عليه السلام have been political by nature, as this is an aspect that distinguishes us from animals.

It is for this reason that many historians like al-Tabari started their historical works with the history of the *anbiya* (Prophets). All the Prophets that we know, and the ones we do not know brought the message of *tawḥīd* (Oneness of Allah) and submission to Allah in the way of worship. Worship is not simply ritual acts but an ethos, ethics, morals, behaviours, and practices. As a result, Muslims make the case that all the Prophets, such as Adam, Nuh, Dawud, Ibrahim, Mūsā, and Isa عليه السلام were Muslims and so were their followers. This is why many Muslim historians included the writing of the lives of the Prophets as part of the corpus of Islamic history.

However, with the advent of Prophet Muhammad ﷺ as the final Prophet and Messenger, Islam came to mean worshipping Allah in the way that the Prophet ﷺ had conveyed in the *din* of Allah. It is worth noting that Islam thus came to humanity as a whole, over a prolonged period of time, in which it took human endeavour to pass on the message generationally. The process of passing on the message of Islam across generations has indeed required immense human effort. Each community of believers built upon the teachings of previous Prophets, embracing the concept of *tawḥīd* (the oneness of Allah) while adapting to the evolving context of their times. This collective journey reflects a deep commitment to preserving and transmitting core beliefs. Maintaining knowledge and belief across generations is a significant challenge. The complexities of culture, environment, and individual interpretation can lead to gaps in understanding or even the loss of certain teachings. This highlights the importance of active engagement with the tradition—through education, dialogue, and community support—to ensure that the essence of Islam remains intact and relevant. This ongoing process of learning and sharing was vital not only for the preservation of knowledge but also for fostering a vibrant, living faith that resonated with each new generation. It called for a concerted effort from believers to cultivate an environment where the teachings of Islam could flourish and continue to guide individuals and communities in their worship and daily lives. Muslim historians should find ways of showing such processes, so that existing Muslims feel connected to the past and can learn from methods of people from the past.

In earlier times, Allah sent Prophets to guide people. Their main role was to remind others about the importance of *tawḥīd*—the belief in the oneness of Allah—and to show them how to worship in a world that was always changing. Some of these Prophets, called *Rusul* (Messengers), were given specific messages from Allah, often in the form of commands or scriptures, to help develop religious practice. Others, called *Anbiyā'* (Prophets), were sent to continue the teachings of previous Prophets without bringing a new message. It's important to note that every Messenger (*Rasul*) is also a Prophet (*Nabi*), but not every Prophet is a Messenger.

This act of sending an intermediary was to help people understand the message with ease and see it manifest in the behaviour and practice of the Prophet ﷺ so that they could see how to replicate it. The Prophet Muhammad ﷺ was the last example for humanity, who brought the Qur'an and his *Sunnah* that would finally become the completion of the *din* of Islam. When Allah says in the Qur'an that He has perfected His *din* and completed His favour upon us, and has approved Islam as our religion, this was not simply with regards to the people of Arabia at the time of the Prophet Muhammad ﷺ, it was for all times. In this manner, humanity going forward would now submit to Islam in the way that it was completed by the Prophet Muhammad ﷺ. Thus, one could say that, in a general sense, Islamic history started with the Prophet Adam ﷺ.

Muslim historians of all generations have written about the life of the Prophet ﷺ known as the *Sīrah* in many ways. These were early works on the life of the Prophet ﷺ including what the Qur'an had mentioned about him ﷺ, *ḥadīth* (his sayings and actions and what he stayed silent about) which shaped the *Sunnah*, and the *Maghazi* literature which were works on battles and expeditions. It was not until Ibn Ishaq (Died 150AH, 767 AD) that a chronological order was put together to show the beginning, middle, and end of the Prophet's ﷺ life in narrative form that provided meaning. These history works provided great meaning for early Muslims, and later Muslim scholars started writing life stories of the *Sahabah* (Companions of the Prophet ﷺ), the next generation known as the *Tabieen*, and the next generation known as the *Taba'al-Tābi'īn*. While naturally much of the life-story of the Prophet ﷺ made him the central person, after his death historians would write about a host of subjects, but primarily when they wrote about power they wrote about Muslim leadership, knowledge producers, and the *ummah* as a collective.

Shaykh Muhammad Ramadan Buti, in his *Sīrah*, explained that he felt that his study of the life of the Prophet ﷺ was needed as a didactic approach to address the questions of students who started to study in Western-style academies. Shaykh Buti would explain that with each new generation, there are a new set of learning methods and different sets of questions that people may emphasise. As a result, he continued that scholars must not stop writing the *Sīrah* but rather continue to write about the life journey of the Prophet Muhammad ﷺ as a way of bringing the life of the Prophet ﷺ closer to every generation. It should come as no surprise that the likes of the *alim* Ahmet Cevdet in the Ottoman Empire and the Nadwi scholars in India also engaged in writing *Sīrah* for the Muslims of their time and nations.

This *Sīrah* paved the way for the development of Islamic history with Muslims first collecting the data to write about the Prophet's ﷺ life, and then of the *Sahabah*. Later, this developed into the discipline of writing history about Muslims. The people who submitted to Allah were now written about as a way of showing how Islam continued to resonate with people as the world kept changing, indicating that the Islam that was finalised by the Prophet Muhammad ﷺ was applicable throughout time. However, as the Prophet ﷺ had passed away, the history of the Muslims after the Prophet Muhammad ﷺ was not an easy one. As it was an act of human endeavour and interpretation, we see a host of challenges that the early Muslims faced.

The first of the *Sahabah* Abū Bakr Siddique (ra) who was elected as the deputy of the Prophet ﷺ was, of course, not a prophet and so was given the title *Khalīfah*, the one who was to shadow *Nubuwwa*, as in deputise in implementing the *Sharīa* rather than replicating Prophethood or replace it. Abū Bakr Siddique (ra) himself laid down the foundations of what it meant to be a *Khalīfah*, as he stated that there would be no Prophet after the Prophet Muhammad ﷺ and that he was simply a man not a Prophet and that he would do his best in such capacity to administer the *Sharīa* and continue to propagate the Islamic call (*dawah*) as part of the Prophetic mission.

The *Khilafah* (or Caliphate) thus emerged as an Islamic form of government led by a *Khalīfah* (Caliph), who is considered a political successor to the Prophet Muhammad ﷺ. The *Khalīfah* is responsible for upholding Islamic law (*Sharīa),* leading the Muslim community (*ummah*), and ensuring the welfare of its domains. In attempting to comply with the Prophetic message of Islam without the Prophet ﷺ, the *Khalīfah* Abū Bakr would seek the support and opinions of the *Sahabah* who would operate as an intellectual, religious and political group of advisors. But Muslim rulership was not a monopoly of a few, but rather a practice in which much of society was required to be able to run itself. The executive branch of the government (*Khilafah*) would deal with the administrative matters, the *Sahabah* would operate as a constituent group that would advise both the *Khalīfah* and *ummah* and help to hold each to account to allow the system to run smoothly. The model of governance was not one of dictatorship but instead provided much agency to the Muslim community to be able to organise their affairs. As such, the idea that authority belongs to the *ummah* reflected this point. As time went by the title of *Khalīfah* remained as a continual line of deputyship as expected, the *Sahabah's* duties regarding religious and spiritual knowledge were replaced by the new learned class known as the *'ulamā'*, and the *ummah* maintained their agency while also having authority as invested participants in the correct implementation of Islam. Thus, Muslim politics and the continuation of Islam depended upon political authority (*Khilafah*), the learned class of scholars (*'ulamā'*), and Muslim community (*Ummah*). These three 'institutions' would now adhere to the principles of Islam and constitute a civilisational outlook based on *īmān* and *iḥsān*.

As Muslim societies evolved so did the institution of the *Khilafah.* I have noticed that many Muslims today conflate the

Khalīfah (Caliph) and the *Khilafah* (Caliphate) as synonyms, and yet it is worth making the distinction for Muslims to understand the historical *Khilafah* (Caliphate). The *Khilafah* is made up of a sum of all of those men who make up the government of the *Khilafah* system. This usually involves the *Khalīfah* as the head of the government and the responsible authority to administer the rules pertaining to governance, the *Ulu wal-amr* are those people who are part of the governing structure or authorities that administer the executive actions of governance, the *Ahl al-Hal wa'l-Aqd* members of authority who are more deliberative and consultative; they are seen as representatives of the community who hold decision-making power, especially during leadership transitions or critical situations. Thus, the *Ulu wal-amr* are people in positions of power and the *Ahl al-Hal wa'l-Aqd* are people of power. The *dawla* in Arabic or *devlet* in Turkish is the *Khilafah* state and it consists of all the administrators, judges, military personnel, subjects or citizens of the state. The *'ulamā'* who are seen as 'Heirs to the Prophets' are the meta-institution of scholars who insure that the *din* (religion) is understood and functions pertaining to it are met, they study and teach *'ilm* (knowledge pertaining to *din*), and tend to the correct application of the *Sharīa* and administrative laws, upholding the *Sharīa* rules in holding the various authorities of the government to account in relation to the various positions they hold such as *qadi* and *Mufti*, and mediate for, and between, state and society. The *ummah* refers to the global community of Muslim believers. Outside the boundaries of the *Khilafah* they are simply part of this broader religious community. Within the *Khilafah*, however, they are also its subjects and active participants who help meet its needs and responsibilities. In this sense, they are stakeholders in the political system. This aligns with the Islamic principle that "authority belongs to the *ummah*." This is based on the fact that all members regarding the *Khilafah* government are both responsible for the *ummah* as a whole but also part of it. Additionally, during times of war, the armies comprise mainly from the *ummah*, they pay taxes for the government to administer its duties and are equally held accountable if the *Sharīa* is not administered. Historically this was expected by the people of authority to act on their behalf.

As previously mentioned, the *Khalīfah* is regarded as "the Shadow of Allah" on earth, meaning he is the designated representative tasked with ensuring the implementation of *Sharīa* and its associated laws. His responsibilities include protecting the lives, honor, religion, and intellect of all those under his rule—both Muslims and non-Muslims. He is also entrusted with upholding the Prophetic mission of inviting humanity to Islam. While he is responsible for safeguarding all citizens, there is a distinction in the way he must address the needs of Muslims, particularly in ensuring their ability to freely practice Islam and in working to create conditions conducive to their success in the *ākhirah* (afterlife). The *ʿulamāʾ*, as the "Heirs of the Prophet ﷺ," are charged with overseeing the correct application and interpretation of Islamic teachings. Importantly, the principle that "authority belongs to the *ummah*" remains central. Viewed in this way, the *Khilafah* was not a rigid top-down hierarchy, but rather a more dynamic structure—more like a matrix—where various stakeholders played interdependent roles.

In addition to that, all facets that made up the *Khilafah*-system such as the government, the *Khalīfah* (leader), the *ʿulamāʾ*, the military and the *ummah*, had to submit to the tenets of the Islamic *ʿaqīdah*, the whole ecosystem submitted to the *Shahādah*. This meant that no authority or individual could monopolise Islam, as all stakeholders were counterbalances to each other. Thus, what held everything together was Islam—meaning the *Sharīa*, and via the *Sharīa*, Islam would influence and shape Muslim civilisation. The *Sharīa* was not just legal rules, or rules regarding worship, but pertaining to good practice, recommended actions and behaviours, morals and values and so on. To translate the *Sharīa* to Islamic law is to reduce the comprehensive role of the *Sharīa*.

In regards to the conditions of governance, the *Khalīfah* would have to pledge an allegiance to the various Muslims who comprised of belonging to the *Ahl al-Hal wa'l-Aqd* to adhere to the precepts of Islam. If he did not, then mechanisms would be used for his removal. In the Ottoman Empire, a *fatwa* known as the *Hal-fetva* (Fatwa of removal) would be issued to depose the *Khalīfah* as an extra measure, meaning that the people of *Ahl al-Hal wa'l-Aqd* would need authorisation from the office of the *Shaykh ul-Islām*, who was the *Mufti* in the highest position of the state apparatus. But even then, the *fatwa* would first go through a process to be examined whether the conditions were met for the *Khalīfah*'s removal by the "*Fetva Emini*". Needless to say, that this was not always the case, as Janissary revolts, at times, used pressure to force *fatwas* out of the office, however, this was the principle. Later, the Ottomans drew up a constitution to regulate all the parts that made up their *Khilafah*. The reason I have explained the make-up of the Muslim governmental structure is that too often, especially during the period where Sultanic rule became the norm, there is an assumption that the *Khalīfah* either was or had the right to be an authoritarian. However, this is a reductional reading of the historical reality as well as the works of theology. The Islamic political culture throughout its history was vibrant, complicated, and still requires a better contemporary treatment. I shall come to the point of obedience later, but for now I want to explain the nature of rule. Unfortunately, even scholars today only focus on *Khalīfah* and his role, rather than examining the roles of the *Khilafah* government and who comprises it.

The early *Khilafah* system of the *Khulafah* Rashidun (Rightly guided Caliphs) is seen as the template after the *Sīrah* regarding the ideal form of governance. It displayed four models of the *Khalīfah* being elected, indicated different styles of governance, indicating the evolving nature of the governmental system, and the different ways in which different configurations of people made up the *Ulu al-Amr*. In the case of Abū Bakr Siddique (ra), he was elected in *Saquifah Banu Sa'ida*. The discussion at *Saquifah* led to a debate about who should lead the community. Abū Bakr Siddique (ra) was nominated by Umar Ibn al-Khattab (ra) and accepted by others present. His close companionship with the Prophet ﷺ and his leadership qualities were emphasised, which ultimately led to his election as the first *Khalīfah*. When Abū Bakr was close to his death, he recommended Umar Ibn Khattab (ra) and consulted with the *Sahabah*. Abū Bakr (ra) did not delegate for Umar (ra) to be *Khalīfah*, but endorsed him, and advised the Muslims that for the continuity of the Prophetic mission that Abū Bakr (ra) upheld so stoically and diligently that Umar was the best next choice. The community accepted Umar's (ra) nomination, but they had the right to reject if they chose to, but such was Abū Bakr's standing that the Muslims knew that, as a key companion of the Prophet ﷺ and then as a *Khalīfah*, he was nothing short of a visionary man of great wisdom whose decision-making was always in the best interest of Islam and the community, and such was his wisdom, that his decision-making was trusted. When Umar (ra) was on his deathbed, rather than delegating who he thought ought to succeed him, he created a council of *Sahabah* to elect one from among them. After careful deliberation and counsel, they chose Uthman Ibn Affan (ra). Ali Ibn Abi Talib (ra)was formally elected as *Khalīfah* during a gathering at the *Masjid al-Nabawi* (Prophet's ﷺ Mosque) in Medina. His election was supported by a significant number of prominent *Sahabah* from the Muhajireen and Ansar and the people of Medina in conditions of great strife.

After this period, following the Umayyad reign of Muawiyya (ra), the *Khilafah* system retained the *bāyah* process, and the political culture went into a phase of hereditary rule, as possibly the safest process of maintaining continuity by keeping power in one place, under one household, so that other power brokers do not challenge for political authority. The system would mean that a member would be chosen from that tribe or household. This method is often criticised as monopolising power into the hands of a few, while others have argued that this was against the principles practiced by the *Khulafah* Rashidun, yet the history of the Umayyads, Abbasids, and Ottomans shows that hereditary rule was still dependent on the *Ulu al-Amr*, and throughout Islamic history, these people changed and evolved depending on the historical conditions. While there is much to criticise regarding hereditary rule, in many ways, it is somewhat akin to interpretations of authority remaining with the tribe of the Quraysh or today's modern political parties in the sense that the main point of these classes is that the people within them adhere to similar principles and values regarding their ideas of politics and life, and that they are trained within a habitat for the sole purpose of leadership.

Such is the nature of politics and power, and the balance of power that throughout Islamic history there are ample examples of power struggles. Whether within the various habitats, or with the various authorities that made up the *Khilafah* system. The political system within the history of the *Khilafah* has shown that the other authorities were reminded to be obedient to the one leading the confederation of factions and authorities that made up the government, but there was also evidence of holding the *Khalīfah* himself to account. In principle, there were a host of laws and mechanisms to make sure that the *Khalīfah* did not become despotic. While the *ʿulamāʾ* wrote works to hold the *Khalīfah* and the *Ulu al-Amr* accountable throughout Islamic history to an ideal standard, practical considerations often reflected a different path and tensions at times. That should come as no surprise, as every

Muslim attempts to live a life in accordance with Islam's ideal, but we are still sinners, we will still make mistakes, and just because one did not stand in comparison to the standard does not mean that the ideal is not important; and just because all the conditions of the ideal are not met does not invalidate their governance, as governance requires multiple 'institutions' not just the one who is leading it. While scholars often examine the history of the *Khilafah* through either the prescriptions of the system from a legal perspective, or from the narratives of the *Khalīfah* only, I think for Muslims today, they ought to be taught how the *Khilafah* system as a complete governmental system is not just one-man rule, and that political cultures are complicated, with many actors.

A few examples of the Ottoman *Khilafah* show a host of moments when works, treaties or documents were written to address the various actors of the *Khilafah*-state. When Sultan Selim I in 1517 was declared *Khalīfah* in Istanbul by virtue of his defeat of the Mamluks, and subsequent house arrest of the nominal Abbasid *Khalīfah* al-Mutawakkil III in Istanbul, works by t*asawwuf*-oriented *'ulamā'* in Istanbul and Anatolia were written in accordance with what the moral characteristics ought to be of good *Khalīfah*, in this case Selim but also in preparation for the House of Osman, which was now being educated to uphold these values. People continue to examine whether Selim's accession was legal or not, but do not examine that his defeat of the Mamluks and making the Arab domains part of the Ottoman world, turning them into the Arab provinces, radically reconfigured the positions of *the Ulu al-Amr* in the sixteenth-century Muslim world that was now under Selim's authority. Istanbul is where all the power lay, and its system of governance could not tolerate an outside *Khalīfah* who was not part of the Ottoman configuration of power, neither in practicality nor in tradition. When Abdulmecid I came to power in 1839, the *Gülhane* Edict was drawn up to remind all authorities that made the *Khilafah*-state, including the ministers of the *Khilafah* government, to uphold the principles of the *Sharīa*. This document was drawn up due to the conflict between the Sultan and the *ayan* (magnates) who made up significant parts of the Ottoman authorities outside of Istanbul. Finally, in 1909, when the Ottomans re-introduced the Ottoman Constitution of 1876, after making constitutional amendments, the document was designed to define the roles of all those who were members of the Ottoman *Khilafah* government. Their roles were designated in the written document of the Constitution, which included the *Khalīfah* Abdulhamid II.

In 1909, the configuration of the *Khilafah*-system was organised for the modern period as:

1) The *Sharīa* and the Ottoman Constitution as a set of rules to administer government.
2) Under that was the Constitutional *Khilafah* Government, which included the *Khalīfah* as sultan and head of state as part of the Ottoman government, the state *'ulamā'* as a constituent group who wrote, amended, and upheld the constitution in law as well as the *Sharīa*, the *Ahl al-Hall wa'l-Akd* who were a specific group within parliament, and the *Ulu al-Amr* in the guise of the Ottoman Parliament and the ministers who held ministerial positions.
3) And finally, the Ottoman *Khalīfah* as the executive authority of the state who adhered to the constitution and advice of his parliament.

When examining the history of the *Khilafah* government rather than the *Khalīfah*, one can understand how, at times, when there were poor leaders, weak leaders, or token puppet leaders in Islamic history, the ecosystem was still able to function. This is not to imply that a *Khalīfah* is not important, because political systems require sound leaders to lead.

Examining the conditions of the role, duty, and ideals the *Khalīfah* should follow is important, but so is the examination of the conditions that make up the *Khilafah* government.

For the Ottomans, the idea that Islam could be implemented without a political culture of governance was unthinkable. We see ample amounts of works pointing to the idea of *Din-ü-Devlet*. The idea here is that the term *din*, which is often understood as religion in Islam, was used more broadly as representing the Islamic ethos or philosophy that regulated the Ottoman world. For the Ottomans, Islam was the worldview that shaped and curated all things Ottoman. Thus, without *din*, there was no Ottoman Empire as the Empire was an Islamic one. The politics of the Ottomans was Islam; Islam shaped their political ideals, and without it, political expressions had no meaning. Just as politics needed *din*, likewise, the idea of the *devlet* in Turkish or *dawla* in Arabic represented the physical implementation of the *din*. For many Ottoman thinkers and *ʿulamāʾ*, the comprehensive implementation of Islam could not be actualised without the *devlet*, which meant the government and administrative systems of the state. While *devlet* in today's modern understanding has often been understood to mean "the state", in fact, in the Ottoman Empire, *devlet* actually meant the political configurations that ran the Empire. The objective of the *devlet* was to actualise Islam as an invitation to the world, and to the people of the Ottoman domains. Thus, upon the collapse of the Ottoman Empire, many *ʿulamāʾ* within Istanbul made the case that without the *devlet*, Islam would simply become a matter of personal worship left to the *ummah* to uphold and would lose its civilisational quality.

The historical *Khilafah* was primarily an institution that was seen as the *Khulafah Rashidun* (Rightly Guided Caliphs), the Umayyads, the Abbasids, and the Ottomans. While other entities may have used the title as *Khilafah*, including in the contemporary period too, and some historians have attributed the term to other dynasties in Islam, the most prominent have been the ones in which there was an attempt to implement Islam, safeguard the interest of the *ummah* within its domains, and offer protectorship over the three centres of *ʿaqīdah* in Islam, which are Mecca, Medina, and al-Aqsa. There are cases where the protectorship over the centres had moments of disruption, such as in the case of Ibn al-Zabayr ruling over the Hijaz during the early Umayyad period, the Abbasids conceding the loss of al-Aqsa to the Fatimids, Crusaders, and Ayyubids, and the Ottomans having a short spell where the Wahabbis took over Mecca and Medina. But overall, safeguarding the three holy precincts in Islam was one of the duties that the historical Caliphates took seriously.

What is worth noting is how the three central cities of Islam, with their three important mosques, represent a unique connection. After the conquest of Mecca by the Prophet ﷺ re-established the Kaaba as the centre in *qibla* (direction) towards which Muslims offer *Salah*, the city of Mecca with the Kaaba as its centre became a place where Muslims go on the *Hajj* and *Umrah* (*major and minor pilgrimage)*, which was built by Ibrahim عليه السلام and then purified by the Prophet ﷺ, representing for Muslims the notion of *Ubudiyya* (Worship). There is no other centre in Islam that represents worship in the way the *Kaaba* does, and it is a pillar in Islam and a centre for Islamic civilisation.

If the Kaaba represents *Ubudiyya*, then after the death of the beloved of Allah ﷺ, Medina is the centre of *Nubuwwa* (Prophethood). It is the centre for all those who come to pay their respects to the Prophet ﷺ. Medina, after the death of the Prophet ﷺ, is a constant reminder of the Prophet as the *Habib* (beloved) of Allah ﷺ. While the Prophet ﷺ could have chosen to stay in Mecca after the conquest of the city, he ﷺ chose to return to Medina, the city where he ﷺ established the first political polity, the city in which the *ummah* had, for the first time, political agency, the first political centre of Islam.

Finally, there is *Bayt al-Maqdis* (The blessed house) where *Masjid al-Aqsa*, the mosque that was the first *qibla*, the place where the Chosen One ﷺ led prayer with all the Prophets, and the place where the Exalted one ﷺ went to the seven heavens, where *Salah* was prescribed from Allah, is located. *Al-Aqsa* is the symbol of the struggle for the Muslim, which we can say is the symbol of *tawḥīd* (Oneness of Allah). The struggle for *al-Aqsa* has been one that evolved around Islam being the *haqq* (the truth) and Islam being the continuation of the calls by the previous Prophets. The Prophet's ﷺ interactions in *Bayt al-Maqdis* all point to making this point. *Al-Aqsa* became part of the Muslim world during the conquest of the second Caliph Umar Ibn Khattab (ra), *al-Faruq* (The one who can distinguish between truth and falsehood), and since then *al-Aqsa* has continued to be a place contested over. The Muslim needs to understand that *al-Aqsa* is blessed in the way the other two places are and is, alongside Mecca and Medina, a sanctuary

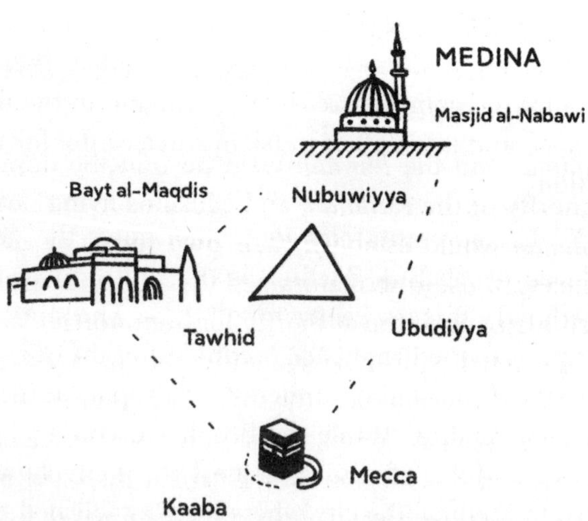

for Muslims. These cities with sacred mosques to which Muslims migrate for specific worship no doubt cultivated a heartland of the Muslim world in regards to geography.

However, these centres of Islam represented more than just places of worship; they became centres of learning and Muslim configuration. Muslims would attempt to replicate these centres by creating centres of learning throughout the Muslim world. Baghdad, Damascus, Cairo, Konya, Bukhara, al-Andalus, Delhi, and Istanbul would all become centres of power and learning, like a constellation joining the Muslim world together. While many centres of Muslim learning would come to exist beyond the domains of the historical *Khilafah*, nonetheless, they would create spaces of attachment to the centre by becoming exceptional centres of learning. In this way, Muslims from around the world would come to *Mecca*, *Medina*, and *al-Aqsa* to worship, study, find a temporary abode, and then return to their centres, thus creating a commonality in practice, law, theology, madrassa curricula, and religious rituals. While Muslims were from many places, cultures, languages, ethnicities, and jurisprudential schools of thought, the plurality of the *ummah* led by the *ʿulamāʾ* was able to establish an imagination and lived reality in which Muslims felt that they were part of a global collective, living their local lived experiences.

The *ʿulamāʾ* and the *ummah* went beyond the domains of the authority of the *Khilafah*, and Muslims living outside of the *Khilafah* would establish their own forms of authority. Nonetheless, those who maintained the authority in the centre often maintained the authority for Sunni orthodoxy. As I said, while not all Muslims were under the stewardship of the *Khilafah* as Islam expanded, Muslims, both Sunnis and Shias, developed an ethical framework of how governance ought to be practised in the Muslim world, which included both local as well as governmental authority. The *ummah* led by the

ʿulamāʾ became an organic mass that lived all around the world, in which the idea of the Muslim world emerged. By extension, the study of the *ʿulamāʾ* was also a study of the institutions that they were a part of, such as the *madrassas*, masjids, law courts, and various other centres of learning. During the Ottoman period after Sultan Mehmet (Muhammad) Fatih's conquest of Constantinople, the *ʿilmiyye* structure—which was a hierarchy of state positions and institutions—became the cornerstone of the Ottoman administration, to the point one could argue that the *ʿulamāʾ* were a meta-institution, meaning they were an institution that regulated every other institution in the Ottoman domains. Through these institutions and centres of learning, the Muslim world became connected as they shared a similar experience regarding life, even if their cultures varied. Islam was the canopy under which life was lived, and the two forms of power, the executive and legal/educational, presented norms that filtered into mainstream Muslim society that not only influenced Muslims but also non-Muslims.

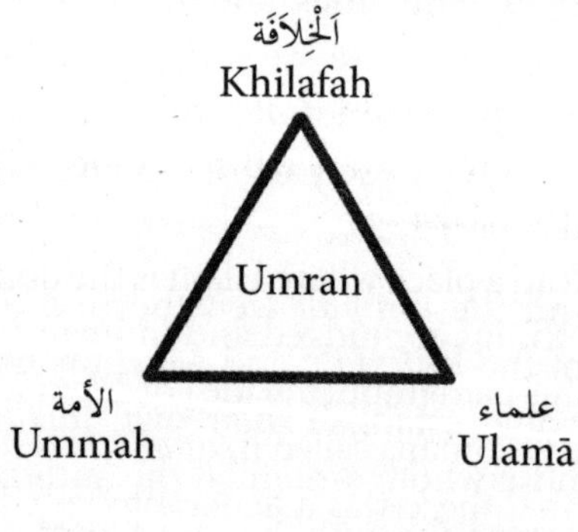

Some academics have tried to question the idea of the Muslim world/Islamic world, suggesting that this is a modern construction, but this idea has existed as long as Islam itself. As I mentioned, the idea of the Muslim world is one of a constellation in which there are connecting node points. The reason they are part of the Muslim or Islamic world is simply due to the fact that Islam was implemented in those places, which included government, knowledge production, and cultural practices. A Muslim from Timbuktu would have few challenges if they went to China and observed how Muslims practised Islam. The primary differences would only be ethnicity and language, as well as Islamicised cultural norms. But as for worship, dietary needs, acts of civility, and so on, one could say that there was a shared commonality in a pluralistic Muslim world.

The issue for some contemporary thinkers is the manner in which the Muslim world has continued to evolve and change, citing, for example, whether today's Spain, which was once Al-Andalus, can be considered part of the Muslim world, and whether the Muslim world is simply a space where Muslims live. Others suggest there is no need to use the term at all. They may also make the case that in the absence of a *Khilafah*, can the concept of the Muslim or Islamic world hold true? One may argue that so long as the *ummah* exists, then so does the Muslim world, but then one may argue about whether European nations like France and Germany or the United States of America are part of this Muslim world? The idea of the Muslim world or Islamic world, which Marshall Hodgson in his *Venture of Islam* tried to call Islamdom is not about where Muslims are present but instead a place where Islam is the dominant authority where most things are judged and influenced by. As I have highlighted in this paragraph, the idea of *Islam Dünyası* (Islamic World) as the Ottomans called it, or *al-Alam al-Islami* as said in Arabic, was that there was a geography in which Islam was the worldview in which all norms of life were judged.

More recently, as a way of attempting to steer away from the idea of the Islamic world or Muslim world, academics have started to entertain an idea coined by Shahab Ahmed, from his book *What is Islam*, where he uses the term "Balkans to

Bengal" complex. "Balkans to Bengal" refers to a vast geographical and cultural expanse that stretches from Southeast Europe (the Balkans) to South Asia (Bengal) and the role of Islam in this geographical space. This phrase often highlights the interconnectedness of diverse cultures, histories, and societies across this significant region. For Shahab, like those critical of the idea of the Muslim world, the main issue is one of how to conceptualise a space where Islam has shaped state, society, law, and culture. But as I have pointed out throughout this book, attempting to conceptualise Islam without Allah is not a conceptualisation of Islam at all, but a manipulation of the essence of what Islam is, no matter how well-intentioned a person may be.

Regarding what makes a place part of the Muslim world, I again argue that this has to do with power and the implementation of Islam. Muslims living as minorities in the West do not make that nation part of the Muslim world, as culturally, politically, and intellectually, Islam is not the dominant worldview through which people judge themselves. This is not an issue of Muslims being a majority or minority, as there are a host of examples where Muslims were the minority people, such as in the case of the early Umayyads, the Ottoman Empire and India during the time of the Mughals. The key point is that the Muslim world was (and is) an ecosystem where religion, knowledge, culture, and politics were parts of an interaction that fostered exchange between Muslims and made them feel part of a whole. That is not to say that Muslims living in the non-Muslim world are not part of the *ummah*; it also does not suggest that the Muslim world is a static concept of geographical space. As I said, it is a fluid and malleable space; at one point Spain as Al-Andalus was part of the Muslim world, and while it may still exist as part of the Muslim imagination as once a centre of Muslim civilisational development, today one could argue that it is no longer part of the Muslim world due to the extraction of power, culture, and Islamic traditions in Spain. All that is left are the historical buildings and a new generation of migrant Muslims.

The historical interplay between authority, the *ʿulamāʾ*, and the *ummah* reveals how Islamic governance and scholarship contributed to the civilisation's resilience and adaptability over time. This historical perspective sheds light on how Islam has maintained its significance amid changing political landscapes. The configurations of authority, whether through the *Khilafah*, local rulers, or *ʿulamāʾ*, created a framework that connected diverse communities across the Muslim world. These hierarchies facilitated the spread of knowledge, culture, and religious practice, fostering a sense of unity among Muslims. Studying these dynamics could better help Muslims in imagining potential futures for the Islamic world. Understanding how power has functioned within Islamic frameworks should help to reframe contemporary discussions about governance, community, and identity. It opens up possibilities for envisioning a future that honours historical precedents while addressing modern realities and concerns.

ب

SECTION VI

THE BLURRING LINES BETWEEN FICTION AND REALITY

The Need for an Imagination – The Thin Line Between History and Fiction

In this section, I shall make the case that studying history is not simply a case of being a historian in academia or to supplement *'ulūm al-Dīn.* The fact that Allah mentions historical accounts in the Qur'an means that this is a vocation that agrees with *insān*'s disposition to reflect on their existence, on what it means to be human, on how we configure as societies, and how we require politics to organise ourselves. With that in mind, it is necessary, in my opinion, that we should study history to enhance other fields, such as sociology, philosophy, political science, international relations, and fiction.

A deficiency in good historical understanding leads people to become deficient in the various fields I have just suggested. For example, how can someone speak of the politics of the people of the Sudan and not have an understanding of their history, not just any superficial history, but the specialised history required for the given place and people of study? Without that specialised history, Muslim countries will lack expertise in fields of politics, diplomacy, and so on, because their understanding of both Muslims and non-Muslims will be skewed. In fact, too often in contemporary politics, people are reduced to simple caricatures without context and meaning. But as truth-seekers striving to better understand human beings, we are *required* to know people and their past better.

It is not only history that shapes future policies but also how narratives are constructed by using the past. Historical narratives by politicians, states, and political scientists are used to push political agendas, shape policy, and influence decision-making. Such narratives are designed to maintain a status quo or consolidate a perception of a nation or power as being all-powerful. But it is Allah Who is the All-Powerful: upon that conviction, counter narratives need to be presented to dispel fictitiously-projected falsehoods.

I have expressed concern when storytellers stand in front of the Muslim community and masquerade as historians. The concern comes from a place of care due to my belief that historians must be sincere and diligent in their quest to examine sources and write history with the best intentions to establish what is true. Part of the vocation is to accept that one may not know everything but nonetheless work to produce scholarship based on evidence and research. However, I am not against storytelling as a medium to convey truths, especially historical truths. My contention is that the work of the historians should not be reduced to mere storytelling.

If storytelling becomes the default way people view historians, it does nothing but diminish the authority of real historians and the vocation as a whole. I appreciate that there is a need for Muslim academics to come down from what is perceived as an "ivory tower" position. This is, of course, a concern as many of us who went into the field went to challenge the established ivory towers and gatekeepers, not to become them. Having said that, the field of history is a painstaking endeavour, and when storytellers provide little evidence, cite only basic works, do not write, and only produce content for mass consumption, then I argue that the community and the vocation are being sold short.

However, I do believe that our imaginative spirit can be appreciated in the field of fiction. I have argued here already that fictional writers, on many occasions, can speak the truth more than us academics, not being constrained by the need to provide evidence in the way we historians do. Fiction is a medium in which one may explore many ideas in an imaginative and creative way and write stories that can resonate with the emotions and experiences of human beings.

It was the famous J.R.R. Tolkien, author of *The Hobbit* and *The Lord of the Rings*, who once said that fiction is about life and mainly death, as the best stories for Tolkien were human stories that reflected the importance of these two aspects, something each human being is connected to. Tolkien, who was a professor of Anglo-Saxon and a philologist—a historian of languages—made the argument for fiction, or in his words "Fairy-Stories". In his essay "On Fairy-Stories," Tolkien made the case for the value of literature. He observes that when humans create, whether by carving a figure from a marble slab or constructing and populating entire worlds from linguistic material, their art is a secondary creation. When artists take the world's primary materials and reconfigure them, a "new form is made; man becomes a sub-creator." According to Tolkien, "God is The Creator, and it is from His handiwork that all art is composed". It is worth noting that Tolkien was a historian, and was able to use his historical knowledge of Anglo-Saxon history and the history of languages to sub-create the world of "Middle Earth".

Not all fictional writers have to be historians, of course, but creative writing requires a repository, and inspiration is often drawn from the human experience. It is my belief that history, if taught well, can inspire a new generation of fictional writers and producers who can tell sophisticated Muslim stories in the way Tolkien did. Tolkien, who was inspired not only by history but was also influenced by *Beowulf*, an English epic poem, wrote his own epics—*The Hobbit* and *The Lord of the Rings*—as epic pilgrimage stories in which the Hobbits, the smallest and weakest people, defeat the strongest symbol of tyranny.

Alongside Tolkien at Oxford University was the academic of English Literature C.S. Lewis, who also became famous for his fictional epic called *The Chronicles of Narnia*. Lewis, who was also an Anglican theologian, would weave narratives inspired by the life-story of Isa ﷷ (Jesus). The main protagonist—Aslan (the Lion)—was a metaphor for the Christian understanding of Jesus. Like Tolkien, Lewis was able to write fictional works influenced by historical accounts and narratives that came from his faith as well as his experiences in WWI. With these combined, both Tolkien and Lewis tried to write works of fiction centred on redemption, with human salvation in mind. Both Tolkien and Lewis wrote their works in order for people to appreciate the "grand narrative" of human existence that will eventually come to an end on the day of judgement.

C.S. Lewis believed that fiction and imagination are powerful tools for grasping abstract truths, especially those related to faith, morality, and the human condition. While reason helps us understand facts, imagination allows us to perceive deeper meanings that logic alone cannot reach. In works like *On Stories*, Lewis argued that fiction, in particularly fantasy which offers new perspectives by presenting familiar ideas in unfamiliar ways, helping us see reality more clearly. He also saw imagination as a bridge between the material and spiritual, and considered storytelling a reflection of divine creativity, capable of revealing profound truths in ways that are emotionally and spiritually resonant.

Muslims did write works of fiction, of course, and they also wrote works that gave Muslims moral meaning on how to live a good life and the dangers of falling into sin, with ideas of destiny and human free will. Today's Muslims should be able to undertake such a task too, as young and old require creative writings in the forms of analogy, metaphor, and narrative to give meaning to their own imagination.

Early Muslim works such as *One Thousand and One Nights* contained moral tales of Aladdin, Sinbad, and even fictional stories of the Abbasid *Khalīfah* Hārūn al-Rashid. So popular were these stories that many people have often assumed that the fictional Hārūn is an accurate reflection of the actual *Khalīfah*. The stories in *One Thousand and One Nights* reflect the moral values, social norms, and imaginative spirit of the time. They often include themes of justice, adventure, and wisdom, serving both entertainment and educational purposes. The narratives demonstrated the oral storytelling tradition of the time, where tales were passed down and adapted, creating a rich tapestry of cultural lore. The tales have had a profound influence on world literature, inspiring adaptations and reinterpretations across cultures, and contributing to the ongoing fascination with Islamic history and culture.

In the nineteenth century, the Syrian Reformist Salafist *ālim* Abdurrahman al-Kawakabi had written a fictional book critiquing Sultan Abdulhamid II. His book *Umm al-Qura* (The Mother of Cities) placed an Islamic conference in Mecca, highlighting the city as a unifying force for the Muslim community, symbolising a gathering point for ideas, discussions, and collective identity. Through the fictional narrative, al-Kawakabi was also addressing contemporary political issues facing the Muslim world at his time, advocating for unity and collaboration among Muslims to address their challenges. While the book was advocating for Mecca as a centre to bring Muslims together, it was also criticising the Ottoman Sultan. The book, as a fictional piece, has been well-read in the Arabic-speaking world, influencing many.

Another work that was popular in the nineteenth-century Ottoman Empire was *Felâtun Bey ve Râkım Efendi*, a novel written by the Turkish Ottoman author Ahmet Mithat Efendi, published in 1910. This work is significant in Turkish literature as it reflects the socio-cultural transformations occurring in the late Ottoman Empire. The novel explores the tension between traditional Ottoman values and Western influences. It presents two main characters—Felâtun Bey, representing westernisation and modernity, and Râkım Efendi, who embodies traditional values and the intellectual depth of Ottoman society. The novel critiques the blind adoption of Western customs without a deep understanding of their implications. It calls for a balanced approach that respects cultural heritage while engaging with modern ideas. Ahmet Mithat Efendi is known for his engaging narrative style, blending storytelling with social critique, making his works accessible to a wide audience. Ahmet Mithat had written many novels during his time. These are just some of the works of fiction that have been written by Muslims in the past.

As shown, fictional works can be used as communicative mediums to express forms of critique as well as provide insights into the conditions in a given society and culture. They reflect the beliefs, customs, and social structures of the time they were written, providing a lens into the cultural context of a particular period. Fiction may reimagine historical events, presenting them through various perspectives. This can help historians see how those events were understood and interpreted by people at the time. Both al-Kawakabi and Ahmet Mithat Efendi's works have been read by wider audiences but have also been works of interest for academics in providing clues on the very aforementioned ideas just discussed. Additionally, fiction can challenge dominant historical narratives, providing alternative viewpoints and voices, particularly those of marginalised groups.

An example of such is that researchers have started to re-examine the novel *The Thorn and the Carnation*, written by Palestinian leader of Hamas Yahya Sinwar who was killed by Israeli soldiers. The work is being examined as an autobiographical work even though it is fictional. The novel reflects the life of a Palestinian in Gaza called Ahmed—Sinwar's alter ego, who faces the challenges of the occupation, while defiantly working for its liberation. It is a work where the realm of fiction and reality become blurred, as Sinwar wrote the book as a way of getting a Palestinian voice to be heard at a time where very little permission—if any—was given for Palestinians to write or read books on Palestinian politics. The book which draws information from Sinwar's life and Israeli intelligence sources thus becomes a form of evidence for researchers and historians alike in attempting to understand Sinwar, his motivations, the struggles of the people of Gaza and the brutality of the occupation. The complexity of Sinwar's use of fiction as a medium to present truth is further complicated due to Israeli depictions of him as part of the Israeli propaganda. In many ways, both present fictitious representations of Sinwar, further complicating the reality of Sinwar from fiction. The parallels between his lived experience and fictional work make a distinction between fiction and reality almost impossible to decipher. But the novel can function as a powerful medium and symbol for the truth of Sinwar's life and the Palestinian people, even though it is fiction. In that sense, fiction can serve as a critique of reality, prompting audiences to think critically about the world around them but unlike in the case of history, authors or creators may exaggerate, simplify, or dramatise aspects of reality to convey a message or evoke emotion, and that is a key difference between history and fiction.

The main distinction between history and fiction is that while history refers to the systematic study and interpretation of past events, particularly those involving human activity, based on evidence and documentation and seeks to inform us about past societies, cultures, and events to better understand the present and inform the future, fiction has no need of such constraints and refers to imaginative narratives created by authors, which may include invented characters, events, and settings. Fiction does not have to adhere to factual accuracy as authors can create scenarios, characters, and worlds that are entirely made up while primarily aiming to entertain, engage, and provoke thought or emotion in readers. In that sense, there are indeed many ways in which the discipline of history and fiction can be useful to each other.

Is History an Art or a Science?

History can be seen as both an art and a science. As a science, it relies on evidence, critical analysis, and methodology to reconstruct past events. Historians use various sources—documents, artefacts, and testimonies—to create an accurate understanding of what happened. As an art, history involves interpretation, narrative, and the ability to convey the complexities of human experiences. Historians often shape their findings into stories that resonate with audiences, emphasising the emotional and cultural contexts of events. So, it blends the systematic inquiry of science with the creative storytelling of art, making it a unique discipline that encompasses elements of both.

Muslim storytellers often claim that the narratives they present are factual, using this as a way to validate points that may actually be open to debate. While facts are important for historians, history itself is largely interpretive. So, the idea that any historical account is entirely factual isn't realistic. Presenting interpretations as absolute facts can become a rhetorical strategy—used to suggest that the speaker's version shouldn't be questioned or is unquestionably true. However, this approach—treating history as only about proving facts—can actually harm how we think about the past. It limits imagination and deeper reflection. That's because facts aren't neutral; they're shaped by how we understand truth (in a theological sense) and reality (in a philosophical or ontological sense). Even if a set of facts seems logically ordered, if the underlying view of reality is flawed, the interpretation can end up being misleading or unjust.

Historians and even people at the time have differing opinions and views. In that sense, the idea of history being factual really makes little sense, as the idea of something being factual, meaning beyond doubt, is usually restricted to indicating whether something took place or not, but it does not attempt to explain the reasons of why things may have happened. That requires the historian to obtain the truth, and truth-seeking is a different enterprise than suggesting something is a fact. Naquib al-Attas responds to this point in his Prolegomena, where he explains in detail that:

> "We do not agree, therefore, that knowledge pertains only to phenomena; that truth is only a property of statements or declarative sentences, or of beliefs and judgements from which statements are derived and which are dependent upon the relation of the belief or the judgement to some fact; that fact is neutral in its relation to truth and falsity. We maintain that truth is also a property of the nature of things in as much as they conform with a suitableness to the requirements of wisdom and justice, that is, to the requirements of the condition of being in their right or proper places. And this does not mean that truth is merely a correspondence of statement or judgement to fact, as that would make fact equivalent to truth. Even though a sentence may be true if it designates a fact, the mere existence of the fact does not necessarily make the fact into a truth. Truth is not simply conformity with fact because facts can be created by man and can therefore be not in their proper places, meaning that facts can be false. That facts can be created by man confirms the truth of our denial that facts are neutral in their relation to truth and falsity, for the very existence itself of such facts is dependent upon values belonging to the particular worldview of their creators."[12]

12 Sayyid Muhammad Naquib al-Attas, Prolegomena to the Metaphysics of Islam – An Expedition of the Fundamentals of the Worldview of Islam, ISTAC, 1995, p130

Insisting that historical accounts must be purely factual has created challenges for historians who argue that interpreting history is a creative process that involves imagination. Some Muslims view the use of imagination in historical writing as equivalent to making things up or being fictional—especially because many have come to believe that imagination is less valuable or reliable than reason.Yet, I have stressed that a dichotomy between the two is to reduce what, in fact, the human being is. According to Imam al-Ghazali, *'aql* (reason) and *khayal/ta'weel* (imagination) which are faculties of the *'firasah* or *ma'rifah* (intellect) and *ruh* (spirit), which are modes of subtle substance that define the essence of man along with the *nufs* (lowerself) and *qalb* (heart). Meanwhile *'aql* refers to the cognitive faculty that allows individuals to engage in logical thinking, deduction, and analysis, it is often associated with the ability to draw conclusions from premises, evaluate evidence, and solve problems. *Firasah* or *ma'rifah*, on the other hand, encompasses a deeper understanding that transcends mere logical reasoning.

For al-Ghazali, intellect involves a kind of spiritual insight or intuitive knowledge that goes beyond rationality. It can grasp truths that are not always accessible through reason alone, particularly in matters of faith and spirituality. Regarding imagination, according to al-Ghazali, there are two types: *khayal* (sensory imagination) and *ta'weel* (rational imagination). *Khayal* refers to the ability to form mental images based on sensory experiences. It is grounded in the physical world and shaped by our direct perceptions. Al-Ghazali emphasises that sensory imagination can be misleading, as subjective experiences and the limitations of the senses influence it. While it plays a vital role in everyday understanding, it can also lead to misconceptions if taken as the ultimate source of knowledge. *Ta'weel*, on the other hand, involves higher-order thinking and the ability to conceptualise and understand abstract ideas. It allows for reasoning beyond mere sensory perception.

Al-Ghazali views rational imagination as essential for deeper understanding, particularly in philosophical and theological contexts. It facilitates the interpretation of complex concepts and texts, such as those found in religious scripture. Al-Ghazali argues for a balance between sensory and rational imagination as sensory experience provides foundational knowledge, while rational imagination is necessary to interpret and understand the implications of that knowledge. He emphasises that true understanding requires moving beyond immediate sensory impressions to engage in rational reflection and interpretation. This distinction is crucial in al-Ghazali's epistemology. He challenges the reliance solely on empirical observation and highlights the importance of reason and intellectual engagement in forming a comprehensive understanding of reality.

The unique aspect of human thought is that its existence is required in order to understand the speech of Allah (The Qur'an), and along with reason, so is the spirit, and hence so is human imagination. Listening or reading the words of Allah helps you reflect over the meanings of what is being conveyed, which moves the soul into emotional expressions at times. A good historian and intellectual requires *'aql*, then*'ilm* followed by intellectual insight, and then sound imagination, which is part of the soul, to make these ideas experiential for people. As I have suggested before, the human imaginative process is not a deficiency but a disposition of human beings.

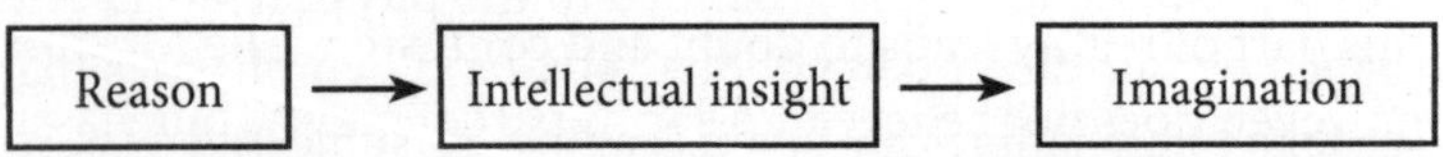

Unlike fiction, the historian cannot make up an unimaginable claim or attempt to assert claims that have no evidence. The first point is an act that is devoid of reality, and the second is one that lacks evidence. An example is that a historian will not make the claim that people were flying or time travelling during the time of the Abbasids. That is neither real nor imaginable. This is because they are understood as an irruptive cessation of the natural laws as observed by us and occur to establish the truth of Prophethood. Aside from Allah Himself mentioning them, they are verified by true testimony (*khabr sadiq*) and the soundness of authority of the recounters. This can be seen when Ibn Khaldun made criticism of historians using hyperbole or exaggerations, such as in the case of the numbers of people who were on the battlefield or the number of people killed in warfare, where those numbers are impossible to have existed. Ibn Khaldun argued that a historian must know the possibilities and impossibilities regarding the realities of the time. An example was when Ibn Khaldun criticised the Muslim historian al-Mas'udi, who mentioned that Alexander the Great going to the bottom of the sea in a glass box without oxygen was impossible. Yet al-Masudi, who probably just transmitted what was narrated before, chose not to challenge this imaginative liberty.

The works of history must be in conformity with reality and must be real. Understanding reality is not simply in what is in conformity with one's sense but also with the *ʿaqīdah* of Islam. A secular *ʿaqīdah* because it rejects Allah, and consequently His word, His Prophet ﷺ, angels, *shaytaan* (the devil), the human soul, heaven, the divine order of things, the divine plan, just to name a few, provides a limited understanding of reality restricted simply to worldly matters. The absence of this part of reality leads to doubt and confusion. The Muslim, however, does not believe in Allah as part of reality, but via rational and intellectual contemplation comes to the conclusion that Allah is the only reality as all things lead to Him and all things have been created by Him, in accordance with the laws He has set. Thus, once a person establishes the reality of Allah, which is a rational endeavour, then they can deduce that the Qur'an is His word and a book of truth, and that He sent the

Messenger ﷺ as guidance for mankind and as an enforcement of the truth of Islam which is in conformity with reality.

An example of such a point can be found in the *Sīrah* when the Prophet went on the Isra and Miraj. When he ﷺ told the people of Mecca at the time of his experience, there were some, including Muslims, who mocked such an idea as it did not conform with their idea of reality. However, when Abū Bakr (ra) was asked about the possibility of this happening, he affirmed with *yaqeen* (certainty) that he had no doubt that this had taken place—gaining the title Siddique (The acknowledger of the truth/truthful one). Abū Bakr Siddique's (ra) conviction was not based on blind belief in the Prophet ﷺ but rather his understanding of reality in accordance with the Islamic *ʿaqīdah*, meaning not only was this miracle possible but it happened as a matter of fact, because the Prophet ﷺ does not lie as that contravenes the principle of Prophethood, which has already been established. When some doubtful minds pressed the Prophet ﷺ, they asked him to explain what he had seen in this world so that it could conform with a sensory understanding of reality. In response, the Prophet ﷺ recounted to them what he saw in *Bayt al-Maqdis* and that a caravan was on its way. Because of their poor understanding of the Islamic *ʿaqīdah*, some left Islam; this was because their understanding of reality was devoid of the ultimate truth of Allah and that which was related to Him. If they had understood the notion of *nubuwwa*, they would have understood that he ﷺ is in conformity with reality. Thus, this narrative is proof of how differences at a foundational/creedal level of understanding reality—and the knowledge pertaining to it—can lead to misguidance. This incident was not only an issue of *īmān* (belief), it was also an *ʿaqīdah* issue in the sense it indeed conformed with reality, and, depending on one's understanding of the *ʿaqīdah*, subsequently shapes one's knowledge of reality. Thus, the Islamic understanding of reality is comprehensive in that it provides a complete understanding of reality, whereas the secular mind will continue to misdiagnose reality as it has restricted itself to foundational parts of understanding it. This in turn not only skews their understanding of reality but also the knowledge they build from it.

We can see this in the example of the cultural and biologist Christian Richard Dawkins, when in an interview with Mehdi Hassan at Oxford University, he rather mockingly relays a similar sentiment to those in the aforementioned narrative above about the possibility of the *Isra* and *Miraj*, by questioning one aspect within the narrative which speaks of the Prophet ﷺ travelling on a horse-like beast. Dawkins questions Mehdi Hassan by saying, "Do you believe that Muhammad ﷺ travelled on a horse with wings?[13]" To that, Mehdi replies, "Yes he does." Dawkins then responds as if Hassan's answer was a case in point in the irrationality of religion, which according to him is simply a set of mythical beliefs. On closer examination, the interaction was no different from the interaction Abū Bakr Siddique (ra) had. This was not a question of Hassan's belief over Dawkins' understanding of reality. But rather Dawkins' "factual" belief was distorted due to his distortion of understanding reality and hence being unable to understand the truth of the *Isra* and *Miraj*. It is understandable that Dawkins could neither imagine nor understand the reality of Buraq, because for Dawkins' *ʿaqīdah* and worldview, he required material proof of Buraq's existence. He had not seen Buraq, he had not found any evidence of Buraq, and there was no fossil proof of Buraq, and so naturally he rejected this idea in the *Sīrah*. However, if one understands reality in conformity of the Islamic *ʿaqīdah*, one can ask, can Allah create a being like Buraq? The simple and conclusive answer

13 *Ulamā* vary in opinion on the details regarding Buraq, with some mentioning it was a beast with wings, and others simply stating it was a mule-like creature that could make large jumps.

is yes, as Allah can create whatever He wishes, and Allah the creator of all the worlds is not diminished simply because Dawkins chooses to reject the truth of the comprehensive Islamic *ʿaqīdah*. Just like Abū Bakr Siddique (ra), we also must affirm that this is true, in conformity with the comprehensive Islamic *ʿaqīdah* and part of *īmān*, attesting to the point of Allah creating angels, *jinn, iblis* (satan) and any other creature he may not have knowledge of, as well as it being part of *īmān* regarding the belief in Allah, in the Prophet ﷺ, in the Qur'an, in the angels, the belief in miracles, the *Qadr* of Allah as well as the unseen—which are certain truths. For Dawkins, we can see that what he presumed as a fact based on his understanding of reality meant that not only did it skew his understanding of the truth but also restricted his imagination. His thought process was restricted at the state of *aql* unable to get to the stage of *firasah,* and his imagination was restricted to the stage of *khayal* unable to get to the stage of *ta'weel.*

Miracles are one of the hardest things to write about for historians. They are rejected by the secular mind as part of the mythology of religions, and thus, will not be taken seriously by any academic venture in intellectual production. For this reason, miracles, the metaphysical and the supernatural, are caricatured to be part of the world of fiction. However, as I said, miracles and metaphysics are part of reality. In the case of writing about the lives of the Prophets ﷺ or the Prophet Muhammad ﷺ we are able to write about such matters due to the Qur'an mentioning them or from the *Sunnah*. Thus, historians writing the *Sīrah* are not only able to write about miracles and the metaphysical as they are conclusively mentioned as proof in the Qur'an and *Sunnah* but also have to mention them as they are a part of the sacred mission. This is what differentiates a secular approach to *Sīrah* writing and an Islamic one.

For a Muslim historian, they need to write about such matters with great care as these matters cannot be simply reduced to the primitive level of the human thought process, nor can they be left to simply a sensory level of one's imagination as these relate to spiritual experiences. Thus, these matters ought to be written with great care and careful scrutiny, lest we make a mistake and misguide the readers. What we learn from the Qur'an and *Sunnah* is that matters to do with the metaphysical were often corroborated with witness testimonies. These testimonies would operate as evidence of such matters taking place and being experienced. We can see this in relation to when the Prophet ﷺ split the moon, there were a host of witnesses, or when Jibril ﷺ came to visit the Prophet ﷺ mentioned in the Ḥadīth Jibril, once again there were many witnesses. The Battle of *Badr* is another example, where while the Muslims fighters on that day experienced a metaphysical experience of Allah's help in sending angels to assist the Muslims in battle, they were unaware of the exact nature of the experience until Allah mentioned in the Qur'an that He had sent angels. This was also the case where the Prophet ﷺ in Ḥadīth Jibril asked Umar Ibn Khattab (ra) if he knew who the man was that was questioning him. Umar (ra) said the Prophet ﷺ knew better, and it was then that the Prophet ﷺ told him that it was the archangel Jibril. These witness accounts are confirmed by Allah or the Prophet ﷺ, making them conclusive proof. However, after the time of *nubuwwa* (prophethood), historians cannot verify metaphysical events or experiences with the same certainty. As a result, metaphysical matters after this period are open to greater scrutiny and interpretation.

As a result, Muslim historians regarding later accounts of possible metaphysical events or experiences after the life of the Prophet ﷺ ought to tread cautiously on the side of documented witness testimonies as a way of highlighting a possible metaphysical moment to the reader. The tradition of Islamic sciences includes many methodologies that use testimony as a form of evidence or proof. We see in *ḥadīth* tradition the examination of a single narration to narrations from multiple people; we see examinations of the witnesses and possibilities of what could bring question to their testimony; we see investigations in the generational chain of the transmitted *ḥadīth* in order to validate the testimony. Then, there is the content, which is to see if it is in conformity with the Qur'an, and then there is the examination of whether narrations contradict one another or if there is a possibility of collective collusion. Witness testimonies in Islam are not only important in the *ḥadīth* sciences but also play a crucial role in legal matters, where they must meet many conditions to ensure the truth with minimal doubt. Therefore, when recording metaphysical events, Muslim historians are expected to apply the same careful standards.

Let's take the matter of a narration from a single author or witness, such as an autobiographical work, memoir or travelogue. It is much harder to prove the validity of a claim from a single source that cannot be corroborated. Singular testimonies without other witnesses are challenging as one is capable of lying, making mistakes, falling on the side of error, misunderstanding experiences or having flaws in memory. An example can be the travel writings of Evliya Çelebi, who mentions that the Ottoman scientist Hezarfen jumped from the Galata Tower with hang glider-like wings across the Bosphorus Sea and to the other side in Üsküdar. There are two challenges for the historian here, firstly that it is not scientifically possible for Hazerfen to make it to the other side jumping from the height of the Galata Tower even if there was a strong gust of wind. Evliya Çelebi concludes that he made it with the help of Allah. But in order to examine such a claim witness, accounts could be used, and in this case, should be used as this happened during the day and this type of spectacle would have piqued the interest of people at the time. But we have no eyewitness accounts, and we do not even have the testimony of Hezarfen himself to validate Evliya Çelebi's claim. That is not to say that Hezarfen did not jump from the Galata tower or that he was not interested in such a scientific venture, but rather one should lean on the side of caution when speaking about this event.

However, I shall use another example to show how Muslim historians attempted to weave in a possible metaphysical moment in Islamic history—Sultan Mehmed Fatih's conquest of Constantinople. During Fatih's conquest, the Muslim armies were struggling to break the Eastern Roman Empire's defences, which was leading to much despondency among the Ottoman armies, as they were starting to lose heart on the long siege they had laid without demonstrable results. In the historical accounts, Akşemseddin had a dream that the Muslim armies would be successful. It was after this that Fatih's troops lifted three ships over the hills of Constantinople and were able to avoid the boom chain and use their canons to shoot the back of the city walls and finally break through. When the men were taking the boats above the hills, many have testified to this feeling as if it were a metaphysical moment, with multiple accounts making such claims. When compared to the example of *Badr*, we see that Allah had not sent angels to wipe out the enemies, but rather they came in assistance to the Muslim armies who were still demanded to fight and take on the physical endeavour. Muslims at the time of Fatih did not suggest that angels helped them lift the ships but simply attested to a feat that was unimaginable for both the Muslims and the Eastern Romans to have actually been achieved, citing that the events of the conquest during a moment of *jihad* had spiritual undertones. This has been mentioned in multiple testimonies. However, without Qur'anic proof, it is impossible for a Muslim historian to verify such claims; instead what many historians have done is record the testimonies regarding what people experienced and leave the claims to Allah knowing best. In doing so, the historian is not denying the experience of the people at the time but also not claiming that this was factual. In my opinion, this is the best way a Muslim historian can write about such matters.

But this point of caution should also be expressed for the Muslim fiction writer. While fiction writers have the freedom to write however they see fit without any restrictions on evidence, nonetheless, Muslim fictional writers should lean on the side caution of writing such fantastical tales that people start to imagine real metaphysical experiences in the same way. For example, a miracle in regards to the Prophets was a sign of proving their Prophethood in that they were chosen by Allah, and it was He, Allah, who created the cosmos, who can also break the natural order of it. By doing so, it is not implied that the Prophets have magical powers, but rather that they are the ones chosen by the One who controls everything, and as proof, Allah provides miracles for people to witness. To understand miracles is to understand reality and how a miracle disturbs that for human understanding. A miracle is not what we see in the Marvel Universe, where the idea of superheroes having superpowers is the equivalent of what we subscribe to, as Muslims of the metaphysical. We must be responsible in the way we write our stories that have restrictions on our imaginations, as we are responsible for not letting unimaginable thoughts contaminate our tradition. It is one thing for non-Muslims to create works of fiction that have ideas that are in contradiction to the truth of Islam, its values and principles; it is even worse if such is done by Muslims. Thus, even our imaginative faculties should be restricted so that our fictional works do not express forms of *kufr*, and furthermore, we ought to be responsible that even if our imaginations do not point to *kufr*, they also do not encourage Muslims to be led astray.

In that sense, I would argue about making sure that when we write fiction, the aspects which are the 'conventions of storytelling' and the 'imaginary world' are in conformity with the Islamic *ʿaqīdah*, which I shall explain shortly. For a historian, their job is to make sure that what they are attempting to establish is real, in the sense that it is an attempt to establish if what has transpired is true. They use and source evidence to validate that truth and use their imaginative faculties to help the reader understand with meaning what transpired in the past. Additionally, the work of the Muslim historian must be in conformity with the Islamic *ʿaqīdah* and reality; it is sinful to spread lies, and it is against reality to make fictitious claims about things that do not agree with the conditions and reality of the past world we are writing about. In that sense, the Muslim historian is bound regarding being accountable in the eyes of Allah, and accountable in relation to the rules of the reality they are trying to explain.

In the case of the fiction writer, however, their imagination applies to two aspects. The first is the imaginary world they create that they have curated, which is not based on any evidence or historical fact, but rather in accordance with the rules of that imaginary world, and the second is the conventions of storytelling that still need to conform with reality for the story to be relatable. The imaginary world thus can be anywhere at any time, it can be 300 years in the past or 500 years in the future, it can be on another planet, or on another world altogether. However, once an imaginary world is articulated, it must have some rules of its reality for the readers/viewers to be able to make sense of it. These rules, while made up, still conform to the basic principle of "natural laws and order" as human beings cannot relate to fictional works that are just mere abstractions. Thus, if an established law of the imaginary world is broken, it leaves the reader/viewer dissatisfied because we are beings who are innately aware that in reality there is a natural order of things.

An example would be Superman. In *Superman*, we have accepted that he is an alien who looks human, from the planet Krypton, who arrived on Earth as a baby on a spaceship. Due to the sun of our solar system, Kryptonians who would be human-like on their own planet when they enter our solar system attain superpowers that allow them to fly, be stronger than steel, have super hearing, and shoot laser beams from their eyes. *Superman*, real name Kal-El on Krypton, arrives on Earth, is adopted by human parents and is told to hide his abilities, but when he gets older, he becomes Superman, the strongest being on the planet. In this work of fiction, the only way to kill Superman is the use of Kryptonite, which is a rock from the planet Krypton that arrived with Kal-El to Earth when he landed. These rocks, which are green, are poisonous to Kryptonians on Earth. Audiences who have now become acclimatised to the "natural order" of this fictitious world expect the story to uphold the rules of the world. If Superman were suddenly to be killed by slipping on a banana peel and smacking his head on the ground, this would be rejected by the audience as an absurdity due to the conventions of what has been invented. The reason why it is absurd is that Superman cannot die like that in this world that has been imagined. Human beings are accustomed to making sense of things in accordance with rules.

The next point was the conventions of storytelling, which are the aspects that are relatable in the fictional story. These are social relations, human emotions, relatable characters and events, universal themes, and concepts such as justice, to name a few. These are what make the story work, and it is these meanings, values, ideals or themes that resonate with the audience that make fictional works relatable as these concepts and human configurations exist in reality. Thus, we see that the imagination of human beings is still restricted to being able to build upon reality or express reality, as it is impossible for human beings to go beyond that. Stories conform to the human lived experience.

If we go back to *Superman*, the reason for this fictional work's success was that it was a symbol of American ideals and values, particularly in the early and mid-twentieth century. Created by Jerry Siegel and Joe Shuster in 1938, *Superman* emerged during a time when the US was grappling with the Great Depression and was on the verge of entering World War II. His character was crafted to embody values like hope, justice, and the fight against oppression, which resonated with the American spirit of the time. The famous motto "truth, justice and the American way" became associated with *Superman*, especially during the 1940s and 1950s. It reflected the post-World War II optimism and the notion of America as a beacon of democracy and fairness in the world. *Superman* was often depicted standing for the rule of law, fighting against tyranny, and protecting the vulnerable, all of which aligned with American ideals. During World War II, *Superman* comics were used as a form of patriotic propaganda. He was portrayed fighting Nazis and other Axis powers, reinforcing America's fight for freedom and justice against totalitarian regimes. This further solidified his connection to American values at the time. *Superman* worked as it was associated with the American way of life, primarily for Americans, and when the US represented the side of "good" during the Cold War, and then Globalisation, the image of *Superman* evolved with that. Thus, for good fiction to work, irrespective of the imaginary world, the key is the convention of storytelling and how that relates to reality, as this is what human beings are searching for.

Thus, in matters of the imaginary world, Muslim writers may choose to be as creative as they see fit so long as they are in conformity with the Islamic ethos. For example, making a fictional life of Muslims in hellfire, or a fictional devil in heaven, or furthermore attempting to depict Allah or the

Prophet ﷺ cannot be part of the world the Muslim fictional writer is trying to curate. Regarding the conventions of storytelling that attempt to resonate with real-life realities, Muslim fiction writers need to be careful that they do not write stories that betray the *ʿaqīdah* or Islam or the Islamic ethos. For example, permitting, normalising or encouraging *haram* (sinful) or *kufr* (disbelief) acts or concepts in their narratives, or encouraging bad moral or ethical behaviour, or seeking to put doubt in the mind of the reader are all against Islam. In that sense, when encouraging Muslims to be imaginative in their fiction works, whether regarding the imaginative world they create or the conventions of storytelling, both forms of imagination must be in conformity with Islam. In that sense, like the historian, the Muslim fictional writer is also bound by the norms of the Islamic ethos and their belief in Islam should treat their imagination.

Thus, for me, Muslim fictional writers and creatives must show the beauty of Islam in their artwork in the ways Muslims have in the past, where we think of Allah's beauty, we love Him and the Prophet ﷺ, that we write and curate beautiful forms, and that we write stories that represent the values of Islam, the ethics of the divine message, and shape the Muslim mind in accordance with the principles of Islam. Even when producing social and political criticism, Muslim writers should try to show Islam as a beautiful alternative, and provide solutions for the reader, as a fundamentally and Islamically inspired fictional project should attempt to provide solutions from Islam, just as any other form of knowledge that the Muslim becomes involved with. In order to curate comprehensive works of fiction inspired by Islam and in conformity with it, a Muslim fictional writer should seek to understand what is permitted and what is not, they must also appreciate the current reality as a way of curating meaningful works of fiction that can help Muslims to find cultural meaning and search for solutions for change. They should seek inspiration from history, especially Islamic history, as a way of seeing if they can use the large repository of lived experiences of Muslims. They should consider whether they can make their work one of *dawah*, not just mere entertainment.

No doubt the line between fiction and history writing can be thin, and it is for this reason that some thinkers argued that historians are the novelists of the scholarly world. But as I have mentioned, historians who are aware of this point know the difference between fictional storytelling and historical writing. While history as a medium shares many aspects with fiction writing, primarily, what is important is that the Muslim community works on both mediums as they are both needed for this *ummah*.

Fiction, as a Way of Speaking Truth

Like history, fiction can have a way of influencing and representing what is happening at a given time in a society. For us as historians, it is not just the archival sources that we read to understand the past, but, in fact, we read works of fiction from a given time to see how, in the creative space, people were attempting to speak truth or reflect a particular problem at the time. Fiction, as explained by Tolkien, is a creative retelling of fundamental truths in reality, with purpose and an end for its characters, that take place in a secondary world of the storyteller's conjuring, and while not necessarily bound by the laws and consequences of the Primary World, i.e. in having the same implications, it is dependent on the elements of truth from the latter.

Fiction can be found in the guise of a host of mediums such as poems, novels, theatre plays, puppet shows, and comedy—all spaces that provide historians with an insight into a society. For society, fiction can have a more powerful impact in providing ideas of the past than any academic work at times. A number of Muslims I have spoken to have said that Mustafa Akkad's movie *The Message*, which was of the life-story of the Prophet ﷺ depicted in cinematic form, is more influential in shaping their lives than the books of *Sīrah*. In fairness to Akkad, he did not present his movie as a work of fiction, but instead history, but what Akkad was able to do was creatively use his imagination to put the *Sīrah* into cinematic form. People I have known have said the same about Spike Lee's depiction of the life of the famous Muslim activist Malcolm X.

An example of fictional creativity that blurs the lines between history and fiction can be seen in Gilo Pontecorvo's *The Battle of Algiers*. Pontecorvo, a leftist filmmaker, made this movie in which he depicted how the Algerians revolted against the French in 1954 and attained independence by 1962. The movie was produced in 1966, only four years after the Algerians attained independence and was banned in France until the 1970s. Pontecorvo chose to show a history from below, where there were no main characters, and how the Algerians resisted the French and were brutally tortured. The movie was reflective of the Algerian struggle but was nonetheless a work of fiction, with many Algerians making the case that what the French had actually done was far worse than what the movie had shown. While the film was based on real events and real-life experiences, it is fiction insofar as the storyteller employs his imagination to deploy fundamental truths that are attested to in reality (e.g. the deaths from French atrocities) in service of the ends of the adaptation (which is largely up to the director). Hence, there can be disagreement as to the gravity of the atrocities that happened versus what was depicted without disavowing the verification, i.e. that it *actually* happened.

It is said that the IRA, PLO, and Black Panthers took inspiration from the movie as art attempting to imitate reality and, in a turn of going full circle, as life imitating art. It is also said that the CIA would use *The Battle of Algiers* to show their recruits during the US invasion of Iraq after 9/11 how to deal with urban guerrilla resistance.

During this period, another work that took ideas from Algerian liberation was Frank Herbert, who would produce his science-fiction book titled *Dune*. In *Dune*, Herbert borrowed many ideas and terms from Islam and the resistance of the Algerians against a greater colonial force. Many themes in the books would later inspire George Lucas and his *Star Wars* movies, in which Lucas would portray how the smaller rebels were able to hold up against the large, technologically sophisticated empires, which symbolised mainly the British and then the Americans. In the book *How Star Wars Conquered the Universe: The Past, Present and Future of a Multibillion Dollar Franchise*, Lucas explained how he had planned to incorporate Vietnam ideology into his blockbuster sci-fi since its inception, having written a note on a draft of the screenplay penned in 1973 that simply stated the overarching theme of "a large technological empire going after a small group of freedom fighters". The portrayal of Vietnam ideology in films often reflects the country's complex history, particularly regarding nationalism, communism, and the struggle against colonialism and imperialism and many Hollywood directors used this as a form of critique regarding American foreign policy. Later in an interview with the movie director James Cameron, while the two were conversing Cameron would state that in Star Wars, "The good guys are the rebels, they're using asymmetrical warfare against a highly organised empire, I think we call those guys terrorists today," with Lucas responding with "The irony is that, in both of those, the little guys won. The highly technical empire—the English Empire, the American Empire—lost. That was the whole point". There is something "*Badr-esque*" in the way both Lucas and Cameron speak about their movies; the narrative of Dawud (David) and Jalut (Goliath) has a deep genealogy in imaginations up until today.

The world of fiction was finding a way of presenting a sense of thematic patterns that resonated with colonised people. While *The Battle of Algiers* and *Dune* were inspired by Algeria, and *Star Wars* by *Dune* and the Vietnam War, a common theme occurred about the nature of colonisation and its abuses. When Lucas, after a long hiatus, made *Revenge of the Sith*, the 3rd prequel and 6th Star Wars movie, he was criticised by American political conservatives who said his movie was attacking the Bush administration and its invasion of Iraq post-9/11.

Since then, James Cameron himself produced a movie of a similar nature titled *Avatar*, in which he made the case of an indigenous group of people with simple weapons resisting the invasion of a large technological empire that seeks to extract the resources of the planet they have invaded. Upon the release of this movie, activists in Palestine would paint themselves blue in the image of the fictional characters in *Avatar*. More recently, the *Dune* books have become movies, and the *Star Wars* franchise has produced its darkest extension of the franchise yet, titled *Andor*, in which the TV series shows how the story of the rebellion of the oft-forgotten regular people. All these themes and ideas today continue, for example, to resonate with people of the Muslim world, as they continue to experience colonial violence.

There are many works of current fiction that are popular and still inspiring, of course. An example is the Japanese manga and anime tradition where the younger generation is reading and watching shows like *One Piece* and *Naruto*. *Harry Potter* was and still is an exceptionally popular franchise that has inspired many young readers, and the Marvel Universe and Star Wars Universe produce shows that people continue to watch and take creative inspiration from.

In the case of the Marvel Universe, they have also introduced a Muslim character—Kamala Khan, but her inclusion in the Marvel Universe is nothing more than a token gesture of liberal inclusivity than anything that provides or learns from the teachings of Islam. While for Western media, Kamala Khan's depiction as a female Muslim superhero is in stark contrast to how Muslims have traditionally been depicted in Hollywood, as terrorists and dehumanised people who either need killing or saving, nonetheless the Western fictional space in regards to Muslim representation is either not relatable for many young Muslims in the Muslim world or is outright antagonistic.

There have been more recent attempts in the US and the UK to create Muslim-oriented stories of Muslims living in the West under the genre of sitcoms. Secular-liberal shows in the US, like *Ramy* and the tamer *Man Like Mobeen* in the UK, have shown that there is a space that permits Muslim representation, but none of these shows have reflected any of their inspiration from the principles of Islam and Islamic history. Instead, they rather reflect forms of more secular-liberal entertainment. That is not to say that fictional shows and dramas have not emerged, especially in the Muslim world. More recently from Türkiye, shows like Diriliş Ertuğrul (Resurrection Ertugrul) and later Payitaht Abdulhamid have become exceptionally popular for Muslim audiences, indicating that at least in the field of historical fiction, Muslim representation on the small screen is becoming noticeable. The success of these shows was less to do with historical accuracy and more to do with the fact that they represented values, principles and ideals that Muslims are accustomed to in relation to the tradition of Islam, as well as Muslims not being vilified as being evil or terrorists. It's not just Türkiye that has produced works of historical biopics, in Iran, the life-story of the Prophet Yusuf ﷺ and in the Arab world, life-stories of Umar Ibn Khattab (ra) and Imam Ahmed Ibn Hanbel have also attracted attention from Muslim audiences. In these matters, there is a clear case that history can be instructive for fiction work. As the need for Muslims desiring more qualitative fictional and historical content increases, the need to produce such works becomes ever more important.

While at the moment, Muslims are becoming acclimatised to narrating historical works on screen, as time goes by, a more imaginative approach, such as in the fields of science-fiction, fantasy, historical fiction and so on should also be attempted, as in this space Muslim creatives are still somewhat lacking. This is not a criticism of Muslims, but just a reflection of our reality as, at times, we have lacked the resources, institutions or technologies. Furthermore, it is my hope that as Muslims engage with the past more, they can find inspiration from history to curate not only historical works but works in all forms of fiction.

Illustrative Narratives as a Medium of Fiction

It was not only the West that curated such fictional expressions of criticism. As I mentioned earlier in the field of animation, the famous anime artist and director Hayao Miyazaki, when making *Howl's Moving Castle*, employed the use of metaphor by way of an analogy to criticise the US invasion of Iraq—the animation had only limited showing in the US as a result. What is worth noting is that Miyazaki had made his movie for children. *Howl's Moving Castle* was not a dark movie, but it was a sophisticated animation that used a host of metaphors in both visual form as well as in narrative to educate his young audience about the perils of war— something that had impacted Miyazaki directly.

In the comic book form, Joe Sacco, a prominent American cartoonist and journalist known for his pioneering work in the field of graphic journalism, has combined his artistic skills with investigative reporting to create powerful narratives about conflict, human rights, and social issues, especially in the Muslim world. In particular, three of his works are worthy of mention here.

1) **"Palestine"**: This graphic novel chronicles Sacco's experiences in the West Bank and Gaza Strip during the early 1990s. It provides a personal and political perspective on the Israeli-Palestinian conflict.

2) **"Safe Area Goražde"**: This work documents the experiences of people in Goražde, a town in Bosnia, during the

Bosnian War. It combines personal stories with historical context, offering insight into the impact of war on civilians.

3) **"Footnotes in Gaza"**: In this graphic novel, Sacco investigates the events surrounding the Gaza Strip and explores the long-standing conflict through interviews and illustrations.

Sacco's style is characterised by detailed artwork and a commitment to authenticity. He often immerses himself in the communities he portrays, conducting interviews and capturing first-hand accounts in conveying the complex social and political issues through the medium of comics that the people of Gaza have faced. Through his unique approach, Sacco has opened up a unique form of political and investigative storytelling, allowing readers to engage with the serious nature of the issue of Palestine in a visually compelling way, which is different from simply reading text. His contributions have made a significant impact on both journalism and the graphic novel genre.

Regarding *Footnotes on Gaza*, the narrative is built around interviews with survivors and residents of Gaza, providing a human perspective on the consequences of the ongoing war with the Israeli occupation. Sacco's immersive approach allows readers to see personal stories and experiences. The graphic novel has been praised for its innovative approach to journalism, bringing attention to underrepresented voices in the context of conflict. As in the case of the novel of Sinwar, it is rare for Palestinians to be given agency or their stories to be told. Sacco's famous works even inspired artists in Gaza, as indigenous artists, to have a voice in illustrating the hardships they are facing. His book serves as an educational resource, helping readers understand the complexities of the Israeli-Palestinian conflict through a narrative that is both accessible and deeply informative.

Today, more and more young people are choosing to read Japanese manga and watch anime, just as many young people have engaged with the works of Sacco. The visual form can be found not only in comic books or animations but also in computer games, infographics, and advertising. For many, animated storytelling may be perceived as simple cartoons with no meaning beyond the obvious of entertaining younger audiences. Others may question the validity of illustrations as a permissible form of expression within the Islamic context. Islamic scholars themselves have a difference of opinion on this matter. Throughout the history of Islam, people have used illustrations to tell narratives to teach Islam to new groups of Muslims. This was especially normalised during the Pax-Mongolica period, where miniatures were painted from as far as East Asia to the Persianate lands. In the Malay Archipelago, stories with morals were presented via puppet shows, while in parts of Anatolia, Muslims were taught the morals from Islam as fables.

From the miniatures tradition that came from the Mongols, manga drawing became a tradition of educating the masses in East Asia. Manga's tradition dates back to the twelfth century when Buddhist monks created Emaki scrolls and illustrated texts that discussed issues such as spirituality and politics in narrative form. These scrolls could be found on the walls of buildings, such as houses of worship. The eighteenth-century Japanese woodblock artist Katsushika Hokusai popularised the term "manga", which comes from the amalgamation of the words *man*, meaning "whimsical", and *ga* meaning "pictures". However, Hokusai's work was anything but whimsical; the artist is famous for his print, *The Great Wave of Kanagawa*, which is one of the most recognisable paintings in the world. He also produced thousands of manga images in a fifteen-volume collection named Hokusai Manga, which was first published in 1814 and mostly contained vignettes unrelated to each other.

The Muslim world was not unfamiliar with the illustrated storytelling traditions, and in the Persianate worlds, the long-established tradition of miniatures blossomed under Mongol Ilkhanid patronage in the thirteenth century which later included the Ottomans, Iran, and Mughal India. These works of fiction, but also history, have continued to shape people today, and the interplay between history and fiction ought not to be marginalised by future Muslim historians. Many young people are watching Japanese anime, with historical and political themes being interlaced into the anime.

Some may dismiss the illustrative medium as a worthy form of storytelling, due to it being associated with the idea of them being cartoons after the emergence of Saturday morning cartoon culture that signalled animation taking off as exclusively an entertainment medium, which Walt Disney by the mid-1950s was largely responsible for and took advantage of. Illustrative forms of storytelling, however, have been part of many societies where images as signs have conveyed meaning to represent ideas, much like symbols or words. This concept is rooted in semiotics, the study of signs and symbols and their use or interpretation. In regards to animation, as the medium improves, the desire to "watch" fiction over reading is gaining equal momentum.

In regards to an emerging young generation that is surrounded with the sophistry of imagery being used in all walks of life, especially on social media, it can be no surprise that the popularity of illustrations and images, along with photography, has become a preferred choice of learning. One could make the case that we live in a world where visual learning has never been as dominant. Equally, many young people engage with fiction by watching it in the illustrated form of animation. This is a space where Muslims have fallen behind, not in its consumption, but creative animators, studios, art schools and Muslim publishing houses are still lagging in comparison to other cultures and parts of the world. At the moment, animated storytelling in the Muslim world is one of simply replicating Western forms, both in visuality and storytelling style. A distinct form of animation that is in conformity with the indigenous visual cultures of the Muslim world is still lacking.

This is at a time when there is a need to teach history to young people not only as a set of narratives but also metaphorically and allegorically in the form of fiction and even illustrated fiction. This is because the young naturally have an affinity to this medium; Muslims thinking about teaching history to their children should consider this point carefully. There is an assumption that children are unable to make a distinction between what they watch on the screen and the real world, but that is part of the modern culture of infantilising children to the point where we do not believe they are mature enough to learn intellectual ideas. Ideas can be taught in stages and in various ways, and visual learning can present intellectual concepts within a story, making them memorable. Characters and plots can contextualise lessons, allowing children to relate personally to the material. There is a need for illustrative storytelling that can be in conformity to the *ʿaqīdah* of Islam while reflecting the various artistic cultures within the Muslim world.

We should try to encourage children to understand concepts in Islam, such as *ʿaqīdah, adab, iḥsān, īmān*, and *taqwā* via these mediums as well as through the traditional books we use. Young people need these ideas inherent within them before we expose them to complex works of Islamic literature. In that sense, it is worth asking if we have the desire or the creativity to work within our own framework of knowledge and create fictional works, including illustrated fictional works, for our children and young people, as illustrations, animation, and cartoons should not simply be seen as primitive forms of storytelling but can, in fact, be a powerful medium of conveying ideas about life.

World Building – One Piece as an Example of Longue Durée Storytelling

In particular, I would like to discuss how the famous Japanese anime/manga fiction series *One Piece* as an epic world building story, in much the same way that Tolkien and Lewis had created worlds, has brought young audiences to be more interested in the history of Japan, colonialism, nation-states, imperial history, as well Japanese mythology that draws on both Shinto and Buddhist traditions. People and scholars may have differing opinions on whether the next generation should engage with anime. My point is not to get involved in a theological debate but rather express how one of the most famous anime shows has been become a powerful medium in influencing viewers and readers, stressing my point in the need for fiction in the animated form needing to be undertaken by Muslims as a form of insightful and deep storytelling.

At first glance, *One Piece* may seem like the average cartoon watched by children, even though it has been running for twenty-five years and still counting. However, on closer inspection, the show has chosen not to infantilise its audience but rather to provide complex ideas in the medium of animation and manga. As the audiences have grown with the show, so has the storyline, which reflects the criticism of the author and mangaka Eiichiro Oda regarding our current predicament. To dismiss Oda as being a mere mangaka is to degrade how, in Japanese culture, manga creators can be viewed in the way any profound fiction writer exists in any other society. This is especially the case when we consider how profound Oda's show is in its criticism of modernity, the nation-state, imperialism, and the hierarchies of structural violence. Finally, *One Piece* is also a show that stresses the importance of history, a theme that runs throughout. An essential point in *One Piece* is how a world built on violence and exploitation has created ignorance, a loss of self, and an assumption that violence in the world has always been this way. In *One Piece*, the idea is that once people start learning their history more, it can be revolutionary in their desire to make change. The will to change the world, along with the desire for justice, truth, and connecting with the past, are just some critical themes of *One Piece* that I will elaborate on below.

I use *One Piece* to make the case that, like other vernacular intellectuals, Oda has found a medium. In this case, the medium is fiction and anime to explain what he thinks can change our current predicament, and that history can be a part of that. Oda, in many ways, is using *One Piece* as a mirror of the world we live in today and hopes that our world can be transformed in the way his fictitious one is in his story. But not only that, when watching *One Piece*, his narratives resonate because we see a repetition of the themes of war, justice, and injustice in a way that people have become accustomed to seeing in their everyday news feed. Oda's work also presents patterns in his narrative writing that we continue to read about in the books of history. In that sense, *One Piece* is a conversation about what history can mean to the audience, and fiction can be the best way of helping the young mind become interested in history.

One Piece is a story about a young pirate by the name of Monkey D. Luffy as the protagonist who is part of a world that is governed and controlled by a world empire that reflects the empires of the colonial period. For the world government to control the world, it has set up a series of coalitions with other nations, some willingly choosing to align with the world government and others forced to do so, creating a hierarchy of violence that has become the world's culture. In doing so, the world government can extract the resources of the ordinary people and keep any alternative powers at bay, using mechanisms of force, coercion, and disinformation spread by the media. Additionally, the show makes the case of the period known as the "void", a period in history that is no longer found in textbooks, where very little trace of a particular ancient civilisation can be found. The ancient civilisation of the people who existed at the moment known as the "void" is viewed as myth, legend, and hearsay. But what was once a reality is now missing from our collective memory and imagination. The show itself pushes the viewer to ask themselves how much of their past do they know, and how much of their past have they forgotten. *One Piece* makes the argument that even the mythologies of old have drawn from some reality, as myths and "fiction" require a repository which is reality.

Another point of the show is who writes about the past and why. When one of the characters known as Donquixote Doflamingo is asked about the notion of justice (or the absence of it), he quips, "Justice will win, you say? Of course it will! Because whoever wins will become justice!" The point Doflamingo was making was twofold: firstly, that justice is not universal, but rather the ideal of those in power, and that while people can feel a sense of injustice, nonetheless, those in power have the authority to determine justice. For Doflamingo, those in power are the victors of war and the ones who control the world we live in, similar to the victory of the Western empires that have shaped our world since WWI and WWII. The second point implied by Doflamingo was that the winners of war control not only the idea of justice but also history, as it is the winners of war who write history, something echoed by the controversial British Prime Minister during the colonial period, Winston Churchill who stated that the "victors of war write history."

Doflamingo was also making the case that the victors tend to be violent and if they write an unchallenged history legitimising violence then it creates a synergy between violence and history, which creates in the minds of the people the notion that violence is the norm of life and human history, as people have not experienced anything else, and that this violence is part of a cycle which is just the disposition of human beings. The point made in *One Piece* is that there needs to be a paradigm shift in which violence is not normalised, both in the past and in real life, and that a different approach to human history may force people to question the actual violence they currently experience.

In *One Piece*, there is a need for a charismatic hero figure that reflects the characteristics of a person of a prophecy. With the help of his crew, who are disciple-like, this individual will stand up against the current injustice to save and free humanity from tyranny and hardship. In the anime, this person is Monkey D Luffy. The second point is that while life has moved forward, Luffy will reignite the cultures of old and even reflect the return of tradition(s) that have been forgotten due to modernity and salvage humanity. In this sense, the ancient world was advanced and still has life solutions for humanity today. Finally, with the aid of his crew, in particular the character Nico Robin, Luffy is in search of reading a set of "*Ponegliffs*" that have been scattered around the world to revive the forgotten history of a previous civilisation. The 'One Piece', which the show is named after, can be considered the loss of knowledge that was once part of human civilisation but has now been evaded from collective memories.

In *One Piece*, history matters! It matters in dispelling falsehood from truth to remind people that the current way they live is unjust, that there is another way, and that the narratives of old constructed to uphold the current status quo are, in fact, not true. While an anime show, *One Piece* is no less sophisticated than, say, George Orwell's *1984*. Oda emphasises the importance of understanding history, not just as a record of events but as a rich tapestry of knowledge that informs contemporary identity and action. The epic weaves together narratives from various cultures, highlighting the wisdom of ancient knowledge systems and their relevance today. What is central in *One Piece* is the notion of fostering trust and responsibility in the next generation, which involves passing down not only knowledge but also values, ethics, and a sense of collective identity. Oda's work clearly critiques the structures and systems imposed by colonial powers, highlighting how these have distorted local knowledge systems and perpetuated cycles of violence. By exposing the hierarchies of violence left in the wake of colonialism, Oda challenges readers to recognise and dismantle these legacies in contemporary society. The epic may explore how colonialism introduced new epistemologies while undermining indigenous ways of knowing, suggesting a need to reclaim and celebrate diverse knowledge systems. Ultimately, Oda's epic serves as a call to action, urging individuals and communities to engage critically with their histories and knowledge. By doing so, they can confront the ongoing impacts of colonialism and work towards healing and empowerment.

In many ways, while *One Piece* is a work of fiction, the truth in it is the fact that the past is not simply a relic and that with knowledge we can overcome our predicament; we need to be action-oriented if we want to change our state. Finally, for someone like me, *One Piece* tells us that history matters. It matters as it is supposed to dispel falsehoods, and in doing so, remove the legitimacy of the structures that are based on that falsehood. It matters because people require attachment to the past to make sense of themselves and the world they belong to. It matters because we seek values in history that can shape and guide us, and finally, it matters because it tells us that change happens as an accumulative process over a considerable lapse of time.

Whether it is the world building works of Tolkien and C.S. Lewis, the sci-fi movies of Lucas and Cameron, or Japanese anime, what is evident is that fictional works rely on history and, at times, can be intellectually complementary to the ideas and truths that historians are attempting to uncover. While both require the use of the imagination, they nonetheless use different methods with respect to their own disciplines. However, where the two are similar is that they are interested in the human experience. Muslim representations in fiction are still based on identity rather than anything that represents the tradition and culture of Islam. Furthermore, teaching young people how to take their ideas and providing knowledge that can give them an intellectual insight to establish a sound imagination and ability to be creative cannot be done with academic books alone. Instead, fiction alongside history works can help to provide such tools by the time the child becomes an adult.

Western Imaginations Are Shaping Our Future

I have tackled thus far how history and fiction share features and how they have been used to shape people, their thoughts, identities and imaginations. In this section, I shall discuss how the secular forms of history writing and fiction are shaping discussions about the future, where there is no place for Islam at the "table". Currently, the idea of modernity shapes the way we see the past, present and future, similar to George Orwell's remark that "He who controls the present, controls the future; and he who controls the past, controls the present". In many ways, the manner in which we interpret the past inevitably shapes the way we place ourselves and the way we see ourselves in the present and in our future. Orwell's statement pertinently suggests that whenever the past is changed, it changes not only the present but how future generations see themselves. This is what is called a paradigm shift, where revisions of the past change the present and subsequently future generations. In the West, the influence of history on fiction and the role of fiction to generate imaginations of the future have led to very bleak imaginations. The secular consciousness, which is devoid of Allah, His divine will, His *Qadr* and life's purpose, which is to worship Him, has meant that human beings have become inward-looking and only see the future in terms of their quest for worldly progress.

We currently see the same in the conflict between the Palestinians in Gaza and Israel. While the conflict is a physical one as the Palestinians are resisting Israeli aggression, it is also a war of historical narratives. The Israelis are aware of the importance of historical narratives and are thus trying to control the narrative of the past in order to control the present, so that the future generations adhere to the official narrative of the Israelis and their partners. The Palestinians, aware of this, are also firstly trying to expose this falsehood and secondly present their own counternarratives. We clearly see here that he who controls the past controls the present and the future. We see the impact of the rewriting of history, as it not only changes one's own collective self-perception, but it is also how one perceives the other in relation to themselves. For example, the criticism regarding the Eurocentric reading of Europe's importance was not only the overemphasis on the significance of Western Europe. It equally downplayed the importance of the rest of the world. As the historian John Goody has commented, by doing this, Europe misrepresented its own history but also imposed its own concepts and cultivated an understanding of its own liking that has been significant to the past as well as the future.

As a result, Muslims by and large are still in a tussle in the post-colonial world, which is dominated by Western secular thought. This has not only created challenges in the present but also how to place themselves and a future with Islam at its centre. This is because over the last century, the dominance of secularism has meant that even the Muslim world has become a victim of the yoke of the global secular order, especially its elites. Western secular institutions have produced many works on Islamic history, explaining how Muslims were. They continue to write about Muslims, objectifying them on how they ought to be. As a result, a response of validation is constantly required from the Muslim that their humanity is in accordance with the way of the secular world. The Muslim world has found it challenging not simply to free itself from the global secular order, but how a future world beyond these confines could be imagined. As a result, by being unable to escape their current predicament, it not only impacts how they view themselves in the present, but it hinders them in generating ideas or taking practical steps to create action plans of how they can make the world a better place for humanity in accordance with the precepts of Islam. Thinking about the future matters, and Muslims need to have imaginations that the current way the world is shaped will not always be this way—history is proof of this. If we can imagine a future that emerges from the current darkness, that is inspired by the Prophetic mission and can be a guiding light for humanity, then we can deal with the way the future is being imagined by the dominant West. In order to do that, we need our thought producers to be able to understand the undertaking, which requires a sound understanding of reality, an adherence to the Islamic *ʿaqīdah* as a foundation, an understanding of history, and practical ideas and steps to strive for a better future. That entails not only understanding Islam but the reality of how secular thought producers are shaping our collective future course into the abyss.

In the West, thinkers have always tried to project imaginative ideas of the future, for the future, both as a creative exercise as well as steering people into a course or direction. The intricacy is always how much of the future emerges due to an inevitable course and how much is steered by those in power and their worldviews and ideas about life. For example, currently, with the emergence of Artificial Intelligence (AI), or "imitative intelligence" as I call it, there are many who fear the planet and humanity in the future will be destroyed by "intelligent machines". The Zionist popular-historian Yuval Noah Harari, for example, in his latest book *Nexus: A Brief History of Information Networks from the Stone Age to AI*, discusses that AI is not simply a tool that we use; it can make decisions and generate new knowledge independently. For Harari, the rise of AI could fundamentally alter the structure of human society. AI and other forms of digital technology, according to Harari, are a new kind of intelligence—what he provocatively calls "alien intelligence"—that could potentially operate beyond human control. In the book, Harari uses examples from human history to make his case as he draws parallels with the invention of steam technology, which includes the modern printed press. The book is not simply a history book; however, he envisions a future world where AI-driven systems could reshape not only human societies, but the entire biosphere, potentially creating new forms of life and intelligence.

It is not only ideas by secular thinkers that are shaping contemporary imaginations, works of fiction, especially in Hollywood, are full of such examples where dystopian imaginations of the future are presented. With the popularity of the entertainment industry, fictional works have become a staple that people engage with, whether at the cinema, online or on television. Hollywood has been the best proponent of facilitating fictional narratives that become internalised by many. Rick Edwards and Dr Michael Brooks have pointed out in their book, *Is Hollywood Trying to Kill Us*, how Hollywood is full of apocalyptic movies, such as nuclear disasters, human beings being wiped out by pandemics, machines with artificial intelligence taking over the world, and zombie apocalypses. It is worth noting how all these ideas in Hollywood are centred around scientific explorations, which is central to the ideas of Western progress. Such has been the influence of these forms of fiction that even Muslim scholars have interpreted the idea that *Yajuj* and *Majuj* (Agog and Magog) found in *Sūrah al-Kahf*, associated with chaos and destruction, as a zombie apocalypse. This chain of thought is no different to when some nineteenth-century Muslim scholars suggested that the *jinn* were akin to bacteria. The popularity of

Hollywood has infected the minds of cinemagoers to a sense that doomsday scenarios are often found in the mainstream press often today—especially regarding AI.

While I encourage us to be imaginative, I also want to stress that our imaginations ought to be in conformity with reality and the Islamic *ʿaqīdah*. For example, when Harari mentions that AI will create new forms of intelligence that may supersede humans, I would argue that this is more in conformity with a fictional imagination of the future than one based on sound evidence. This is because firstly, Harari's examination of human history has taken very little, if any account of Islamic history, or Islamic thought and his secular *ʿaqīdah* is imposed upon the notion of a history of humanity not driven by religion and the truth of Allah's existence but rather when joining the dots of his meta-history of humanity one can only sense a secular material human experience. When he talks of religion, he simply suggests that they are good for societies for myth-making. Harari, who is an atheist, is unable to realise that his concerns about AI taking over humanity are based on an erroneous understanding of the capability of technology as well as the natural laws of the universe. His position shows the depravity of such hubris in thinking that human beings can create something more elevated than themselves. Furthermore, as Allah created human beings as the best of creation, it not only denigrates human beings below technology but also implies that we can invent something better than Allah.

On the one hand, thinkers like Harari are in full admiration of the handy work of human beings, and yet at the same time believe that human beings will become secondary to the things they invent. No human invention will ever be able to replicate the complexity of the human being, let alone a fly, and no machine will ever be able to have *ruh* and *aql*. I'm assuming that Harari's rejection that he has a soul means he sees machines in his own image, nothing more than matter that produces information.

I want to mention a point made by Allah in the Qur'an that is worthy of mention in addressing the above point. Allah says in *Sūrah al-Hajj*, "*O people, a parable is set forth: pay heed to it. Those who call upon aught other than Allah shall never be able to create even a fly, even if all of them were to come together to do that. And if the fly were to snatch away anything from them, they would not be able to recover that from it. Powerless is the supplicant; and powerless is he to whom he supplicates.*" (TQM – *Sūrah al-Hajj* 22:73). This *āyah* has two points worth noting, the first is the idolators' arrogance in their foolishness, the second is that they could not even create a fly. The idol worshippers during the time of the Prophet ﷺ were warned by Allah that the foolishness from which they seek the gratification of their desires is so utterly helpless that all of them together cannot create a humble thing like a fly. One cannot help but say that the foolishness of today's secular paganism is similar in the sense that their belief that they can create something exemplary from their handiwork is nothing but arrogant and misguided and that in reality they cannot even create something in comparison to a fly, such is the complexity of all that Allah has created. Thus, the doubts raised about the possibility of AI taking over humans are similar to the mindset of those who question Allah's creation of even a mosquito. These minds of disbelief, even in their imagination, are drained of all power to see things in a proper perspective, while such empty misgivings never touch the minds and hearts of true believers. Naturally, a Muslim thinker can recognize that AI may have the potential to be harmful, but to assume it is purely destructive is both irrational in light of reality and contrary to what Allah has revealed.

While technology is primarily designed to make human life easier, and there is a current trend to make it faster and more powerful, the imbalance it is causing in the world suggests that unchecked technological progress—especially when it harms nature and human tranquillity—should be reconsidered or even slowed down. Furthermore, currently, technology which is being made within the purview of secular ideology needs to be restrained by different ethical standards and principles—I would argue, Islam. If we take a more responsible approach with technological development, a different path can be formed and imagined regarding the course humanity is taking. Human beings have been given agency and free will, and they can make better decisions regarding technology and its benefits. My point here is not to suggest that I do not share Harari's general fear that AI needs regulating, but rather how Harari has curated imaginations of the future due to his poor understanding of reality, which is devoid of Allah but also human capabilities. If human beings trod down the path to destruction, it will primarily be down to their lack of knowledge masquerading as intelligence rather than the supremacy of AI.

In an interview on *The Late Show with Stephen Colbert*, George R.R. Martin—the author of *A Song of Ice and Fire*, which was adapted into the TV series *Game of Thrones*—expressed his pessimism about the future. Both Colbert and Martin noted that during the "Golden Age of Science Fiction," the genre, influenced by Enlightenment ideals, tended to be much more optimistic. This "Golden Age," typically defined as spanning from the late 1930s to the 1950s, was a transformative era for science fiction writing. "The Golden Age", typically defined as occurring from the late 1930s to the 1950s, was a transformative period for the genre. During this time, science fiction became a respected literary form and gained widespread popularity. Writers began to delve into speculative concepts, such as space travel, time travel, alien civilisations, and the implications of technological progress on humanity. But when Martin was asked about today, he said that after mankind stopped going to the moon, he can no longer imagine these types of futures, but rather, in his own words, he had "lost faith" in such imaginations, like losing faith in religion.

During this Golden Age of science fiction, two important dystopian works emerged, challenging readers on how new technologies in the hands of modern governments could be detrimental to humanity. In 1931-32, Aldous Huxley wrote his famous dystopian piece *Brave New World*, in which in a futuristic world in the year 2540 AD, technological advances were able to make citizens be born in artificial wombs and then be indoctrinated by the government's educational program into classes. Society is kept peaceful by a drug that facilitates a consumption culture until the main protagonist realises that this world is not fair. This type of social commentary, while set in the future, was based on how Huxley viewed where the world was going. Like Huxley, George Orwell wrote his book 1984, in which he warns of the direction modernity was taking regarding totalitarianism and surveillance culture. Written in 1949, Orwell wrote about an imagined future and what the world may look like if we continued the path that was being fashioned post-WWII. It was a cautionary work, one in which Orwell was creatively anticipating as well as predicting the future. The works of Huxley and Orwell challenge people to imagine and then fashion a different future perhaps, although the works never really stated solutions or hopes of real change. More than half a century on, and the sense of despair in the Western secular mind has found no solutions nor found solace, as they rather fatalistically accept their fate and convince the rest of us to accept it also.

Some may say that both authors were correct in the way they had predicted the nature of modernity, and many of the themes mentioned in these two books have become actualised today. These authors were able to aptly examine and criticise Western society and then imagine creative ideas to place complex social and political themes within the genre of science fiction, nonetheless, their works of fiction have not been able to stop the things they were warning the reader about, because in order to do that, solutions need to be provided. Some may say that this is not the aim of fiction, but rather its main objective is to provoke thought. I can agree with that sentiment, but in the case of Muslims I would argue while we too can learn from the social criticisms from the works of Huxley and Orwell, but unlike Harari, we need to search for different solutions, and imaginations, ones that are in conformity to the Islamic *ʿaqīdah*, and built on the Prophetic mission. In light of the works of Huxley, Orwell, Harari, and even the sentiments of Martin, what we are seeing is that all is not well in the world that is dominated by secular thought and imagination. Muslims need to become thought producers and challenge such imaginations by trying to provide alternate thoughts and take on the collective responsibility to once again become a civilisational people as an alternative to the way the world is today, including in our works of fiction.

Muslims Need Future Imaginations

I was in a workshop with the eccentric Ziauddin Sardar when he got me thinking about imagining the future. Ziauddin is a man of many ideas and thoughts, and can push to the edges of the boundaries at times, and while I do not agree with all of Sardar's proposals, I do not doubt that it was he who made me think of this matter, and it was my conversation with him that leads me to jot down some of my thoughts on this matter.

As I have mentioned above, people from the West, many of whom have no belief in Allah, are providing imaginations not just for themselves but for all of us. Their imaginations and visions evidently lack soundness, but it does not lack in hubris.

I would argue that it is time that we, as Muslims, attempt to envisage a different future for ourselves and humanity that is based on the teachings of Islam and with full effort with the responsibility that Allah has bestowed on this noble *ummah*, the ones who worship Him and Him alone, who tread in the path set out by our beloved Master Muhammad ﷺ. It is a path that has a history full of people of exceptional character, of survivors, of piety, of uprightness, those who had visions for themselves and hopes and aspirations for the *ummah* of the future. There have been many throughout the history of Islam who have sacrificed in the way of Allah so that we are Muslim today, and in that same spirit, we need to do the same for the *ummah* of the future, who should see better days than we see today. I have continuously written about Muslim scholars who have been solution-driven to resuscitate this *ummah* from its slumber and work to change its conditions. But in order to do that, there has to be *niyyah* (intention), and then a vision, and then a plan of action.

The future vision for this *ummah* needs to be one where collectively we want a better future together. We have a treasure trove of ideas from the past, we should learn from it and find ways that it can give us inspiration for our ambitions that are under the protection of the One who has created us. In Allah I trust, and so do I trust in His protection. Our history should be able to inform us that we can change our collective condition and that just as people have in the past, so shall we. History tells us that change is not easy, and indeed, there are many obstacles that will emerge on this journey. We learn the same from history that all those from this *ummah* who worked for change, faced challenges, trials, tribulations and difficulties. But we also learn that throughout the history of this *ummah*, there were those who did succeed in making change. Allah has already told us in the Qur'an that He does not change a state of a people until they change themselves. If we want to see change in our current disposition, then we need to change first.

In our everyday lives, we see individuals having imaginations for their future, whether that be about marriage, having children or becoming a doctor. We even have examples of parents who have visions for their children. So, should we not have imaginations for the future of this *ummah*?

If this *ummah* wants to have a better political future, they need to imagine it. If they want a better world for their children, they need to imagine it, and if they want a better world for humanity—they need to imagine it!

In order to have a better imagination of our future, we need some practical goals. This means Muslims need to work collectively in supporting each other's goals. This means that we need local goals and global goals. But what we need is a global vision that is ambitious, practical, and achievable, and aware that there will be many who will be working to obstruct that.

When we examine cyclical theories of human history, we learn that change is generational. This means that we not only need plans for changing our conditions but also setting generational ambitions and goals. That means that rather than raising children to be whatever they want to be, or rather than raising children to simply go to university and get an education, encourage them to study and learn about the tools that will help this *ummah* in its mission to change. This means we need to see in which areas we are deficient, and in which areas we have a surplus.

I accept that the world may seem far more complicated now than we read about in the past. But each generation has its own complexities, and we need to diagnose ours correctly, and then find solutions from Islam that are in accordance with Allah's *din*, and that are practically applicable. This means not only do we need to set visions for ourselves, but we need to inspire the next generation to both believe in them and then educate them with the necessary skills and tools specifically to achieve them.

To envision a sustainable future, it's important to set realistic and achievable goals while also fostering a tangible sense of imagination. Asking people to imagine 500 years into the future is impractical, as it's beyond most people's capacity to conceptualise, and it lacks a clear direction. Instead, I propose creating a three-generation plan, which is both feasible and relatable. The Prophet Muhammad ﷺ spoke of the three generations of the Salaf (Pious Predecessors), which were familiar and tangible to the people of his time: the first being his *Sahabah* (companions), the second the *Tābiʿīn* (followers), and the third the *Tabaʿ al-Tābiʿīn* (followers of the followers). These three generations—spanning roughly 90 to 120 years—form a bridge that connects the past, present, and future. In this framework, the first generation represents the grandparents, the second the parents, and the third the children. Not only are these generations interconnected, but they also provide a century-long vision for progress. It is no surprise that Muslims in the past referred to the concept of a "renewer" or renewal occurring every 100 years, symbolising the completion of a three-generational cycle.

Muslims should not only develop plans for the present but also create a vision that extends to future generations, rooted in the foundational principles upon which the vision was first established. Such visions demand the cultivation of healthy narratives and stories, both from our history and from fiction. These narratives can provide a space for creative thinking, allowing Muslims to envision their future and, from that vision, set concrete goals to bring it to fruition.

Thus, we need to have our own imaginations of ourselves, we need to have our own imaginations of our future, of the future of our children, and the future of this *ummah*. I realise that I have not offered a solution to this in this section, as it lies beyond the scope of this essay. What I can say is that I have made the intention to speak and write about it, and I ask you—the reader—to do the same.